AF607991

John Paul II

AND THE LEGACY OF *Dignitatis Humanae*

John Paul II

AND THE LEGACY OF *Dignitatis Humanae*

Hermínio Rico, S.J.

Georgetown University Press
Washington, D.C.

Georgetown University Press, Washington, D.C.

Printed in the United States of America

10 9 8 7 6 5 4 3 2 1 2002

This volume is printed on acid-free offset book paper.

Library of Congress Cataloging-in-Publication Data

Rico, Hermínio.
John Paul II and the legacy of *Dignitatis humanae* / Hermínio Rico.
p. cm.—(Moral traditions series)
Includes bibliographical references and index.
ISBN 0-87840-889-4 (cloth : alk. paper)
1. Vatican Council (2nd : 1962–1965). Declaratio de libertate religiosa. 2. John Paul II, Pope, 1920– 3. Freedom of religion. I. Title. II. Series.
BX830 1962 .A45 L587 2002
261.7′2—dc21 2001040806

Contents

Preface

This book is about encounters and a consequence of encounters. It is, in general, about the encounter, as old as the revolutions of the end of the eighteenth century, between the Roman Catholic Church and the ideas and practices of liberal democratic societies. This has been an encounter often confrontational, sometimes cooperative, which continues to be negotiated today in many debates about the role of religion in the political sphere and the rules for the formation of a social consensus on standards of public morality.

The stimulation for the research for this book resulted from an encounter between my own personal experience in Portugal and the widening of intellectual perspectives on these matters offered by an extended time of study of theology in the United States. To my long-held interest in the relationship of the church with society and the presence of religion in public life, the acquaintance with the writings of John Courtney Murray and the developments of his thought by some of his disciples offered an attractive systematization, enlarged views, and suggested paths for exploration of new possibilities.

Read in this light, *Dignitatis Humanae* appeared at once as a particularly interesting component of the church's teaching. It had undoubtedly been a milestone, settling, on the part of the church, a point of bitter contention with fundamental values of modernity. But, for historical contexts of still-latent conflict between Catholicism and secularist liberal forces, its doctrine continued to look to be a useful charter for defining necessary boundaries and fostering useful cooperation. Moreover, the declaration of Vatican II seemed to offer promising general guidance for a fruitful presence of the church in the public sphere of contemporary pluralistic societies, whatever the brand of liberalism these have initially evolved from.

In addition, most of the substantial content of the document had been, in great part, the official in fact consecration of Murray's contribution, involving his own redactional work. It was, thus, formally already a fruit of the encounter of the American constitutional experience with the sequels of old Southern European incidents in church-state relationships. *Dignitatis Humanae* presented itself to me, therefore, as a point of confluence of all these encounters, with all the weight of conciliar authority added to it.

At the beginning I was confronted with questions about whether it was still possible to develop a research project about a document from Vatican II, thirty years after the closing of the council. One could presume, however, that a statement so important and so difficult to elaborate and approve by the church had to yield more durable orientations for its life in the world. Such inference was supported by the recognition that many of the basic quandaries *Dignitatis Humanae* tried to deal with seem now to be recurrent. Consequently, the principles uncovered then may be of use again in questions affected by similar fundamental issues. In the end, the central argument of this book contends that renewed in-depth study of the declaration on religious freedom is not only possible but necessary, because its continued critical actuality may have not yet been adverted in its entirety, let alone explored. I conclude, then, that although *Gaudium et Spes* is the great orienting document of Vatican II for the relationship of the church with society, *Dignitatis Humanae* is equally crucial and no less rich of implications and consequences for that same relationship.

The book deals with problems raised by the situations of pluralism and secularization common to Western liberal democracies. Nevertheless, my own personal primary interest on the ecclesial Latin European context led me to focus first and foremost on the role and responsibility of the institutional Roman Catholic Church, in regard to the possibilities of productive encounters with secular liberal culture. A consequent slight stressing of the liability of the church cannot mean any absolution of the secularist forces from their responsibilities past and present in creating and sustaining the political-religious conflict. It is true, however, and the Latin context makes it unmistakable, that, even today, greater progress in church-society relationships continues to depend significantly on a credible evolution of attitudes on the part of the official church.

Because of this focus on the role of hierarchical structures, in this book, "Catholic Church" or simply "church" more often than not refers to the official institutions of the Roman Catholic Church. I do not want to imply that the Catholic Church is really only, or even primarily, the hierarchy, the institutional structure or that the church of Christ is limited to the Roman Catholic Church. Catholic laity and other Christians are obviously equally part of the community of the followers of Christ. They too are the church. But, I am dealing with an issue restricted to the Catholic realm, in which the hierarchy is the decisive actor on the side of the church. For reasons of economy of language, in order not to burden the text with repeated qualifiers, I take the liberty of addressing the part by the names that, in all accuracy, belong properly only to the whole.

Furthermore, the utterances and conduct of the Vatican continue to be decisive in shaping the public image of the Catholic Church, wherever it has a significant institutional presence, in a greater degree even in Latin Europe. Therefore, the focus on the role and responsibility of the institutional church cannot dispense with an attentive consideration of the position of the papacy, the attitudes and lines of thought it has been favoring. This way, the goal of a renewed exploration of *Dignitatis Humanae* coalesced, finally, in a plan of research that gives a particular weight to an analysis of the teaching of John Paul II, regarding the way he has appropriated, interpreted, and developed the doctrine of the conciliar declaration.

The argument of the book unfolds in four chapters. The first one tries to justify the insight about the continued relevance of *Dignitatis Humanae* for church-society issues. To respond to the question, Is now the time for a reconsideration of its content and import?, it proposes a sequence of three moments in the history of the application of *Dignitatis Humanae:* three different consecutive social and political challenges for the church gave form to three opportunities for different emphases in the reading of the declaration. The first moment corresponds to the conflict, concluded at Vatican II, between Catholicism and liberalism about the right to religious freedom; the second was the time of confrontation with communism in Europe; and the third consists of the present challenges to the life and the teaching of the church mounted by the heightened cultural pluralism of Western societies. The second moment diverted somewhat the fulfillment of the expectations of the end of the first; and now, in the third, the church finds itself again at similar crossroads, having to choose between alternative strategies to better accomplish its social mission.

The second chapter differentiates and classifies what is in *Dignitatis Humanae.* It will start by looking at three typical structured interpretations of the declaration. After their comparison and critique, it will identify a set of fundamental assertions that try to represent faithfully and completely the letter and the spirit of the declaration as a doctrinal systematic whole. These principles can serve, it will be argued, as parameters to guide church-society relationships in pluralistic contexts.

The third chapter will look to uncover the practical standing of the declaration in the current doctrinal framework of the church's official social teaching. It will concentrate exclusively on the teaching of John Paul II by making a detailed analysis of his uses, interpretations, and developments of *Dignitatis Humanae.* Starting from a basic particular interpretation of essential issues of the doctrine of the declaration, John Paul II has applied and expanded that same fundamental approach into some currently contentious areas of the public role of the church. This way, he has directed the church to a kind of positioning before moral challenges of pluralistic societies, which will be possible to characterize in reference to the guiding principles of the declaration.

Finally, in the last chapter, the conclusions of these two analyses will be brought together and contrasted over the implications of the principles affirmed by *Dignitatis Humanae* for a concrete set of challenges in the realm of the church's advocacy in matters of public morality. Judgment will be proposed about which kind of interpretation and expanded use of the doctrine of the declaration will be most helpful to the church in its search for a way to engage secular liberal and pluralistic societies that is effective and fecund, as well as faithful to the gospel and the Catholic tradition.

This study marked the conclusion of a course of studies of theology at Weston Jesuit School of Theology, Cambridge, Massachusetts, and Boston College. I am grateful to faculty and fellow students at those schools for their teaching, inspiration, and encouragement. In a very special way I want to thank David Hollenbach for his enormous support and expert guidance in the planning and writing of the whole research project. The anonymous readers who evaluated the initial manuscript for publication made very valuable suggestions about the organization of the text. Needless to say, the responsibility for the many shortcomings of the work continues to rest entirely with me. Special thanks go to Jim Keenan, series editor, and Gail Grella, from Georgetown University Press, who made the publishing of this book possible.

One

Three Moments for *Dignitatis Humanae*

Dignitatis Humanae, the declaration on religious freedom of Vatican II, "in itself did no more than clear up a historical and doctrinal *équivoque,*" wrote John Courtney Murray in one of his many commentaries on the document.[1] This looks like a surprisingly dismissive comment,[2] especially coming from someone who had been a major participant in the drafting of the declaration and, moreover, who had worked for almost twenty years (and even through painful hardships)[3] to develop and defend this new doctrine, and make such an official statement possible. "None the less," Murray immediately continues, "the document was rightly called by Paul VI 'one of the major texts of the Council.' "[4]

The duality of the full assessment seems paradoxical. However, it is an appropriate description of the singularity of the conciliar document. *Dignitatis Humanae* primarily and directly addressed, in the area of church-state relations, the confined issue of the civil right to religious freedom. Here, it radically reversed the long-held official position of the Roman Catholic Church. On this account, it was a document that dealt primarily with the past. But, it had also a significant impact on the understanding and the practice of the relationship of the church with society—and thus it opened, in this wider domain, exciting new possibilities for the future. It is this dual character that Murray wants to highlight, as we see in another, more clear, formulation of the same paired judgment on *Dignitatis Humanae:* "*Formally,* it settles only the minor issue of religious freedom. *In effect,* it defines the Church's basic contemporary view of the world—of human society, of its order of human law and of the functions of the all too human powers that govern it. . . . [It] lays down the premise, and sets the focus, of the Church's concern with the secular world."[5]

Murray truly believed that *Dignitatis Humanae,* in closing a long and protracted controversy, had also set the Catholic Church on the path for a new, qualitatively different, encounter with the temporal order. He thought that it had marked the acceptance and alliance of the church with the movement of history toward "a rightful secularity of civil society," neither sacral nor laicist, which would transcend the present dichotomy of sacred and secular in a new higher unity respectful of the integrity of each of these two orders of human life.[6]

More than thirty years later, how much of Murray's expectation has been realized? Today, is *Dignitatis Humanae* a document definitively of the past, or does it still have relevance and something to teach to the church at the beginning of the twenty-first century?

If *Dignitatis Humanae,* at the time of its publication, was already interpreted as having two different, although complementary, functions (the closing of old church-state controversies, and the promise of new progress in the relations with democratic societies), the historical context of the time soon assigned it a third one. For a Catholic Church facing a strong ideological challenge by communism, and suffering, in many parts of the world, including some traditionally Catholic societies, severe oppression and drastic constraints on its freedoms, the declaration was a most valuable doctrinal resource for the denunciation of, and resistance to, religious persecution. This last use quickly configured the main focus of attention on *Dignitatis Humanae.* And so it remained for twenty-five years.

The sudden collapse of communism in Eastern Europe has, however, cleared the way for a new concentration of attention on the relationship of the Catholic Church with liberal, democratic, pluralistic societies. Will this be also an opportunity finally to explore further the paths *Dignitatis Humanae* seemed to have opened at the end of the council? In favor of the declaration's renewed relevance, one cannot but notice how the basic challenges put to the church by these secularized societies today are in remarkable continuity with many of the points of contention raised by nineteenth-century liberalism. It is equally striking that the typology of present diverse Catholic reactions evokes the divergent kinds of attitudes toward liberal freedoms that competed within the church up until Vatican II. Hence, the question: *Dignitatis Humanae* brought some resolution to the lagged nineteenth-century polemic, and set, at the closing of the council, a fundamental new direction for the attitude of the church toward civil religious pluralism; can the same principles still be of use for the new, or not so new, contemporary challenges of a more acute and extensive pluralism in the area of church-society relationships? After all, what is taking place now is, in great part, the direct continuation of the old contest between Catholicism and liberalism, both now significantly changed. And *Dignitatis Humanae* has so far been the most serious attempt, on the side of the church, to establish the terms for a fruitful encounter between them.[7]

There are, thus, three moments in the short history of *Dignitatis Humanae,* each associated with one of three sequential historical phases: first, Vatican II and the past to which it brought closure; second, the years of the cold war after the council; and, third, the present situation. These moments are defined by the encounter between, on one side, three predicaments in the area of the relationship of the church with secular politics and culture and, on the other side, the use of *Dignitatis Humanae* as a fundamental doctrinal resource to respond to those problems. Each moment is both a specific occasion of challenge to the church and an opportunity for a new examination of the document as a source of direction for the role of the church in society. I use the term moment to designate both the set of challenges raised by each of the predicaments and the kinds of focus on the conciliar declaration that the addressing of those challenges has highlighted. The three moments are, thus, phases both in the recent history of church-state and church-society relationships, and in the interpretation of *Dignitatis Humanae.*

This typology is a heuristic device to organize a complex development of historical and doctrinal issues. It pretends to stress the richness and continuing relevance of the declaration to the contemporary development of the encounter between the Catholic Church and secular society. The differentiation of the moments is not, therefore, strictly exclusive, neither thematically nor chronologically. The basic questions of each moment, and the functions to which *Dignitatis Humanae* is primarily assigned, coexist within the other two. Nevertheless, at different times, each set of issues has gained particular ascendance. Consequently, each has highlighted, within the complex of themes addressed directly and indirectly by the doctrine of the declaration, different functions and dimensions of *Dignitatis Humanae.* Hence the distinct moments.

As historical phases, each moment organized itself around a political and/or cultural ideological adversary of Catholicism, one that quickly gained the status of designated main ongoing threat to the mission of the church. Each highlighted distinct, even if all related, conceptual issues, stressed different points of doctrinal dispute, and, most importantly, imposed particular demands on the public practice and posture of the church. These distinct historical contexts have asked different dominant questions to *Dignitatis Humanae.* Each, in consequence, has prompted different hermeneutical approaches to the declaration, determining, correspondingly, different emphases on its reading and distinct focal points for its application. Thus, each has created, both within the church and in the eyes of the world, a novel perception of the value and relevance of *Dignitatis Humanae.*

On the side of the church, the moments have consisted of reactions to challenges coming from outside. The kind of response that has prevailed in each case fashioned different dominant moods, different basic attitudes—of more confidence or more distrust, more openness or more self-sufficient rejection, more cooperation and dialogue or more opposition and denunciation—of the church toward the world. Because the responses relied significantly on characteristic uses of *Dignitatis Humanae,* readings of the declaration helped to form, or lent their support to, the kind of impulse and momentum in the social mission of the church typical of each moment.

Until recently, the document approved by the conciliar fathers in December of 1965 has been used to deal primarily with two different historical problems faced by the Catholic Church—the first and second moments. Adding to, and sometimes in contrast with, these two past approaches, this book wants to explore the potential for contemporary church-society relations of a new reading of the text from the perspective of the historical challenges of the present-day situation of the Catholic Church in liberal pluralistic societies. That constitutes the third moment for *Dignitatis Humanae.*

However, to understand the potentialities of this third moment, we need first to understand better the significance of the other two by considering their main features and lasting legacies. It will be particularly important to become aware of the way they have helped shape attitudes still determinant for the positioning of the church before the challenges it now has to confront in its mission to the world.

First Moment: Religious Freedom Replaces Established Catholicism

The first moment of *Dignitatis Humanae* consisted basically of the clearing up of the *équivoque,* the resolution of the "minor issue," in the words of John Courtney Murray. It took care, primarily, of the past. The Catholic Church, finally, after more than one and a half centuries of resistance, accepted constitutionally guaranteed religious freedom as a human right not to be denied to any one. With such an affirmation, Vatican II radically developed Catholic official doctrine: It dismissed the long-favored thesis/hypothesis formulation, reversed the strict condemnations of religious freedom and separation of church and state by the nineteenth-century popes, and stated, with the authority of an ecumenical council, the definitive renunciation of the church to the ideal of a juridically privileged status in a confessional state.

Dignitatis Humanae concluded the reconciliation with liberal political freedoms.[8] It resolved the last obstacle to a full alignment of the church with modern democratic societies, which, since the end of the eighteenth century, had elected religious freedom and separation between church and state as cornerstones of their political philosophies and constitutional practices, even though their initial motivations and ideological foundations were not as pure and honorable as the principles themselves.

The ideological adversary associated with the problematic of this first moment—an enemy that many in the church still continued to fight uncompromisingly at the time of the council—had been Jacobinic secularist liberalism, the political theories and practical policies that issued from the French Revolution.[9] The church did not miss that the revolutionary liberal proposal of religious freedom was grounded on an extremist rationalist philosophy of absolute self-determination for the individual conscience, which acknowledged no objective truth, no transcendent order of morality, no law higher than its own subjective imperatives. As a consequence, religion was seen as a purely private affair, exclusively of the realm of the individual conscience, without any claim to challenge the absolute control of the state over all aspects of public life. Absolutism of individual freedom and totalitarian social monism under an omnipotent state, the two dogmas of sectarian liberalism,[10] provided the philosophical foundations of religious freedom and separation of church and state, as they were proclaimed initially by the modern revolutions in continental Europe.

To the rejection of ideas were added the consequences of the violence against Catholic institutions with which liberalism introduced itself at the time of the French Revolution. For a long time, anything liberal would immediately evoke, in the church's imagination, the terrible grievances of the first encounter in France. Similar attacks, supported by a very aggressive anticlericalism, would take place in other countries of Europe all through the nineteenth century. They further confirmed and reinforced the impact of the conflictive French experience, not just on the understanding and the development of Catholic theory and practice of church-state relationships,[11] but on the whole attitude of Roman Catholicism toward modernity. Circumstantial historical factors helped create the depth of antagonism and put the church in a path of vehement and uncompromising confrontation by the mid-nineteenth century.[12]

If the church could not but repel the initial revolutionary claims, the problem became that, after the first impact, it crystallized its position and did not recognize the later possibility of clearly separating the political institutions from the ideological basis on which they had been first grounded.[13] Such intransigence showed firmness on fundamental doctrine, but complicated the adaptation to the movement of history.

The difficulties of the Catholic stance were plainly represented by the weaknesses of the thesis/hypothesis theory,[14] the official Catholic position on church-state relations since the middle of the nineteenth century.[15] This doctrine stated an ideal—the thesis—arrived at by abstract deduction from the starting axiom that only the truth deserves freedom and its corollary that error has no rights. It affirmed, in principle, that only Catholicism, the only true religion, should be allowed public freedom by the state: the Catholic Church should be the established religion of the political community and, in order to protect its citizens from error, no other religions should be allowed public expression. Wherever the conditions to enforce this ideal were absent, the state might, in the name of public peace, suspend its application. The church could, in these particular cases, reluctantly admit religious freedom and separation of church and state as lesser evils—the hypothesis. Imposed by the circumstances, such freedom and separation were never approved as principles, but just accepted as prudential exercises of tolerance.

If, in the beginning, this formulation reduced the conflict and gave some leeway for the accommodation of the church to different historical contexts,[16] it soon became a source of uneasiness. The formula was too vulnerable to the accusation of being a mere opportunistic expediency. The council finally broke the impasse and granted full credibility and moral authority to the church's defense of human rights and opposition to any form of totalitarianism.

Dignitatis Humanae, thus, had a dramatic effect of liberation in the church. It created the conditions for a new impulse in the church's social mission, radically revamped the image of the church in the eyes of the secular world, and opened there a whole new receptivity for its message. Roman Catholicism took itself out of the doctrinal dead end in which it had been cornered (or had cornered itself) on the area of church-state relations.

The espousing of the personal right to religious freedom involved the stressing of a clear distinction of the spheres of church, state, and society, with the consequent redefinition of the relation of each one of them with the other two. In this political philosophy, the sphere of society becomes the great space of freedom, where democratic discussion takes place. *Dignitatis Humanae* set up a new normative model for the coexistence of church and state, based on a clearly delimited new understanding of the competencies of each one. The church respects civil freedoms by relinquishing any claim to control society through the instrumental use of political power, specifically in matters of religion publicly expressed. It rejects any interference of the political power in the church's internal affairs and mission, and only asks of governments safeguard of its own freedom. The competencies of the state are also redefined. Its main duty is to provide the conditions for the exercise of the various freedoms in the social sphere. In matters of religion, the state is declared incompetent, and, therefore, must respect the immunity of persons and religious communities from any encroachment on their freedom to seek, profess, and express their faith, privately or publicly, individually or corporately. It has only to see that individuals and religious communities are free to live privately and publicly their religious faiths, with the only limitation that public order of society be not endangered.

In a longer historical haul, *Dignitatis Humanae* meant that, in a solemn way, the church proclaimed its renunciation of what—in many different forms, some very obvious, others more subtle—had been very much part of its life since the time of Constantine: the idea of a certain instrumentality of the secular power in the service of the spiritual power, the reliance on the help of the temporal authorities to promote actively the goals of the church's mission. The church definitively forsook any claim to a privileged juridical status, even in "Catholic countries." From now on, the only thing it demanded from any government was respect for its freedom as part of the respect for the religious freedom of every human being.[17]

The concept 'religious freedom' took over the center stage from two other related but more limited concepts: 'tolerance' and 'freedom of the church.' Tolerance meant a compromise, out of necessity, with difference and pluralism. It was a concession, by the church, to a lesser evil for the sake of public peace, a mere option not to seek repression.[18] Religious freedom affirms, instead, the positive intrinsic value of freedom as an inalienable human right: it recognizes it as necessary, declares it unassailable, and promotes it as fundamental in the search for religious truth. Its claim applies equally to people and institutions of any faith. The dignity of the human person, of every human person of any religious faith or of no faith at all, is the foundation of the right.

Religious freedom is, thus, not a church-centered concept. While, before, the freedom of the church was a special institutional privilege claimed in the name of the exclusive rights of the truth, now it is seen as the intrinsic institutional dimension of the personal right to religious freedom, the two inseparably connected because of the social character of the human person. The new central concept shifted the focus to the good of the person, and turned the Catholic Church away from too self-centered claims of exclusive privileges, to a service of herald and defender of the rights of all human beings. It shifted the focus of engagement for the mission of the church, from the state and the political power, to society, its culture, and the democratic social debate. The intervention of the church could now appear more clearly motivated by the defense of the rights of human persons and not so much by the interests of institutions.

The remarkable impact of *Dignitatis Humanae* on the world outside the church ultimately had to do more with issues of image and attitude than with drastic changes in tangible ecclesiastical practices. In its basic doctrinal statement—affirmation of the civil right to religious freedom and consequent renunciation to the ideal of established Catholicism—the council just caught up formally with an already widely observed praxis. A situation of generalized *de facto* recognition of religious freedom became now fully legitimized by official church doctrine; what had been just prudential became normative.

If we focus, then, exclusively on this confined result and take it at its face value, *Dignitatis Humanae* will look today as a document simply of the past, its possibilities having been exhausted with a first moment narrowly considered. However, equally part of the significance of this first moment is the promising new impulse brought about in the life and presence of the church in the world. The novelty and promise actually resided more in the potentialities of both the substance and the mode of the new doctrinal thinking advanced to support the right to religious freedom than in the affirmation of the right itself. It is these potentialities that continue to make the principles of the declaration relevant today for the present and the future of a Catholic Church committed to engage the secular world.

Dignitatis Humanae signaled a consequential change of public demeanor on the part of the church. For a Catholicism so long seen as conceited and arrogant, "it was a major act of humility on the part of the teaching Church."[19] The burden of the situation of impasse had long been on the church, and the church was able to assume the correction. It came around to adopt an institutional development that it had not promoted, and which it had strongly resisted for a long time. In a considerable measure, the church was led by others to the acceptance of values and institutions very much in conformity with the Christian view of the person and of society, but to which the church had been blinded by historical distractions and also a certain loss of the right sense of direction in its mission to the world.[20] *Dignitatis Humanae* was a tacit recognition by the church that its view of the dignity of the human person and of the rights intrinsic to it had been made richer and more explicit through the stimulating encounter with secular movements, namely the Western liberal tradition, in their concrete historical contexts.

The first moment of *Dignitatis Humanae* substantiated a very important change in the whole disposition of official Roman Catholicism toward modernity. It constituted a decisive moving away from the culture of "integral Catholicism" that had gained roots in the nineteenth century. Equipped with a new doctrinal framework, enlivened by a new attitude, and enjoying a very positive external image, the Roman Catholic Church came out of Vatican II ready to embark on a new era of dialogue, cooperation, and fruitful engagement with the temporal order. The stage was set for what Murray envisaged as the great leap forward promised by the resolution of the "minor issue" of religious freedom. History, however, was already presenting more urgent challenges, and *Dignitatis Humanae* soon came to be looked at from the perspective of that pressing reality. This turn could not but provide a slight diversion to the just described impetus of the first moment in the use and interpretation of *Dignitatis Humanae*.

Second Moment: Freedom of the Church against Atheistic Communism

The second moment of *Dignitatis Humanae* corresponds, in terms of historical phases, to the period of the great confrontation of the Western world with communism, which, replacing nineteenth-century secular liberalism, became, in the second part of the twentieth century, the foremost ideological enemy of Catholicism. Communist governments had imposed violent restrictions on the Catholic populations of Eastern Europe after the end of the Second World War. Then, communist regimes steadily spread into other parts of the world, where they immediately curtailed the activity of the church and repressed any practice of religion. In the West itself the communist menace was also felt at other levels. There was the alarming growing influence of communist parties in some of the Western democracies,[21] and the seduction of a good part of the European intellectual elite by Marxism or Marxist-inspired methods of analysis. Most of the long-standing philosophical anticlerical opposition to Catholicism suddenly adopted the Marxist credo as its fundamental inspiration. At this ideological level, there were different strategies of response by the church, many based on efforts to engage in dialogue. At the level of political practices, however, the denunciation of its systematic disrespect for the right to religious freedom took the foreground of the condemnations of communism by the church, especially with the papacy of John Paul II.

Once again the church mobilized itself in defense of its freedom against this new political threat. *Dignitatis Humanae* was the obvious and very capable doctrinal instrument for this battle.[22] That, however, implied a slight shift of conceptual emphases and of the foci of application of the doctrine of the declaration.

This was no illegitimate appropriation against the intention of the declaration itself. With the exception of the schismatic Bishop Lefebvre, there was no intent, by those who championed the fight for religious freedom against communism, to cancel the acquired results of the first moment. The threat of communism was real and momentous, and could not be ignored or downplayed. It had actually already been taken into consideration in the process of the redaction of the declaration.[23] Paul VI dedicated one long paragraph of his speech marking the opening of the second session of the council to the victims of religious persecution, calling attention to the empty places in the *Aula* belonging to those who could not leave countries where the church was being persecuted, where religious freedom was suppressed by principles and methods of intolerance, political and antireligious.[24]

The role attributed to *Dignitatis Humanae* in the second moment—the defense of religious freedom as a universal human right—is actually the *prima facie* application of the text of the declaration. It is a permanent and fundamental function that continues today when the Catholic Church denounces religious persecutions by antireligious governments, or addresses the delicate situation of Christians in countries where they cannot profess publicly their faith. It will always be opportune whenever the church finds the need to speak up in defense of the human right to religious freedom.

The argument of this book, however, intends primarily to discern the consequences for the tone and manner of the relationship of the church with society derived from the kind of consideration given to *Dignitatis Humanae.* From that perspective, what this second moment did was to reorganize the balance of the reception of the document, putting more emphasis on what it demanded from governments than on what it committed the church to pursue and promote by example. The second moment refocused the import of the declaration on church-state issues, on conflicts of institutions, and deferred, in good part, the drive to explore its implications for the mode of participation of the church in the public dialogue of democratic societies. And it certainly toned down the dynamism of humility on the part of the church, particularly characteristic of the first moment.

The first moment was primarily an episode of conversion of the church. During the second moment the pressure was again on the states, and the church reappeared as both innocent victim and righteous judge. The struggle against communism, in what concerned the kind of challenge put to the church, was not substantially different from previous historical battles against oppressive temporal powers. This defense of religious freedom could well be done with an attitude and demeanor in essential continuity with Gregory VII or Pius IX, as they fought for the freedom of the church. In this whole predicament, the church was not confronted in its ways or invited to any degree of adaptation; it just had to close ranks, assert its principles, resist the intimidation, and wait for the weakening and collapse of the adversary.[25]

While in the first moment the freedom primarily at stake was that of non-Catholic believers in countries in which there was a privileged juridical status recognized to the Catholic Church, now it was the freedom of Catholic faithful under oppression by atheistic governments that the declaration was called above all to defend. This second moment assigned the declaration to a narrower role, running the risk of diverting attention from its wider potential implications perceived in the first moment. It created a more limited hermeneutical approach to the purpose and significance of *Dignitatis Humanae,* and, in a certain way, defined a context in which some of the most demanding challenges that its doctrine had put to the church itself could easily be pushed to the background. The risk of a too reductionistic reading of *Dignitatis Humanae* was to limit the potentialities of its full teaching and to reinforce, at least temporarily, the natural resistance, within the church, to the path of change to which it had pointed. It may have also provided the opportunity for the restoration, and subsequent preservation in the practice of some groups, of elements of the old views and ways of a distrustful and hostile relationship with modern society.

The replacement of secularist liberalism by atheistic communism as the perceived main enemy of the church had the effect that religious freedom passed very quickly from being a topic reviled by the more defensively antimodern Catholic forces to becoming one of the basic supports of their mobilization against the foes of Catholicism. The menace of totalitarianism led these groups to value more the freedoms and human rights proposed initially by the long-opposed liberalism. In the first moment, the conciliar declaration had been a promising sign highly regarded by those who wanted the church to continue to grow in openness to the modern world. In the second moment, *Dignitatis Humanae* became also, and not without much irony, a document of great utility for currents of a Catholicism much less open to the world and in general very suspicious of modernity.

At the same time, the context of general social and cultural crisis in the years immediately after the council, of which the social turmoil of 1968 was emblematic, affected also the confidence of the church and cautioned its promotion of freedom. This had an impact on the effects of *Dignitatis Humanae.* It quickly became a great preoccupation of the official interpretations of the conciliar doctrine on religious freedom to avoid possible misapplications of its propositions that could seem to justify concepts and practices of unbridled freedom and rejection of all authority.[26] In those years, these corrections accounted for many references of Paul VI to *Dignitatis Humanae;*[27] in the later period of his pontificate we find more frequently all-out denunciations of the limitations imposed on religious freedom by some governments.[28]

The serious challenge of communism and the postconciliar sociocultural context compelled mainstream Catholicism to add elements of a more cautious, or even defensive, attitude to the optimistic openness of Vatican II.

However, if the second moment may have tamed some elements of the impulse of the first moment, it did not cancel the teaching nor erase the experience from the memory of the church. It did not make it impossible, therefore, that the direction of growth for the practice and the attitude of the church in the world envisaged at the conclusion of the first moment of *Dignitatis Humanae* might be resumed with refreshed eagerness after the dismissal of the momentous threat that defined the second moment.

Third Moment: The Challenges of Secularism and Relativism

The third moment is now unfolding. It is made, on one hand, of the challenges to the Catholic vision of the human person, individual and social, by the dominant culture of democratic, pluralistic societies; and, on the other, of the rivalry, within the church, of different views about what is the best approach to respond to those challenges.

The basic roots of most of the present points of contention in the area of church-society relations are in continuity with the old issues to which *Dignitatis Humanae* tried to give a modern appropriate answer. What we see now is a new encounter of Catholicism with an evolved liberalism, in which, again, conflicting views on human freedom, the ultimate significance of pluralism, and the universality of values related to an objective order of truth, raise questions about the kind of presence and the amount of influence the Catholic Church is allowed to have in the public sphere of democratic societies. The church-*state* conflict, centered on constitutional structures of freedom, has been basically resolved. But the central issue of confrontation between Catholicism and liberalism returned under the form of a church-*society* debate about the place of religious principles and the public role of the church in the formation of a public consensus on the values and rights that constitute the substance of human society.

Here, again, the church opposes indifferentism and laicism, not anymore of a state seeking the monism of absolute power, but of a society and culture threatened by the ideology of a new monism of democratic procedures that limits itself to formal notions of freedom, indifferent to questions of truth and value. The challenge is to strike the right distinctions between the positive values of the liberal tradition and the ideology of doctrinaire liberalism, and find the right balance between inalienable democratic freedoms and rights and the need for a substantive consensus in society of which religious values are an integral component.[29] How much *Dignitatis Humanae* may still be relevant in providing answers for these new challenges remains to be seen, but there is, at least at the level of the questions, a sequence that justifies a possible third moment—a novel role through a refreshed interpretation from a new perspective—for the conciliar declaration.

RELATIVISM AND PRIVATIZATION OF RELIGION

The collapse of communism in Eastern Europe and the Soviet Union, symbolized in the fall of the Berlin Wall, marked the transition of historical phases. In the immediate term, the change raised hopes in some that the heroic strength of the Catholicism that had endured and helped defeat communism would burst in a great renewal of Christian values, a tide that would expand beyond the newly liberated countries of the East. It did not happen. The vanishing of the communist threat, however, certainly freed the church for a new unimpeded attention to its relation with democratic societies. But it could not be expected that the church would automatically resume the same motion to which it had seemingly been set into by the impulse of the end of the first moment. The diversion of the second moment had been more than just a parenthesis endured with impatience. Twenty-five years after the conclusion of Vatican II, both protagonists found themselves quite changed. Liberal democracies have evolved and the alignment of forces in the church is also different. Not just have each of the two sides remade itself in its moods, dominant trends, and governing preoccupations, but the status of their mutual relationship has also been altered. The momentum of mutual goodwill has dwindled considerably, as it is manifest in prominent stances on either side. The gains of the council, both in terms of the tone and clear direction for the engagement of the church in the world, and as receptivity on the part of secular society, need to be consolidated and, in some aspects, to be acquired anew, if the auspicious prospects of the end of the first moment are to be fulfilled now.

On the side of secular society, the most obvious thrust in the area of church-society relations today is the growth of a secularism carried through from the nineteenth century, which wants to reduce religion to a purely private affair and denounces as inappropriate any public position of the institutional church on social and political issues.[30] Although there are also signs of a revived public influence of religion,[31] the secularist push to privatization continues to be the great challenge put to the church in the Western world. Present-day secularism is less a threat by its direct aggressiveness toward the institutional church (as was the nineteenth-century kind, although animosities still remain in many circles), than by its promotion of indifferentism and relativism. Relativism has become, in the Catholic Church, the last "ism" to attain the status of "central problem for the faith."[32]

Two reasons make the questions and challenges of this third moment look more like those of the first than the ones of the second moment. First, many of them are reruns of old points of disagreement with liberalism.[33] The issues raised by a libertarian culture and an idolatry of individual autonomy have again to do with the status of the truth, the character of human freedom, and the possibilities of pluralism, questions that the church had also to deal with in the run up to *Dignitatis Humanae*. Second, they cannot be solved with an easy judgment between incompatible models of society and ideologies set clearly apart, as in the second moment. The church opposes not a clearly delimited external aggressor, but the more diffuse dangers of extreme forms of many modern cultural tendencies, not all of them bad in everything they propose. One more time, there is the need to carefully understand, to formulate distinctions,[34] and to make nuanced judgments in the determination of what is acceptable, what can allow for compromise, and what is irredeemable.

Moreover, these mentalities and inclinations make inroads also into the church, their ambiguities echo within it, and so the lines of attrition cut through it, too. It is impossible just to stay apart, proclaiming principles, defending rights, and delivering judgments, as in the second moment. The challenge to be in and with this new world confronts the church with important choices also about its own self-understanding, its relationship to the not inert deposit of revealed truth, the image it chooses to project of itself, and even about issues of internal organization. As in the first moment, the duty of facing an external provocation forces the church to look at itself and the church cannot avoid being changed in the process.

The great immediate task of the third moment is, thus, for the Roman Catholic Church to find an effective way to resist, denounce, and help to transform this culture of relativism and secularism. It has to do so guided by the doctrinal resources of its tradition, in continuity with the behaviors and attitudes to which it has committed itself in similar situations in the past. Equally important, or even more in the long run, is the form of this engagement at the official hierarchical level, both in the substance and in the demeanor of the pronouncements. This form will determine in great part how the church will position itself before its own as well as before secular society for its role of a lasting, active, and credible participation in public affairs, a central requirement of its mission to the world.

COMPETING RESPONSES

Most agree about the external threat. But in what concerns the preferable kind of response, Catholicism finds itself also internally at a crossroads. There is no easy accord about which of these modern and postmodern tendencies have redeemable potential and how far they can be pushed until they become unacceptable extremisms. Some prefer a kind of encounter with society that favors a receptive accompaniment of cultural transformations, pushing forward and deeper the views and strategies of dialogue and adaptation to modernity typical of the closing of Vatican II. Others, instead, moved by a defensive attitude of suspicion, favor a clear distancing from contemporary cultural trends and opt for a recovery of older "traditional" approaches of less openness and more uncompromising prophetic denunciation.

Such diversity in itself is not new nor is it negative. A plurality of degrees of involvement with the secular world by different groups within the Catholic Church has always been part of its tradition and, in their complementarity, a source of richness for the witness of the church. However, present differences seem to be resulting more in rivalry and some antagonism between movements than in harmonious contrast and enhancement of the multidimensional Christian witness to the world. Contrarily to the time of the conclusion of Vatican II, under the unifying impulse of the conclusion of the first moment, it is now more difficult to discern a clear overall direction for the attitude of the church regarding the dominant culture of secularized societies. The public voice of the church appears sometimes hesitant about the fundamental route to take. If, on the side of secular forces, we can again identify some recycling of themes typical of the nineteenth century, within Catholicism too, attitudes and types of discourse from a church before *Dignitatis Humanae* are being occasionally revived.

At stake is a fundamental strategic choice for the path the church will take in the near future in its relationships with the modern secular world. The consequences will be immediately visible in the effectiveness of the presence of the church in the public cultural debate. But the stance cultivated now will also have lasting consequences for the sustained long-term credibility and relevance of a church confronting the challenges set to its social mission by pluralistic societies in accelerated transformation. In this regard, the lessons of encounters and confrontations in the long historical period of the first moment continue to offer unavoidable actuality.

These inconsistencies and tensions in the practice and the thinking of the social mission of the church, thus, reflect themselves on the present standing of the broader implications of *Dignitatis Humanae.* Its emblematic character for the encounter of the church with modernity and the importance of the historical and substantial issues implied in the declaration make it suitable for an indicative role. The way its principles continue to be used, interpreted, and developed, gives a particularly apt indication of the direction the church will take in its relation with society. The prominence given or denied to *Dignitatis Humanae* may be, therefore, a good sign of the prevalence of either of the competing tendencies.[35]

The historical parallel of internal lines of fraction in the church, together with the resemblances of external predicaments, calls, thus, for a reconsideration of *Dignitatis Humanae* in its manifold historical significance, complete doctrinal scope, and fullness of implications. In return, the new exploration of the declaration may help clarify what is now demanded of the church if it wants to confront again in an earnest, credible, and fruitful way the cultural and moral challenges of contemporary liberal societies. This is what constitutes the great challenge of the third moment for *Dignitatis Humanae* and for the Catholic Church.

As a matter of fact, even if only implicitly, each of the two very general basic dispositions toward the secular world referenced above entails a tacit judgment on the larger significance, and present relevance, of the conciliar declaration. The inclination to expect a mutually enriching encounter fits with the understanding that *Dignitatis Humanae* has effected a definitive break, set an irreversible direction of openness and dialogue in the attitude of the church toward the world. The potentialities opened by the first moment, therefore, need to continue to be developed as they were envisaged then. The challenges of the third moment are not seen to be fundamentally different from those at the end of the first. Concomitantly, the accuracy and aptness of the doctrine of *Dignitatis Humanae* is not considered to have been significantly questioned by the developments in the last thirty years. The better response, from this perspective, is still further insistence on the declaration's principles and strategies. Here, *Dignitatis Humanae* is even now seen as a breakthrough document with great consequences for the church itself, still waiting for the implementation of its full implications.

For the opposed disposition, it is as if the second moment's restrictive interpretation of *Dignitatis Humanae* was the most adequate. The first moment's excitement with unlocked possibilities would have sought to go too far. The preferred, continued traditional attitude of the church had always been much more prudent. In this view, today it is possible to avoid those misjudgments because we have a much more sober appreciation of the negative consequences of secularist freedoms than was anticipated at Vatican II. Thirty years after, the presumption is that a correction in the direction of the approach of the declaration is necessary. On this side, *Dignitatis Humanae* is now seen as an opportune solution for a limited external issue, a document arrived at with maybe a little bit too much compromise with secular tendencies, which now needs to be adjusted so the church can return to the accustomed stand against the modern trend of indifference toward God and natural morality.

This correspondence between dispositions toward secular culture and interpretations of the declaration on religious freedom is not an arbitrary attribution or just a matter of coincidence. The key issues determining the basic disposition toward modern society have to do with basic evaluations of pluralism and secularity, and with the way freedom and truth relate fundamentally to each other. *Dignitatis Humanae* dealt precisely with these issues and, therefore, in the measure it established clear principles about them and their mutual relations, it has determined with the same clarity the concrete direction for the church's presence in the contemporary world. It is warranted, then, to explore the connection between different interpretations of the declaration on religious freedom of Vatican II and the essential character of competing views on the role of the church in contemporary pluralistic societies. That is the orienting idea of this book.

To complete the laying out of the problematic and direction of inquiry of this study, however, it is still necessary to add to the framework of the three moments an adequate distinction of the particularities of the two historical-geographical contexts more directly implied in the framing of *Dignitatis Humanae*. The interaction of these two quite different historical experiences of the Catholic Church created some of the problems, helped in devising the solutions, and continues to be central for the understanding of the emphases of the different interpretations and for the appropriate application of useful lessons from *Dignitatis Humanae*.

Two Defining Historical Experiences: Latin Europe and the United States of America

Although the Roman Catholic Church continues to be a highly centralized institution, there have been, in the last centuries, especially in the area of the relationship of the church with the social and political orders, diversity, polarities, and creative interactions in the experience, and consequent attitudes, of different local churches. The matter of religious freedom is a typical case of how particular local circumstances had a crucial role in shaping Catholic official teaching and the way it has evolved. The theoretical and practical context of *Dignitatis Humanae*—creation of the problem, formation of the church's attitude and initial doctrine, and, later, the development that produced the conciliar declaration—unfolded as an interaction between the two different political, juridical, and ecclesiastical historical experiences of the United States and Latin Europe.[36] It was not a coincidence that, right before the council, the recognized protagonists on each side of the doctrinal controversies on religious freedom were the

American Jesuit John Courtney Murray and the Vatican's Cardinal Ottaviani; nor that Spain and the United States were the alternative contemporary models being proposed as normative constitutional arrangements for the relations between church and state.

A Dual Legacy of Liberalism-Catholicism Relations

The polarity goes back to two eighteenth-century revolutions—the French and the American—that shared many ideological roots but also exhibited significant differences. They were both made in the name of enlightened liberalism but they actually referred to two kinds of liberalism distinguished, namely, by two significantly different attitudes toward religion: the French, bitterly anticlerical and antireligious, based on extremist rationalist philosophies of human autonomy; the American, of Anglo-Saxon inspiration, generally respectful of religion and careful in protecting pluralism and equality of churches and religious expressions. These two new political realities generated, for obvious reasons, opposite reactions on the part of the local Catholic Church: total rejection in one case; overall peaceful coexistence on the other.

The contrast originated, therefore, in Western Europe, in a disparity of political and ecclesiastical initial contexts. The areas covered by the two political traditions of Anglo-Saxon and Continental liberalism coincided geographically with two groups of nations with historically quite different traditions of church-state relations. Where there had been experience of an established Catholic Church, liberal modernity and Catholicism fought each other, and the transition to democracy, civil rights, and tolerant pluralism was difficult and protracted; where there had not been Catholic establishment, the Catholic Church adapted much more easily to the new political principles.[37]

There have been, thus, at work in the encounter of Catholicism with modern liberalism two reinforcing cause-effect circularities: close traditional ties of a socially hegemonic Catholic Church with the state were challenged by a liberalism profoundly anticlerical, which reinforced and justified the opposition of the church, which, in turn, radicalized the anticlericalism; Anglo-Saxon liberalism, not fundamentally anticlerical or antireligious, met a minority Catholic Church with little problem adjusting (it actually often profited from the new, freer conditions), and neither one raised obstacles to the development and expansion of the other.

This double heritage shaped two cultures of liberal-Catholic relations, different both in the way secular liberal institutions relate to religion and the social mission of the Catholic Church, and in the attitudes of the local institutional church toward the temporal order, be it the political and juridical establishment or civil society at large.[38] Today, these two legacies are still best represented, on one side, by the United States, the prominent case of a mostly tranquil acculturation of Catholicism to modern liberal political institutions; and on the other side, by the nations in which the most acute conflicts of the nineteenth and the first part of the twentieth centuries took place and where, for this reason mainly, the adaptation of Catholic institutions to modern politics has been more complicated: Italy (with the Vatican), France, Spain, and Portugal. These two secular liberal cultures put today only slightly different challenges to the Catholic Church in their respective countries; but each local church carries a quite different historical burden of responsibility for the success of the present encounter.

DIFFERENT CHALLENGES BY *DIGNITATIS HUMANAE*

The problematic of the first moment centered on one main point of contention, the official Catholic position on religious freedom upheld by the Vatican. This was a doctrine of the universal church, but it had also been greatly influenced by particular historical experiences. It crystallized under the determinant influence of circumstantial factors that took place in Latin Europe,[39] the geographic and cultural context of the papacy. For the approval of *Dignitatis Humanae*, however, it was the historical experience of the church in North America that constituted the primary influence, inspiring the new normative model of the official church-state doctrine.[40] As the new universal doctrine was adopted, the challenges put to the Catholic Church in the United States and in the countries of Latin Europe were quite different.

For American Catholicism the document meant primarily that the universal doctrine of the church was not anymore in contradiction with the practical mode of relating to the social and political order that the church in America had generally followed for many years, with satisfying results both for the church and for secular society. The theological status of the established preferences of the American church changed within the universal church but their actions or attitudes did not need to change.[41] *Dignitatis Humanae* for the United States really signified the clearing of just a "minor issue" that had been an obstacle for full acceptance of Catholic participation in political life.

For the churches of Italy, or Portugal, or Spain, the challenge was much greater. *Dignitatis Humanae* was a groundbreaking event requiring in many instances a process of internal adaptation by the church. In some cases they were summoned to procure changes in the still privileged juridical status of the Catholic Church;[42] in others, any claims for restoration ceased to make sense.[43] All had to adopt a new theological basis, a new paradigm in the doctrinal framework for the church's engagement in social and political affairs, one that demanded a significant change of mentality and attitude. They were now called to a wholehearted engagement in rebuilding mutual trust between Catholicism and political societies that had been at odds for a century and a half, while there were still in either side very deep feelings of antagonism and suspicion. In this context, time and perseverance were necessary for the church to assimilate the evolution. And there was certainly a real risk that the change would remain too superficial, that the church would not completely mature to the new attitude, and that the old habits might recur in response to new propitious situations.

The difference of these two Catholic cultures was significant not just to the first moment of *Dignitatis Humanae*. It continues to be important for the understanding of the issues of the third moment. The advances of secularization seem to put very similar challenges to the present-day Catholic Church on both sides of the North Atlantic. There are, however, relevant differences. Both regional churches need to resist the trend of declining receptivity to religion and religious values in public life, and fight for their presence and relevance in the public arena. But the level and kind of secularization they face is quite different,[44] and they arrive here coming from two substantially different starting points and with two different historical burdens.

The discrimination the Catholic Church suffered historically in the United States came more from prejudices of other Christian churches, as a lingering Reformation conflict, than from any variety of liberal nineteenth-century continental European anticlericalism.[45] American Catholics had to battle to be accepted as full participants in the democratic dialogue, not because there was animosity against religion but because there were suspicions about their commitment to tolerance and freedom of religion. This conditioned them to mold their public role in a way that did not threaten other groups, religious or secular, making always clear their unreserved allegiance to the values of the American constitution. The current tendencies for the privatization of religion affect Catholicism together with all the other religious confessions. It has to strive to maintain its public role, but, because it has never tried to control society, it just needs to continue to claim its rights to be a full participant, with the fullness of its identity and message, in the pluralistic dialogue, resisting the dominance of principles of pseudo-neutrality and impartiality, which are, in reality, forms of active secularism.

In the Southern European context, the present condition evolved from a situation in which the church had too much influence upon public power (paralleled by the interference of the temporal power in the internal affairs of the church), and, through that influence, exercised control over society. The whole process, because of the heritage of strong political centralization and weak civil society coming from royal absolutism, took place as a power conflict between institutions—the hierarchical church and the state. In the nineteenth century, the church was stripped of its direct political influence by anticlerical governments supported by secularist ideologies. As a result, it had to let go of its close institutional links with the state, a condition that it definitively accepted with *Dignitatis Humanae.* The only option to keep its public role was to develop its relationship with society, establishing itself as a participant in the democratic process. But, because of historical inertia, the image of the church continues to be, for many, that of a feared powerful social institution, which, therefore, now needs to show exceeding restraint not to jeopardize its credibility and to be successful in its social mission. The opposition to the public voice of the church in political and social affairs in Latin Europe relates to traumas of a past for which the church is not totally blameless. The burden of self-criticism and change lies here also with the church institutional, even if it is the hard to defend secularist ideologies that are primarily under challenge. No balanced pluralism may be achieved if the church does not conclusively dismiss all doubts about possible recurrences of its old authoritarian tendencies.

It is in both these societies that the challenges and promises of the third moment present themselves more vividly to the church. It is, thus, also with their particularities in mind that the competing lines of interpretation of *Dignitatis Humanae* will be analyzed. The difficulties directly posed by the secularist and relativistic culture of democratic, pluralistic societies arguably are not, in themselves, the gravest threats to the dignity and well-being of people, nor the greatest obstacles to the mission of the church in the world today. Its human rights ministry has confronted in recent times, and continues to do so, more critical challenges in many other parts of the world.[46] Even within the domestic contexts of these developed societies there are dilemmas of economic and social justice that may compete in straight importance and urgency with the described church-society problems of the third moment.

The handling of the latter, nevertheless, beyond the concrete issues directly at stake, is crucial for the ability of the church to continue to intervene and influence the cultures, social values, and policies at the national and international level, of nations that have the power to affect for better or worse the lives of virtually every human being on the planet. The obstacles mounted by the culture of these societies, profoundly Christian in its roots and tradition, are also a test case for the capacity of the church to maintain the relevance of its public voice and the social impact of the Christian worldview even when constrained by the radical secularization of modern social and political structures, a trend that seems now to be irreversible.

John Paul II has made of the issues typical of the third moment one of the more frequent themes of his social teaching and has consistently referred them, too, to the social and cultural contexts of the United States and Western Europe. In spite of the growing importance of the local churches, especially through regional episcopal conferences, in a Roman Catholic Church still heavily centralized in its authority structure, the great impelling (or restraining) force for the unfolding of the consequences of the doctrine of *Dignitatis Humanae* for church-society relationships continues to be the way it is interpreted and applied by the papacy and the Roman curia. A consideration of the possibilities of the third moment of *Dignitatis Humanae,* thus, cannot but give a central place to the way the teachings of John Paul II have appropriated and developed the doctrine of the conciliar declaration on religious freedom. The analysis will reveal that the dominant tone of what has been his approach to church-society relationships and the way his magisterium has shaped the generally perceived demeanor of the church before the social and cultural challenges of the third moment, have, in great part, evolved and affirmed themselves from particular interpretations of central themes of *Dignitatis Humanae.*

The uncovering of the ongoing importance of *Dignitatis Humanae* for the role of the church in contemporary pluralistic societies will now proceed, then, with the study of selected alternative interpretations of the doctrine of the declaration and, after that, of the use and development of its teaching in the pronouncements of John Paul II.

NOTES

1. Murray 1966f, 592.
2. The comment is in continuity with a previous judgment of his, given at the end of the third session of the council: "[R]eligious freedom is not the most important issue before the Council, nor the most difficult. . . . More noteworthy is the fact that religious freedom is not the most urgent issue in the world at large today. . . . An argument about religious freedom might almost be called a distraction from the real issues at the moment. . . . It is to be hoped that the Council will quickly conclude its distracting debate on religious freedom, finish the Church's long unfinished business, and get on to the deeper issue of the effective presence of the Church in the world." Murray 1965c, 43.
3. Murray wrote his first articles on issues of religious freedom in the mid-forties. He did extensive research on church-state relations until, in 1955, his religious superiors, at the urge of Roman ecclesiastical authorities, forbade him to make any more public

statements on this topic. For a detailed account of the *affair* Murray, see Pelotte 1976. A brief outline of the succession of events can be found in Noonan 1998, 26–29; 331–33.

4. Murray 1966f, 592.
5. Murray 1994b, 193 (emphasis added). In another place, Murray combines the two formulations: "The issue of religious freedom was in itself minor. But Pope Paul VI was looking deep and far when he called the Declaration on Religious Freedom 'one of the major texts of the Council.' " Murray 1966c, 674.
6. Murray 1966f, 592–93.
7. "It was over the text of *Dignitatis Humanae* that the contest between liberalism and Catholicism was most dramatically fought at the Council." Komonchak 1994, 84. Douglass 1994 makes the case for a new and fruitful "encounter in the making" between the two intellectual traditions of Catholicism and liberalism in the American political and cultural context, in the same collection of essays.
8. For a summary of the evolution—from opposition to formal commitment—of the relation of the Catholic Church to liberal democracy, see Sigmund 1994, 217–41; 1986, 3–21. And also Hehir 1993, 15–30; Papini 1993, 47–63.
9. For a sharp denunciation of its errors, see Murray 1952b, 525–63.
10. Murray 1993b, 51–52.
11. Murray stresses the decisive role of the French experience by pointing that the Revolution came in the sequence of the equally determinant French ancien régime: "one could say without great exaggeration that for centuries the problem of Church and State has been the problem of the Church and France. And 'France' here means two things—royal absolutism and Revolution, both of which, after the French example, became international phenomena." Murray 1952a, 43–44.
12. See Steinfels 1994, 19–44.
13. This criterion of discernment would be formulated by John XXIII in a famous sentence of *Pacem in Terris,* no. 159, but, in the nineteenth century and beyond, was still far from being grasped: "It must be borne in mind, furthermore, that neither can false philosophical teachings regarding the nature, origin and destiny of the universe and of man be identified with historical movements that have economic, social, cultural, or political ends, not even when these movements have originated from those teachings and have drawn and still draw inspiration therefrom." John XXIII 1976, 235–36.
14. For the history of the formula, see Lecler 1953, 530–34.
15. Murray 1993d, an article written at the time of the second Vatican Council, gives an orderly description of the theory, from which this paragraph is a very succinct summary. See also Murray 1993b, 96–101. For a zealous defense of the theory, see Ottaviani 1953, 321–34.
16. Félix Antoine Dupanloup (1802–78), the progressive bishop of Orléans and, later, outspoken voice of the minority at Vatican I, used the formula to provide a moderate and nuanced interpretation of the *Syllabus of Errors.* See Gonnet 1994, 30–32. Dupanloup was even able to obtain a papal brief that in effect formally approved his interpretation. See Aubert 1965, 20–21.

17. This is what the fathers underlined in their message "to all those who hold temporal power" read by Cardinal Liénart at the closing of the council, on December 8, 1965: "And what does this Church ask of you after close to two thousand years of experiences of all kinds in her relations with you, the powers of the earth? What does the Church ask of you today? She tells you in one of the major documents of this Council. She asks of you only liberty, the liberty to believe and to preach her faith, the freedom to love her God and serve Him, the freedom to live and to bring to men her message of life. Do not fear her." Vatican II 1966, 730.

18. "Tolerance is a concept of the moral order. It implies a moral judgment on error and the consequent adoption of a moral attitude, based on charity, toward the good faith of those who err." Murray 1993b, 150. For a development of the contrasts between the theories based on tolerance and on religious freedom, see Murray 1965b, 131–40.

19. Murray 1966d, 566.

20. Martina 1971, 93–101.

21. This was especially the case in Italy, where the Communist Party was, for many years, close to achieving electoral majority. The demonization of international communism served the purpose of cooling down possible enthusiasms at home and keeping the political balance favorable to parties more congenial to Christian values, as was, in Italy, the Christian Democratic Party, which enjoyed great support from the Catholic hierarchy. See Riccardi 1987, 37–51.

22. Cardinal König, one of the leading figures of Vatican II, writing in the mid-eighties, defends the position that it was the Marxist-Leninist threat to religious liberty that initially prompted the declaration, giving, thus, priority of intention to the second moment. "At the Second Vatican Council the Catholic Church took a decisive step forward in its transition from defensiveness, characterized by apologetic, to a much more positive and outgoing attitude towards the world and mankind, characterized by the will to engage in discussion and collaboration. . . . This readiness to enter into dialogue can also be seen in the Declaration on Religious Freedom, *Dignitatis Humanae,* although this document is intended primarily as a defence of human rights in general, and religious freedom in particular, against the attentions of Marxist-Leninist régimes." König 1986, 284.

23. Murray, for instance, had already very much in mind the communist threat when he was still trying to break open the traditional Catholic church-state problematic. See Murray 1954b, 11–32. The same threat was also an important factor in the conciliar debates on religious freedom. See Murray 1993d, 129; O'Donnell 1992, 411.

24. Paul VI 1967, 275.

25. For the style of ecclesial resistance to state power in Eastern Europe in this phase, see Hehir 1996, 114–15.

26. See, for the way the events of the late sixties and early seventies prompted Paul VI to call attention to misinterpretations and misapplications of the doctrine of *Dignitatis Humanae,* Mistò 1995, 20–23.

27. See, for example, Paul VI 1969, 53–55; 1970a, 25–28; 1970b, 183–87; 1972, 125–29.
28. An extended treatment of the issue is Paul VI 1979, 92–99. See also Paul VI 1992, 317; 1978, 547–48.
29. See Komonchak 1994, 89–95.
30. For a survey of different positions on the public role of religion within current liberal democratic theory, see Hollenbach, 1991, 1993.
31. See the widely commented essays Huntington 1991a, 1993. Each was then expanded into a book: Huntington 1991b, 1996. Also Kepel 1994. For the coexistence of processes of "deprivatization" (revival of the public role of religion) with the tendency toward privatization, see Casanova 1994.
32. Ratzinger 1996, 309, 311–17.
33. Komonchak 1994 elects the opposition to the privatization of religion as the common thread of all Catholic condemnations of liberalism since the French Revolution.
34. Sigmund 1994, 235 points out the dangers of lumping all liberals into the camp of "procedural" or "non-value" liberalism, indiscriminately accusing all contemporary liberalism of being relativistic and skeptical, and loosing sight of substantial points of agreement with many of the liberal tendencies. This would be a rerun of the unfortunate nineteenth-century identification by the church of all and everything in liberalism with the Jacobinic brand behind the French Revolution.
35. For the way this tension and shifting of attitudes was present in the Synod of Bishops of 1985, see Ruggieri 1986, 131–37. On the same topic, Tillard, commenting on the final report of the synod, points to a movement toward *inwardness,* correcting the "opening up effected at Vatican II." And then he points, at the end of the text hereafter quoted, to the reception of *Dignitatis Humanae* as a central issue of this whole matter: "The document as a whole is strongly marked by a tendency to centre the Church *in itself*. . . the emphasis is no longer that of Vatican II, disposed rather to take the risks associated with 'dialogue', cooperation, welcoming questions, and 'sympathy' (in the etymological sense) with all men and women who try to release humankind from harsh suffering. It is significant, for instance, that the declaration *Dignitatis Humanae* on religious freedom is not referred to. . . ." Tillard 1986, 70.
36. There were other geographical contexts in which religious freedom was also an issue for the Catholic Church (e.g., Latin America, the case of Mexico in particular, and Eastern Europe), but none had been originally as relevant for the creation of this predicament of the church, nor was any other more influential in the framing of *Dignitatis Humanae* than these two. After that, although the second moment shifted attention to a different part of the world, the agenda of the third moment focused again primarily on problems typical of these same Western societies. This work, therefore, will confine its analysis to the interactions of the social, political, and ecclesiastical contexts of the United States and Western Europe, with especial attention to the specificity of Latin Europe.
37. This thesis was defended by Moody 1953, 10. More recently, the same assertion was made by Casanova 1994.
38. See, for one of his more extended discussions of the contrasts between the two

political traditions of continental Europe and the United States, Murray 1953, 145–214.

39. See Murray 1952a, 43–48.

40. See Murray 1967a, 668–76. And, for a detailed report on all interventions in favor of religious freedom made by Americans at the council, Yzermans 1967, 617–42. Gremillion 1982 gives a summary of the origins and development of the theology of religious freedom in North America. For the history of the tensions between the American church and Rome on this topic, see Fogarty 1986.

41. There was strong resistance to the development of doctrine on religious freedom in the United States too, both in the hierarchy and in the theological community (see, for the American opposition to Murray, Pelotte 1976, chapters 1 and 2), as there also were committed promoters of the same development in France or Italy. When I contrast the United States with Latin Europe, I am not claiming uniformity and exclusiveness. What I am pointing at are prevalent public attitudes, especially on the part of the hierarchies, favorable leanings pro or con, based more on historical experiences than on theological groundwork, that generally predisposed these churches either to fear or to welcome the change.

42. Jiménez-Urresti 1966 illustrates how reluctantly the changes mandated by the council were heeded by many Spanish Catholics; he even attempts a revisionist interpretation of *Dignitatis Humanae,* which would legitimize the strict intolerance of the standing Spanish constitutional arrangement. For the evolution of the juridical status of the Catholic Church in Spain in this century, see Hughey 1981. For historical background and an evaluative account, see Casanova 1994, 75–91.

43. For the support of the post-conciliar Portuguese church to a new legal status of non-Catholic confessions, see Leite 1970. Leite 1978, 265–320 gives a brief history of the constitutional arrangements on church-state relationships in Portugal. See also Braga da Cruz 1991a, 1991b.

44. For the way the different patterns of modern decline of religion in Western Europe and no decline in the United States may be explained by different traditions of church-state relationships, see Casanova 1994, 26–32; 213–15. The differences of the two conditions of secularization, as it is seen from a European perspective, can be summarized in the contrasted concepts of "cultural secularity" *(laïcité culturelle)* and "civil religion," characteristic of the social and political status of religion in Western Europe and the United States, respectively. See Willaime, 1994 and Marienstras 1994.

45. For a general summary of the encounter of Catholicism with American liberal republicanism, see Gleason 1994. In spite of the hostility of what Gleason calls "the American form of sectarian liberalism," the assault suffered by the Catholic Church in America cannot be compared to what has happened in Latin Europe.

46. See Hehir 1996, 107–19.

Two ❧

Interpretations of *Dignitatis Humanae:* Circumstantial Factors and Essential Conclusions

The declaration of Vatican II on religious freedom had a long and tortuous process of elaboration. The way to its final approval was paved with spirited arguments, constant tensions, and skillful tactical maneuvering and countermaneuvering by disagreeing factions. At each stage of the discussions there were groups opposed to each other on the basis of entrenched conflicting views, either on the fundamental goals or on the methodologies. It was necessary at first to overcome the impasses created by the clash of two irreconcilable approaches to the issue: the vocal and powerful group who objected to any development of the standing official doctrine of the church on religious freedom as it had been expressed by the nineteenth-century popes on one side, and, on the other side, the group—finally, the overwhelming majority—who wanted to overcome the limitations and liabilities of the thesis/hypothesis theory.

But then, among the majority favorable to an unequivocal recognition of the right to religious freedom, there were also, during the redaction of the declaration, divergences at other levels. In terms of what kind of pronouncement it should be, some thought that it would be better just to make a pastoral statement, without presenting any doctrinal justifications for it. This position was quickly rejected. Next, there was disagreement about the kinds of justifications that should be advanced. The division was mainly between those who defended the primacy of strictly theological arguments starting from Scripture and those who gave priority to arguments of political philosophy and natural-law ethics.

In the end, the document was the result of many compromises. Only that way could an overwhelming majority finally adopt a text that was the object of so much controversy. Once it was clear that the declaration had already guaranteed the support of the majority, the commission charged with the final redaction elected as a goal to win approval by the greatest possible number of the conciliar fathers. That had actually been the policy of the leading sponsors of the document all through the years of discussion of the successive drafts (maybe because they initially felt they were on the weaker side in terms of the balance of power in the council): As long as their essential goals were not compromised, there was openness to concessions in order to diffuse possible obstruction based on less nuclear questions. Even in the very final stages of the process, they continued to accept suggested corrections, which qualified statements or, in the area of the justifications offered for the right to religious freedom, added concurrent arguments to the text.

The final text was a declaration for which, with the exception of the intractable conservative minority, no other significant group could justify an unfavorable vote. Not only were all the groups in basic (and for many, enthusiastic) agreement with the fundamental statement of the declaration, but each could also find in the text some kind of acceptable reference to their own preferred ways of justifying and framing the endorsement of the civil right to religious freedom by the Roman Catholic Church. Even if the views of some had not been completely received, they had at least been recognized.

However, if all were sufficiently pleased with the document to give it their approval, nobody was totally satisfied with it. It was not the ideal of any one group. *Dignitatis Humanae* signified and effected a momentous change in the official position of the Roman Catholic Church in a very short time. The initial promoters were able to marshal widespread support for the central object of the declaration among the fathers of the council, but there had not been enough time to work out a deeper confluence of views about the best ways of formulating and justifying it. In the end, most were pleased with the practical change operated by the council, but many among these had reservations about this or that aspect of the text itself, be it the general methodology and type of language used, the hierarchy of the arguments grounding the right, the insufficient attention given to one point or another, or even the presence of statements about which they had serious misgivings.

Right after the council, the interpretations and commentaries on the declaration by the major contributors to the process of formulation and redaction continued to wrestle with the unresolved issues. Because of their dissatisfaction with aspects of the text, particular care was taken in recounting the story of the redaction in order to explain the origin and, thus, the weight of the general options and the more controversial phrases. Everyone looked to establish a general hermeneutical key for the whole of the document, under which some passages would be relativized and others stressed. On another front, though, and balancing this attention to the genesis of the text, there were also efforts to advance quickly the theology of religious freedom beyond the council's formulations.

In reporting the debates that took place during the conciliar process, two main approaches, or schools, have been commonly identified within the majority. One—ultimately the one that prevailed in the overall structure of the declaration and in the basic conceptual definitions—was personified in John Courtney Murray. The other, the French school, referred to a group of French-speaking theologians. In the aftermath of Vatican II, these two views continued to distinguish themselves in their ways of dealing with the document.

Murray looked at *Dignitatis Humanae* primarily as a stepping stone, a resolution of a significant but quite limited question that had long been an obstacle for the church's effective confrontation of far more urgent and important challenges. Basically, he stressed the relevance of the declaration's fundamental statement, and looked forward to developing further implications of the change in ecclesial attitude regarding religious freedom and to seeing the church engage the new opportunities created by *Dignitatis Humanae*. In his short life after the end of the council, however, he could not go much beyond commenting on the text, mostly giving his evaluation of the stated arguments, defending his conceptual and methodological options, and trying to clarify points that, in his view, could actually be a source of ambiguity.

The French school was less satisfied with the approved text. Concerned with the methodology and the doctrinal justifications, they considered that the essential content of the declaration still needed more compelling and complete theological grounding. Thus, having more than just an interest in exploring the implications of the actual text, they tried to develop a theology that might serve as the supportive framework and larger background for the stated right. Without questioning the basic assertion of *Dignitatis Humanae,* they tended to highlight those passages more according to their views and use them as a basis to make a stronger case for their own approach.

This dominant concentration on limited contrasting partial elements, aided by the external context of the second moment—which, by itself, induced another kind of particularized and limited focus on the declaration—has meant less attention to the interpretation of the whole of *Dignitatis Humanae,* its intricacies, complications, and maybe apparent contradictions. The declaration on religious freedom of Vatican II certainly did not present clear solutions for all the issues it confronted. However, the whole complexity and even occasional ambiguity of the document, which resulted from the encounter of different perspectives and goals not always put together seamlessly, is not such an insurmountable obstacle to finding in the declaration clear doctrinal direction. Parallel and, perhaps, even apparently conflicting remarks responding to the same basic question may sometimes seem to be difficult to keep together. From another perspective, though, these tensions in the text may be taken together in combination as attempts at setting boundaries by defining the unacceptable extremes. This way, the result can function as a set of guidelines to point to what is to be rejected and what is to be upheld in similarly conflictive situations, even if the way of doing both of these things harmoniously is not indicated by the declaration. The challenge to find the continued relevance of *Dignitatis Humanae* has to pass through an honest confrontation of the tensions and ambiguities of the document itself, but it also has to move beyond them. The promise of greater fruitfulness rests with a hermeneutical approach that looks primarily to identify in the text the unifying dominant thrusts and the fundamental doctrinal options affirmed by the council, looking to uncover ever richer and broader implications.

This chapter will deal first with accomplished interpretations of *Dignitatis Humanae* that represent the different approaches to the text and the issue of religious freedom. It will conclude by summarizing the fundamental assertions made by the declaration, setting them as bases for inferences to be applied in presently controversial areas of the social mission of the church, beyond the issue of the civil right to religious freedom.

John Courtney Murray: The Focus on the Juridical

John Courtney Murray had a determinant role in the redaction of the declaration.[1] The definition of the object and content of the civil right to religious freedom in *Dignitatis Humanae* is mainly due to him and fully consecrated his views. However, after the council he had serious questions about the actual way in which *Dignitatis Humanae* made the argument to ground this human right and to justify the church's recognition of it. In the essays in which he more systematically deals with this question, he is careful to distinguish the two aspects: The affirmation of the human right to religious freedom by the Vatican II declaration is "clear, distinct and technically exact" but the "more difficult question of how to construct the argument—whether derived from reason or from revelation—that will give a solid foundation to what the Declaration affirms" is not satisfactorily resolved in the document—"[T]his argument has pleased or pleases no one in all respects."[2] Murray thought, nevertheless, that "it was altogether necessary that the Declaration should make an argument,"[3] even if it would be very difficult to find general unquestioned support for one, since the discussion, regarding the arguments to ground the right, was still, in his opinion, far from having reached widespread points of agreement.[4]

THE ARGUMENTS IN *DIGNITATIS HUMANAE*

To understand his critique, it is crucial to note how he defines the question at stake. In the twofold immunity from coercion that constitutes the right to religious freedom as it is defined by *Dignitatis Humanae* (not to be compelled to act against one's conscience and not to be impeded from acting according to one's conscience), Murray remarks that only the second immunity was historically problematic for the church in the time before *Dignitatis Humanae*. So he evaluates the arguments by the criterion of whether or not they successfully warrant this second immunity.

The argument from the duty to follow the dictates of one's conscience even if erroneous, central in the first two drafts of the declaration, is thus rejected. The reason is that "from one human being's erroneous conscience no duty follows for others."[5] This moral argument does not demonstrate the incompetence of the state to prevent people from acting according to their erroneous consciences in matters religious.

Equally insufficient is the first argument proposed by *Dignitatis Humanae*, in the second paragraph of number 2: the attempt to ground ontologically the right to religious freedom on the universal human obligation to search for the truth. Again, Murray considers that "man's natural and moral links to truth [are not] powerful enough to engender a political relationship between the human person and the public power so that the latter is duty-bound not to prevent the person from acting according to his conscience."[6] This argument

> does not deserve the fundamental place in the structure of a demonstration of the right to religious freedom. The reason is that it fails to yield the necessary and crucial political conclusion, namely, that government is not empowered, save in the exceptional case, to hinder men or religious communities from public witness, worship, practice, and observance in accordance with their own convictions.[7]

On this argument alone, therefore, there is still space for the state to evoke the defense of society from error and so repress the public expression of beliefs it judges to be erroneous without impeding the continuation of the private personal search for the truth and the acting according to the truth. The argument would not stop, for instance, either the classical Catholic confessional state or a communist government. In each of these cases, the government sees itself as representative of the truth, and, because of that,

> does not greatly bother about man's duty to search for the truth. They simply maintain that they already have the truth; that they represent the truth, which is also the good of the people; that consequently they are empowered to repress public manifestations of error.[8]

Actually, one may add, this repression may even be presented as a service to the common good: By preserving them from the pernicious influence of error, it ensures that people do not go astray in their search for the truth.

The second argument in *Dignitatis Humanae* is introduced in number 3. It starts from the obligation to follow divine moral law, as it is accessible to all by human conscience. The pivotal element in this justification is the appeal to the social nature of the person, which demands both that the free inquiry for the truth be made by a free exchange and discussion and that the allegiance to the religious truth acknowledged by one's conscience be not only affirmed through interior religious acts, which no human power can command or prevent, but also expressed externally and communally. Murray finds the argument begging the question. An extension of the immunity of internal acts of religion to their external counterparts, based on the necessary connection between the two, presupposes that, just as no human power can force human conscience, "in society no power exists with authority reaching far enough to warrant its legitimately forbidding public acts of religion, even acts that transgress objective truth or divine law or even the common good."[9] But, in his interpretation, this is precisely what the argument needs to establish. One more time, the appeal to the social nature of the person in the context of the obligation to search for and follow the truth, by itself, does not establish the incompetence of the state to interfere with public expressions of religious convictions; rather it presupposes it.

Finally, in the last paragraph of number 3, introduced almost as an afterthought, the declaration proposes a third argument. It states that, because the acts of religion (both private and public) belong to a transcendent order, they are above the competence of the state, which is restricted to the earthly and temporal level. For Murray "this political argument is of primary importance. Without it any other argument would not sufficiently settle the question."[10] This way of grounding the personal right to religious freedom on the limits of public power had been his favorite all along. The third draft, of which he was the main redactor, introduced it as the basic argument and set the document on a basis substantially different from that of the previous drafts.[11] In the later stages of the redaction, though, a phase in which he, for health reasons, could not actively participate, this argument was relegated to a secondary place and others were shifted to more prominent positions or even added to the text.

In Murray's evaluation, "the final text of the Declaration is inadequate in its treatment of the limitations imposed on government by sound political doctrine."[12] It does bring itself to make the assertion of the incompetence of the state on religious matters but does not explicitly provide reasons for it.[13] The essential, however, is secured in the whole of the document: there are clear enough statements on the "essentially juridical function of government" (number 6) and on the limitation of its competence to the temporal sphere (number 3) that allow Murray to say that *Dignitatis Humanae* presents a political doctrine of which the most significant element is the

> disavowal of the long-standing view of government as sacral in function, that is, as invested with the function of defending and promoting religious truth as such. . . . In this development the function of government appears as the protection and promotion, not of religious truth, but of religious freedom as a fundamental right of the human person.[14]

Faced with this limitation, Murray, then, in his commentaries, undertakes the outlining of an in-depth reconstruction and development of the political argument for religious freedom, as it can be done from the principles stated in the declaration.[15]

MURRAY'S POLITICAL ARGUMENT

The center point of his reasoning is that, in order to ground the civil right to religious freedom, it is necessary (and also sufficient) to establish the duty by the state "to refrain from keeping the human person from acting in religious matters according to his dignity." It is true, he acknowledges, that the right is constituted *ultimately* by the demand of both freedom and responsibility inherent to the dignity of the intellectual nature of the human person as moral subject. Such dignity requires that, in what concerns the goods of the human spirit, religion being first among them, "a person should act by his own deliberation and purpose, enjoying immunity from all external coercion so that in the presence of God he takes responsibility on himself alone for his religious decisions and acts."[16]

Inherent to human dignity there are, thus, two exigencies: personal autonomy and personal responsibility. The latter consists of conformity between the transcendent order of truth, the inner imperatives of the person's conscience, and his or her external action. In regards to the fulfillment or not of these personal responsibilities, the subjective moral dispositions of the person within the social order are, however, juridically irrelevant. "The major reason is that no authority exists within the juridical order that is capable or empowered to judge in this regard."[17] Because of his concern with the argument of the incompetence of the state, Murray leaves behind the implications of the personal responsibility aspect and focuses exclusively on the other exigency of human dignity.

What undeniably is juridically relevant, according to the same judgment, is the element of personal autonomy. This exigence, that the person act on her own initiative and responsibility according to her nature, constitutes the basic ontological foundation of the right to religious freedom, and defines it, thus, originally as a basic demand of immunity from coercion. Such demand lays a moral claim on others to abstain from coercion but "a right, as a moral claim on others, is not fully constituted, until it is established that no one else may validly enter a counterclaim—in our case, legitimately to invade an asserted immunity."[18] Therefore, the immunity from restraints to acting according to one's religious beliefs is *actually* guaranteed as an objective right only when it is juridically established in society, only when it is recognized and constitutionally acknowledged under the form of a limit upon the power of the state. Only then is the public power bound to respect that immunity.

The issue then, in practical terms, is political, not moral. "The question is, whether some special characteristic or attribute attaches to government that empowers it to repress erroneous religious opinions or practices from public life. And if not, on what principle is this power denied to government?"[19] Murray points to two principles stated in the declaration: the political principle of the free society ("as much freedom as possible, and only as much restraint as necessary") and the juridical principle of equality before the law ("all men are equal by reason of their natural dignity"). Murray claims that while neither the argument from the obligation to search after the truth nor the argument from the social nature of the person proposed by *Dignitatis Humanae* successfully justifies the right to religious freedom as the declaration defines it in its twofold immunity, his political argument, developed from these two principles, provides solid ground for it, especially for the second immunity.

> These two principles, political and juridical, furnish the solution to the political issue raised by the question of religious freedom as the immunity of the person from coercive restraint of action in accordance with his own beliefs. Together they require that government should be "constitutional."[20]

A Narrow Delimitation of the Issue

The critique by Murray of the arguments grounding the personal right to religious freedom spells out one of the most important reasons for his reservations regarding the final text of *Dignitatis Humanae.* But the discussion also makes explicit how extremely focused his way of defining the problem at stake was. Plus, behind this strict delimitation of the question are disclosed the main motivations of his deliberate approach to the challenge of developing the nineteenth-century official position of the Roman Catholic Church on the right to religious freedom.

Murray purposely compacts the issue into a narrow kernel in order to focus the question, sharpen the argument, and avoid the pitfalls of complex interrelated controversies. He defines the right to religious freedom as an immunity with two dimensions, then underscores that it is only the second immunity that is still problematic, and finally circumscribes the hindrance from which this immunity needs to be protected against to the juridically warranted claim of interference by the power of the state.[21] The core issue at stake was the Catholic doctrine that, in particular (ideal) sociological conditions, the government could and ought to restrict the rights of public expression of other religious confessions. Murray restricts his argument against that presumption to the ambit of the juridical relationship between the persons in society and the state, a relationship in which the rights of these persons impose a duty upon the state.

Such strategy is summarized in his statement that "to establish, then, that the human person enjoys a right to full religious freedom, one must *first* establish that the public power has no right to restrict religious freedom but has rather the duty to acknowledge and protect it." He moves, thus, the focus of attention from the first part of the sentence to the second in such a way that he can say not just that now "the inquiry is not about the moral but about the juridical order" but even conclude more forcefully that "clearly our inquiry, although of its nature ethico-juridical, is nevertheless finally and formally political, or what is called constitutional. By this I mean that it deals with the duties and rights of the public power—their nature, their extent, and their limits."[22] Murray's heuristic option locates the decisive discussion squarely in the camp of political philosophy. It is from the declaration's political principles that he will evaluate the efficacy of all arguments and the pertinence of objections.[23]

The civil right to religious freedom as an immunity is constituted by the conjunction of a right of the person with the correspondent duty on the part of the state. Murray concentrates his attention on the side of the state. The essential term of the juridical relationship is its passive subject, the civil power.[24] This way, although his ultimate starting point is the dignity of the human person, in terms of the civil right to religious freedom, he does not try to ground it immediately on the natural impetus and entitlements of the person in matters of religious faith, which would demand, then, respect and support from the state in order to be fulfilled and expressed. Instead, he supports the personal right on the intrinsic limitations of the power of the state, incompetent to judge and, therefore, to repress or authenticate personal religious options and actions. Rather than pointing out that the person's conscientious choice does not allow for interference, he asserts that the public power has no political competence, and, thus, should not have juridically recognized capacity to interfere. He describes the immunity as a juridical definition of a sphere of human activity protected from "coercive intrusion from without," but secures the inviolability of that sphere by stressing the constitutional impossibility for the state to intrude in it.[25] The argument for the universal right to religious freedom almost resolves itself in a defense of the constitutional government.

This strategy, as convenient and appropriate to deal with the concrete historical situation as it may have been, also gives rise to some questions. One is whether this restricted definition covers all the possible threats to religious freedom in society. Even if the state's juridical power is the pivotal aspect, it seems that there are other ways and other powers that are capable of hindering the second immunity. Murray himself suggested so at times.[26] By concentrating the claim almost exclusively on one passive subject of the right (the juridical order of the state), such support of the right may be a weaker instrument to defend and promote freedom of the person against other threats, either not juridically backed or not from the state. Another problem with this approach is that it seems to make the effective upholding of the right to religious freedom dependent on the existence of one particular form of government, constitutional democracy.

For as long as the focus is exclusively on the potential of the state to impede the free exercise of religion, setting a categorical restraint upon the state guarantees religious freedom. However, if the capability of imposing coercion on the person in religious matters is also recognized in other powers active in society, there is a need to affirm and secure the right in a way that constrains also those other powers. To expand the consideration of threats outside the narrow area of the juridical relationship of persons and communities with the state makes it necessary to go back beyond the political and juridical principles in the direction of the ultimate foundation, the dignity of the human person, and to make its practical claims more explicit. The focus would shift again from the state to the person itself, to the defense of the individual human sphere of autonomy against any sort of threat to this immunity from coercion that may be found in society. This is the approach taken by Pietro Pavan, as we will see.

Why these methodological options? Murray offers no direct explanation. At one point, he seems to justify his insistence on the narrow juridical scope by the recognition of the crucial importance of this dimension of the problem for the whole end of religious freedom in society. In the essay in which he comes closer to attempting a clarification of this tension in his argument, he says that, "in its juridical sense as a human right, religious freedom is a functional or instrumental concept." It is, therefore, at the service of a larger goal, the actual living in fullness of the ultimate purposes of human freedom, which reaches beyond the ambit of the juridical relationship between persons or communities and the state.

> The function of religious freedom as a legal institution embodying a civil right . . . is to create and maintain a constitutional situation, and to that extent *to favor and foster a social climate,* within which the citizen and the religious community may pursue the higher ends of human existence without let or hindrance by other citizens, by social groups, or by government itself.[27]

This elucidation assures that the emphasis on the juridical will not be harmful to the final extensive goal, but it does not explain the preoccupation with the narrowing of the question to which he devoted a greater effort. I suggest two (certainly interrelated) lines of exploration for the reasons that moved John Courtney Murray: the situation of the Roman Catholic Church, and the historical and political context of Murray's life and ministry.

AN OPTION OF ECCLESIASTICAL PRUDENCE

The development of the Catholic doctrine on the right to religious freedom faced a long and hard resistance within the church. Many controversial theological issues were implicated in the discussion, each adding different possibilities for doctrinal objection by those opposed to any change. The greater the distance kept from not yet settled theological polemics and the simpler the formulation and arguing of the question, the greater would be the chances of gathering consensual acceptance. Murray understood this very well, and so he tried to define the issue in as restricted and indisputable a way as possible.[28] By moving from the moral to the juridical order and by stating the argument more in terms of political philosophy than theological anthropology, he distanced the debate from the ineffective controversies about the rights of the erroneous conscience (still the main argument in the first two drafts at the council), and avoided the problems of the relation between Christian freedom and civil freedom[29] and of personal freedom within the church.[30] He realized that it would be easier for the church to accept the desired change, once it was presented as a change in the social and political doctrine espoused by the church, rather than in its own ecclesiology or ethics. A somewhat "external" argument had greater chances of breaking open the entanglements of the official position of the church with its own traditional theological principles and methodologies.

In fact, all along, the primary challenge for those arguing for the right was to convince the church itself, especially those powerful conservative circles more attached to a static understanding of the nineteenth-century papal teaching. In the world, there was a general presupposition for the truth of the teaching of the declaration: the civil right to religious freedom was already "supported by the sense and near unanimous consent of the human race."[31] The arguments were more a way to clarify and strengthen support. They were actually not so much trying to convince the world of something new, as they were attempting to make a case within the church for the acceptance and formal adoption of already common views on human rights. In as much as it addressed secular society, however, the task of the declaration, if there was one, was to construct a credible, unequivocal statement, capable of abating suspicions and prejudices and opening doors to ecumenical and social dialogue. A language and logic based on common reason were, therefore, very important for this communication.[32] It happened that it was also the best available means to construct the new teaching, owing to the insufficiency of direct support for religious freedom in Christian revelation, as *Dignitatis Humanae* itself recognizes, and the lack of consensus in Catholic theology about ways of constructing a strictly theological claim for the civil right.[33]

Murray, starting many years before the council and through the council itself, painstakingly researched, developed, and refined his argument for religious freedom, looking for the most effective way to steer the church beyond the limitations of its own traditional teaching without openly antagonizing it. In spite of serious setbacks, he was able to sidestep within the Catholic Church the most serious obstacles, and, finally, his basic approach and many of his methodological options were incorporated in the conciliar document. The search for what he thought was the best argument but also the ecclesiastical tactics of finding the most effective argument in the concrete circumstances of the time drove many of his methodological choices. In addition, there is still another factor equally crucial to explain his approach: his own experience and understanding of the North American social and political context.

The Influence of American Constitutionalism

If there was another issue besides religious freedom to which Murray dedicated special attention in his thinking and writing, it was the Catholic posture before the American constitutional tradition. Facing anti-Catholic prejudices from large sectors of the American society and an official Catholic doctrine (which an American Catholic minority did not cease to recall) that formally questioned the principles of the First Amendment, Murray committed himself to show that there was no incompatibility between fidelity to the American Constitution on one side, and adherence to the Catholic tradition and an active presence of the Catholic Church in American society on the other. American Catholics, for reasons of their faith, were not lesser American citizens nor were they in any way interested in subverting the Constitution. In fact, the Catholic tradition had much to offer to the strengthening of the American consensus.[34]

The kind of focusing of his religious freedom argument served positively the goals of his involvement in the debate about the American constitutional tradition on church and state. To bring the Catholic Church to declare officially a political doctrine of limited government as the decisive argument grounding the immunity of human persons from any interference by political powers of the public expression of their religious faith was in fact equivalent to making it espouse one of the fundamental tenets of the American constitutional tradition.[35] The denial by American Catholics that they would consider desirable the enlisting of the power of the state at the service of their religious faith against believers of other faiths was now not just shakily grounded on their vowed unwillingness to do so even if, in a hypothetical circumstance, they could. It became firmly supported, instead, on the clear profession by the universal Catholic Church of the position of principle that, in order to respect the dignity of the human person, the state cannot, in any circumstance, assume that function.

Even more determinant for Murray's reliance on the political argument was the remarkable flourishing of immigrant Catholicism in America. Speaking of the crucial support offered to the declaration by the North American bishops, he explains that such "support derived its basic inspiration from the American experience, from which the Church has learned the practical value of the free-exercise clause of the First Amendment."[36] American Catholics knew first hand how a political arrangement of constitutional separation of church and state under the principle of limited government, instead of being an obstacle, had actually been a very positive context for the church's mission. It guaranteed religious freedom for all, and, at the same time, provided the Catholic Church with every freedom it needed for its ministry. What had served the Catholic Church in America so well could serve too as an inspiration for the universal church. Murray makes no secret about the sources of the concepts for which he fought at the council (and before) and which eventually prevailed in the declaration.

> The technical definition of religious freedom as an idea and as a legal institution has long been established in the literature of constitutionalism. The definition is commonly accepted, and it is not only technically correct from

> a juridical point of view but also unexceptionable from a moral point of view. Religious freedom is freedom from coercion; it is an immunity; its content is negative. Historically, the First Amendment to the Constitution of the United States launched this conception.[37]

If that is where it found direct inspiration, it is no surprise that Murray would affirm that "the object or content of the right to religious freedom, as specified both in the Declaration and in the American constitutional system, is identical."[38]

The theoretical borrowing was not opportunistic or arbitrary, but justified by the historical Christian roots of the American tradition. In fact, the American constitutional experience had been uniquely faithful to the "organic development of the liberal tradition of the West, whose matrix was the Christian and medieval doctrine of man," in which were already present the ideas of inalienable rights of the individual derived "from his personal dignity as disclosed by the Christian revelation."[39] British history and, much more, French revolutionary theory failed to recognize religious freedom as one of these rights. But,

> the development was again set on its right course, and fuller formulation was given to the right to religious freedom, by the American constitutional system. Caught in the more disastrous aberrations derivative from the French Revolution, the Church long failed to recognize the validity of the American development of what was, in fact, her own tradition. The Declaration accords the belated recognition.[40]

Of course, for Murray and the American bishops it was easier to rely solely on the strength of the political argument. They were living in a situation in which the church had every reason to trust the power of constitutional guarantees to support its freedom and protect the rights of citizens to practice their faith. The American separation of church and state was not set against a legacy of instrumental use of the public power by the church, nor was there much precedent to fear that the state, moved by antireligious ideologies, could be led to interfere, directly or indirectly, with religious convictions and practices of persons and communities.

This was far from being the case in some other places, especially in Latin Europe. The reigning political philosophies and constitutional practices in continental Europe had been much less inspiring and trustworthy in this regard than their American counterparts. Here, separation had very recently meant serious attacks on the freedom of the church by secularist governments.[41] While the issue, for the American context, was primarily to dismiss polemic insinuations of hypothetical Catholic menaces to a solidly established freedom of religion and separation between church and state, in a place like France, for instance, the first preoccupation was still to defend the freedom of the church from undue interference by the public power. In a context of a very interventionist state and of a society where anticlerical forces had significant power, it was more difficult to trust the political argument à la Murray to ground the right to religious freedom.

There was, thus, a very important historical-geographical factor behind the disagreements about the best arguments to be appealed to in *Dignitatis Humanae.* "The conciliar Fathers were oddly reluctant to make much use of the political argument for religious freedom, scil., from the notion of limited constitutional government; they seem to have considered it 'too American.' "[42]

The French School versus the American School

This difference of historical and political sensitivities crystallized in a division between two schools, the "American" and the "French." While both equally supported the proclamation of the right to religious freedom, they disagreed on what would be the best way of explaining and grounding it. The lines of division showed most visibly in the attempts by the French to have a more positive definition of the object of the right (against Murray's, and the declaration's, strict immunity) and also in their reiterated preference for a doctrinal starting point in revelation and a more theological kind of exposition.

The differences did not cease with the approval of the declaration. Actually, much of Murray's commentary on the declaration, especially his defense of the primacy and indispensability of the political argument, was done in contrast to the positions of the French school. In turn, in the aftermath of the council, French-speaking theologians continued to manifest their disagreements with central tenets of Murray's approach.

In their accounts of the genesis of the document and their commentaries on the text, they lamented the small reception of their more theologically and scripturally rich views. Jérôme Hamer, at the end of his historical account of the process of redaction of *Dignitatis Humanae,* summarizes the French feeling of disappointment. He speaks about "missed opportunities" and approves of the questions posed by some: Why didn't the council give a positive definition of religious freedom and why didn't it try to ground it in Scripture? Although he agrees that this could have been possible, in terms for instance of the reciprocity of consciences, he also concedes that neither of these approaches had yet reached theological maturity to be accepted by the council. Still, what the council settled for, he concludes, works as "a source of a new dynamism" for further research on what it was not able to agree upon.[43]

French-speaking theologians took this clue more decisively than any others. Some eventually published systematic theological treatments of religious freedom, in which they attempted to clarify, complement, and expand the doctrinal content of *Dignitatis Humanae* according to the lines of the French approach.

Murray, on the other hand, continued to recognize explicitly these lines of fraction in his commentaries but tried primarily and from several different perspectives to uncover the deeper roots of discord and to point to some of their larger implications. The appropriation of *Dignitatis Humanae* has thus maintained alive the contrast of positions between these two characteristic approaches to religious freedom that vied for prominence during the council.

The Preference for a Theology of Religious Freedom Grounded in Scripture

The place of Scripture in the arguments to justify the right to religious freedom was a particular point of contention between Murray and his French counterparts. Philippe Delhaye, an active participant in the council and commentator of *Dignitatis Humanae,* accuses Murray of some stubbornness in this regard. In the preface to the long and in-depth postconciliar study on religious freedom by René Coste, he praises the author for giving priority to revelation over philosophy (inverting thus the order of the arguments in the declaration), for practicing a Christian ethic that gives priority to faith over natural law. And he immediately decries Murray for having resisted suggestions in the same direction:

> How many times haven't we said this same kind of thing to certain members of the Secretariat for Unity, responsible for the declaration on religious freedom. But the most active among them, Fr. Courtney Murray, did not want to listen. Moral teaching had to be based on natural law and he could not see how to include the gospel in it.[44]

We can see here how the disagreement about the order in which the argument for religious freedom should preferably be founded and expressed was clearly influenced by a larger debate about the relationship between Christian faith and moral theology, a particularly active discussion that took place before and after the council among moral theologians.

Murray is well aware of the critique. In his treatment of the issue of religious freedom he opted to "sharply accent the notion itself as a juridical notion whose immediate foundations are in the order of reason." That, he recognizes, opens himself to a criticism he rejects. The French-speaking school contested his approach, he says, because its

> proponents are not content to defend religious freedom simply as a juridical notion. To do this, they say, would be to fail to pursue the matter *à fond*. . . . They wish therefore, to radicate religious freedom in religion itself—concretely, in the Scriptures, and in the traditional doctrine of the necessary freedom of Christian faith. Moreover, they feel—perhaps a bit confusedly—that a conciliar statement on the subject should be theological in tone. It should draw primarily on the sources of faith, not be content simply with rational argument, and not assign the primacy to rational argument.[45]

The study by René Coste is avowedly a forceful attempt to radicate religious freedom in Scripture. He does not see *Dignitatis Humanae* as having provided a definitive response but rather simply as a starting point setting up further work for theologians.[46] He feels even a certain dissatisfaction with it, convinced as he is that the church had available much richer resources in revelation.[47] Although he recognizes reasons to opt for a priority to natural reasoning (it was addressing all humanity not only Christians), he still believes that even the goal of dialogue would have been better served if the council had stated up front the implicit theology and evangelical inspiration behind its rational thinking, thus reversing the order of the two parts of *Dignitatis Humanae*.[48] In accordance with this view, Coste proposes, then, a thorough theology of religious freedom. While the council limited itself to the consequences in the political realm, he will attempt a complete synthesis dealing also with the philosophical, historical, psychological, sociological, and pastoral aspects of religious freedom. But it will be an ethic not just philosophic or humanistic but, rather, Christian and evangelical, entirely based on the demands of the word of God.[49] His starting point will be Trinitarian *agape,* primal source of religious freedom through the commandments of love of God and neighbor.[50] He wants to distinguish himself from other theologians who keep dealing with religious freedom by reasoning essentially as philosophers and jurists.[51] His study is not a commentary on the declaration but an attempt to go beyond it, methodologically and in content, into a systematic theological treatment of the topic, including a full historical survey and explanation of the issues in the past experience of the church.

From his reading of the whole Bible,[52] Coste is able to uncover the basic principle for religious freedom, that human beings ought to respect the freedom of conscience of other people because God does the same. This is a lesson learned already from the Old Testament,[53] developed in an insurmountably eloquent way by the practice and the teaching of Jesus[54] and continued by the apostolic church. Through the priority given to the data of Scripture, he recovers the concept of freedom of conscience in the act of faith as the starting point and anchorage for all reflection on religious freedom, the approach favored in the first two drafts of *Dignitatis Humanae.* For him, "freedom of conscience is the absolute and sacred core of religious freedom."[55] It is significative that the subtitle of the book is *Liberté de conscience, liberté de religion.*

Coste concludes that it is evident in Scripture, at least in the New Testament, that the word of God demands freedom of conscience and freedom of religion.[56] Why, then, did many argue, and the council heed, that revelation does not establish the right to religious freedom? He blames an interpretation of Scripture constricted by a restrictive conception of the literal meaning of texts and argues for the notion of a "*sens plénier de la Révélation,*" a "convergence of meaning" from different texts all pointing in the same direction, which allows, as he claims to have shown, the grounding of religious freedom in Scripture. The problem with this heuristic process is that he does not seem to be able to dispel the suspicion that the search for such "convergence of meaning" is guided by principles already previously defined. Scripture, then, through a choice of the texts and the setting up of interactions between them, would be called to support what, in truth, had been formulated on nonscriptural bases. If this is true, ultimately Coste would not be doing with his revelation-grounded theology of religious freedom much more than *Dignitatis Humanae* did. It is worth noticing as time and again his analyses conclude with an exact endorsement by Scripture of the statements of the conciliar declaration.[57]

In the end, although he concedes that the *civil* right to religious freedom is not explicitly prescribed in revelation, he refuses to admit that revelation does not categorically affirm a *fundamental* human right to religious freedom,[58] which he, however, describes in a way that does not equally reassure both sides of the twofold immunity of Murray's definition of the right—not to be compelled to act against one's conscience and not to be impeded from acting according to one's conscience. And the one that comes out on the weakest side is precisely the latter, the immunity that is most at issue—the freedom to express one's beliefs.[59]

In spite of all his effort it does not seem that René Coste has been successful in presenting a specifically theological, scriptural argument for religious freedom able to question the contention of *Dignitatis Humanae,* number 9, that "revelation does not affirm the right of immunity from external coercion in religious affairs in so many words." In the end, although he adamantly defends a theological approach from revelation, it appears that his goal is not so much to do away with the rational approach in favor of an exclusively scriptural basis, but rather a mere inversion of the order of the two parts of *Dignitatis Humanae*. It is much more a matter of primacy than of exclusivity. In the first part of the book about foundations, the two chapters on Scripture are followed by a third dedicated to a rational and philosophical treatment of religious freedom, following the several arguments proposed by the first part of *Dignitatis Humanae* to ground the right to religious freedom. Here, he balances some of his previous stronger statements against the method and language of the declaration and puts the two approaches as complementary and necessary.[60]

Although he tries to distance himself from the methodology and the kind of reasoning privileged by Murray to justify the adoption by the church of the right to religious freedom, it is clearly apparent that Coste reaches the same substantive conclusions and stresses very much the same consequences that Murray does. The disagreement is centered on the means of reasoning and explaining, but there is almost no argument about essential conclusions or established results. The debate is more about pastoral strategies, rhetorical preferences, and lines of epistemological development in the discipline of moral theology.

Whenever Murray acknowledged these opposing views, he tried to defend his position primarily by explaining the root causes of the disagreements. For him, the really important differences had to do with both fundamental epistemological choices and pastoral considerations deeply conditioned by particular historical experiences in the past, experiences, which, he thought, continued to determine opposed readings of contemporary social and political reality. We have seen the terms of the disagreement between Murray and Coste as an instance of a larger debate about the kind of language to be preferably used in moral theology—whether to start from Scripture and revelation or to continue to rely primarily on natural law reasoning. What Murray considered to be the fundamental differences, however, were more visible and much more consequential in the significant disputes about the best way to define the civil right to religious freedom and to ground it.

INVERSE METHODOLOGIES INDUCED BY OPPOSITE HISTORICAL EXPERIENCES

Murray calls attention to the distinct, fundamental epistemological approaches of the two schools. His emphasis on the political argument highlights what he considers to be one of the great developments in the social doctrine of the church in the years before the council: the embracing of historical consciousness.[61] It accounted for the shift in the structure of the argument from the level of abstract principle to that of political reality, which happened from the second to the third draft of what would become *Dignitatis Humanae.* Explaining, at the end of the third session of the council, the new process of the third draft, he says:

> The method followed by the Declaration in approaching its subject is governed by historical consciousness. The starting point is not abstract or ideological, but factual and historical. The initial appeal is to the fact that today man is growing more and more conscious of his own dignity, personal and civil. The Declaration does not lay as its premise the abstract truth of human dignity and then take to deduce from it the affirmation of religious freedom as a human right. In the general matter of human rights, this procedure is both logically perilous and also unconvincing. The truth of human dignity is as old as Christianity, and in a sense, even older. The new thing today, and the thing that matters for the argument, is the newly common human consciousness of this truth.[62]

The majority of the council supportive of religious freedom did not unanimously approve this change "in methodology and focus of argument." Murray acknowledged that "[m]any French-speaking theologians and bishops considered their view to be richer and more profound. They were therefore displeased by the third draft Declaration, which relinquished their line of argument in favor of a line more common among English- and Italian-speaking theorists." To them, "this view of the matter seemed 'superficial.'"[63]

Murray, in the essay being quoted, describes also the general orientation of the opposing approach:

> The argument common among French speaking theologians . . . began, not in the order of historical fact, but in the order of universal truth. The truth is that each man is called by God to share the divine life. This call is mediated to man by conscience, and man's response to it is the free act of faith. The essential dignity of man is located in his personal freedom of conscience, whereby he is truly a moral agent, acting on his own irreducible responsibility before God. Thus religious freedom was conceived to be formally and in the first instance an ethical and theological notion. The effort then was made to conclude, by inference, to the juridical notion of religious freedom—man's right to free exercise of religion in society.[64]

He signals this inference as the weak link of this argument: "It is not obvious that the inference from freedom of conscience to the free exercise of religion as a human right is valid."[65] He would later stress this point in his critique of the final form of *Dignitatis Humanae,* as we have already seen.

If the change of the third draft marked a definitive shift in prominence between the two schools, it did not end the discord. The split continued to be present in the discussions and the final document would eventually adopt elements of both. In the balance of the final compromise, regarding the part of the arguments advanced to ground the right, Murray actually found himself on the losing side of the dispute.

To evaluate the final content of the declaration after the council, Murray borrows from the scholarship on the American constitutional tradition on religious freedom a framework of two possible ways of approaching the grounding of the state's duty of abstention from interference in the religious sphere. This duality parallels, in the case of *Dignitatis Humanae,* the two different fundamental manners of arguing for the right that vied for prominence during the conciliar debates. One manner is utterly political, based on the principles of liberty and equality before the law. Another manner is religious in its perspective and in its basis, starting from the church and its spiritual nature, which warrants reverence and cannot admit compulsion from the temporal power. While the first (the one Murray thought could best solve the problems of the church's position) was the one adopted in the American political system, the council went more in the other direction:

> [T]he appeal of the Declaration is to arguments that may fairly be characterized as religious in some broad sense—the moral obligation to seek the truth, the function of conscience in mediating the divine law, the social nature of man (which establishes a necessary link between the internal moral imperative and the external religious act), and the transcendent nature of the religious act. From these heights the argument descends to the political order only in the laconic statement that government "would clearly transgress the limits set to its power, were it to presume to command or inhibit acts that are religious."[66]

Why was Murray's approach not able to prevail? To suggest an answer, he goes beyond the mere description of methodological approaches and tries to uncover the motivations behind the French epistemological preference. The prevalence of the religious approach to the grounding of the right, determined, finally, the structure of the arguments advanced in *Dignitatis Humanae,* in particular

> the prominence given to man's moral obligation to search for the truth, as somehow the ultimate foundation of the right to religious freedom. The notion occurs four times in the text. But behind this insistence on it, one may suspect, there lay a preoccupation that was rather more pastoral than theoretical. . . . [T]he concern was lest religious freedom be misunderstood to mean a freedom from the claims of the truth—in particular, as these claims are declared by the Church. This pastoral concern may well have been legitimate. But it seems to reveal that some of the Conciliar Fathers were still living in the long shadow of the nineteenth century. The fact is that this misunderstanding of religious freedom is impossible for anyone who grasps the twentieth-century state of the question.[67]

In Murray's opinion, many Europeans were still caught in the nineteenth-century state of the question, dominated by old fears of laicist indifferentism,[68] and lacked a correct understanding of the American experience.[69] This explains also their resistance to Murray's definition of the right to religious freedom as an immunity from the power of government.

> In the American view, religious freedom is, in first instance, an assurance against government; in this sense it is properly a civil liberty. In the second instance, it is an assurance against coercions attempted by other powers in society; in this sense, it is a social freedom which will be vindicated by government. Some of the conciliar Fathers seemed unwilling to accept this conception of the problem. They wished to attribute the primacy to the social freedom[70]

and, therefore, were uncomfortable with the primacy given to the formally political aspects.

Murray did not look sympathetically at their position on this point. He suspected they had failed to grasp the true position of the problem.[71] He explains that the definition of the right as an immunity based on "the notion of governmental incompetence in matters religious," signifies that

> the constitutional provision for religious freedom is a self-denying ordinance on the part of the government. That is to say, government denies to itself the competence to be a judge of religious belief and action. But this denial is not an assertion of indifference to the values of religion to man and to society. Nor is it a reassertion of the outworn laicist creed that "religion is

> a purely private matter." It is simply a recognition of the limited functions of the juridical order of society as the legal armature of human rights.[72]

In no way was the council accepting now the liberal laicist ideologies against which the church had combated and under which it had suffered in the last century.

Much of the confusion was created by language. The same terms evoked quite different historical experiences for the Americans and the French. For the Europeans it was difficult to envision the securing of the right on the juridical self-restraint of the state. Any suggestion of a neutral government in matters of religion evoked the avowed neutralism of nineteenth-century liberal regimes, which, in reality, distinguished themselves by an intense antireligious ideology and the persecution of the Catholic Church.

Murray keeps insisting on the distinction between the nineteenth- and the twentieth-century political doctrines and corresponding situations of the church in the face of them. He defends that

> it is possible to see the vast difference between religious freedom in its contemporary meaning and "freedom of conscience" and "freedom of cult" in the sense of nineteenth-century continental laicism. These latter formulas were not simply juridical; they were ideological. Inherent in them was the moral judgment that the individual conscience is absolutely autonomous, and the further theological-social judgment that religion is a purely private affair, irrelevant to any of the public concerns of the political community. In the laicist view, freedom of conscience and freedom of cult were instrumental concepts—but concepts instrumental to an ideological negation of the public status and of the social function of religion. On the contrary, in the contemporary constitutional conception religious freedom is still an instrumental concept, but instrumental simply to the freedom of religion as a public phenomenon, whose manifestations are of a transcendent order, and consequently of such high personal and public interest that no repressive coercion may be brought to bear upon them.[73]

For the success of Murray's endeavor and, for that matter, for that of *Dignitatis Humanae,* these distinctions are absolutely crucial. To fail to grasp them and keep them in mind in the reading of the declaration creates misunderstandings about the proposed solutions and makes it much more difficult to clear the way out of the old controversies.

Nevertheless, finally, the American Jesuit concedes the wisdom of the conciliar options. It was more prudent to let the political principle take secondary position and give primacy to religious arguments.

> In any event, there is no question that vast confusion and opposition, compounding confusion and opposition already existent, would have arisen if the major political argument for religious freedom—from the principle of equality before the law—had been pressed. Minds and emotions conditioned by the Continental experience of nineteenth-century laicism would surely have seen it as a concession to, if not an outright embrace of, the indifferentist principle of the equality of all religions before God.[74]

In spite of his criticism of the fixation of the French view on the nineteenth-century state of the question, he acknowledges the importance of the "preoccupations that gave rise to their view" when these concern present challenges, namely, "the need to go to the depths of the religious problematic of our age, of which atheism is an important integral part, not only as a personal conviction but as a social force. . . . [A]lso the need to center all attention on the problem . . . of religious truth in its relation to human society in its full sweep."[75]

In the end, John Courtney Murray settles for the declaration as we have it. The main reason for his acceptance was that, amid the competition of the two views, the efforts of Anglo-American bishops, nevertheless and in spite of opposition, enabled the inclusion in the text of an explicit statement of the principle of equality before the law, "the essential basis of religious freedom" in American constitutional history.[76] Murray gladly welcomes this inclusion, not just because it is a sound principle but especially because this way "the commentator on the Vatican Declaration can find a footing in the text from which to enlarge its argument and to make a more balanced and convincing case for religious freedom by appealing to political as well as to religious or moral principle."[77] This sentence describes with precision the whole hermeneutical strategy of Murray's commentaries and interpretations of *Dignitatis Humanae*.

Unfortunately, he had time only to do little more than defend his positions at the council. His commentaries in the near aftermath of Vatican II kept the focus on the workings of the political-juridical argument and, for the most part, continued to operate within a narrow delimitation of the question. Because of the difficulties the correct understanding of the declaration was facing, Murray insists on the explanation of the core issue, perhaps purposely avoiding distractions of further explorations until the essential point had reached such widespread acceptance and clear comprehension that it could be considered to be above challenge. This effort to attract all the attention to the simple, fundamental doctrinal statement of the document may also explain his apparently lessening comments on the importance and reach of *Dignitatis Humanae:* "[A] document of very modest scope,"[78] dealing with "the lesser issue of the free exercise of religion in civil society,"[79] "in itself minor,"[80] whose "achievement was simply to bring the Church abreast of the developments that have occurred in the secular world."[81]

Nevertheless, Murray saw also *Dignitatis Humanae* as a text rich of further consequences. He did not have the opportunity to start exploring them in detail. All he left are some pointers scattered through his commentaries, which promise important implications for the conduct of the church, to be uncovered by a fuller engagement of the text of the declaration in the line of his views. Such implications continue to have full actuality to open the way for a third moment of renewed exploration of *Dignitatis Humanae,* as we will see later.

André-Vincent: Ontological Grounding in the Order of Truth

A book by Philippe André-Vincent provides a typical development of the more radical tendencies of the approach Murray described as characteristic of the French school.[82] In his argument, a clear preference for abstract reasoning in search of an ontological foundation displaces reliance on the political and the historical. He puts great emphasis on the relationship to ultimate truth, and the whole argument is developed in sustained confrontation with modern liberal ideologies, keeping the predicaments of the church at the hands of nineteenth-century liberalism as the dominant background reference.

In terms of the interpretative approach to *Dignitatis Humanae,* André-Vincent follows a strategy similar to Murray's, although in a quite different direction. He, too, attempts to enlarge the statements inserted in the text of the declaration that are more favorable to his views into a systematic argument for religious freedom fully consonant with his methodological and conceptual preferences.

CONCEPTUAL PRECISION AND ACCURACY OF HISTORY

André-Vincent's first preoccupation is to distinguish the recent adoption by the Catholic Church of the right to religious freedom from a mere cooptation of the modern brand of individualistic freedoms. He does that in two steps, the first being conceptual demarcation. To the language of "human right," typical of the liberal declarations, André-Vincent prefers the concept of "fundamental right" with an objective rooting in the traditional conception of natural law, thus avoiding any connotation of an absolute foundation in the individual conscience.[83] The twentieth-century adoption of this "modern freedom" by the church is not an affirmation of an individualistic right but of a right of persons, an individual right which cannot be separated from its intrinsic communitarian dimension and transcendent grounding.[84]

The second step challenges the common assumptions about the historical genesis of the concept of religious freedom. The true foundation of the new doctrine of religious freedom, he argues, is to be discovered not in the eighteenth century, but in a tradition that goes back to the apologists and martyrs of the early church. This tradition continued to grow, although still enveloped in a communitarian fashioning, in all the collective assertions of the freedom of the church throughout its history, up to modern times. The martyrs "do not witness to themselves, but to the Truth" (12); "they never claim their freedom for its own sake but for the Truth" (13). It is their encounter with the truth in Christ that makes them free and this interior freedom demands external expression for the service of that truth. The truth by its own nature excludes interior constraint and the spiritual freedom it creates demands external freedom, rejecting thus any constraint also exterior. It is here, thus, in the experience of the truth, that rests the foundation of the conciliar right to religious freedom:

> The *"social and civil freedom in religious matters"* (the one defined by the Council) emerges at this point—at the same source of spiritual freedom. It springs up from the living relation of the human spirit to the Truth, relation entirely personal and yet necessarily social: it is a freedom that must be exercised by each individual and of which each individual will be the subject (12; see also 143–44).

How, then, does the modern claim for human rights fit in this story? André-Vincent responds by proposing an interpretation of the sequence of political turns set off by modernity. The eighteenth century reacted against the centuries-old conflation of religion and civil society and the consequent social pressure upon individuals sustained by the power of the state, a social arrangement that valued the rights of the truth above individual freedom. However, the reaction, in France, was made in the name of an absolute individualism, merely adding to the absolutism of the state the new claim of absolutism of the individual. Moreover, this "religious freedom became a machine of war against religion" (22–23). In Catholic countries, liberalism took the form of laicism, and, whenever it became the state ideology, tried to remove the church from any kind of social presence. The imposed separation between church and state was in reality, through the total privatization and individualization of religion, an attempt of domination of the church by the state and an attack against the freedom of persons. The modern turn may have been well intentioned, but in the short term it only created further problems.

The outcome of the modern revolutions, André-Vincent continues, gave rise to a demand for a third autonomy, that of the person (to be added to the imposed autonomies, vis-à-vis each other, of both the state and the church). The popes of the twentieth century undertook that claim by invoking the right of the consciences against totalitarianism. In the church, the right to religious freedom appears, thus, under the guise of an individual right, a necessary move to distinguish it (without separating it, though) from the traditional communitarian envelope of the right of the church to freedom.

The development took place, in terms of a spatial metaphor, as a movement of distancing from the extreme of the all-absorbing communal in the direction of the personal. Another danger, however, lurks on the opposite end of the path on which this motion of differentiation takes place: the also extremist individualistic understanding of liberal rights. All hangs, then, on the ability to find the balanced middle ground. The personal right to religious freedom only achieves its goal if it preserves its communitarian dimension. History has shown, both with nineteenth-century laicism and with twentieth-century communism, that the negation of the social dimension of religion, the individualistic notion of religious freedom, serves the absolutism of the state and hinders the rights of persons (29–30). The way to absolute individualism returns the person to totalitarian domination.

For André-Vincent, and a whole line of thought that continues to be very influential in the interpretation of the teaching of *Dignitatis Humanae,* only an alliance with the Absolute can sustain human freedom. The law of God is the unique foundation of freedom in the interaction of the three autonomies of the state, the church, and the person (31–32). Religious freedom has its foundation in the Truth (with a capital *t*), and, on that basis, this view claims a particular status for the right to religious freedom among human rights: "The Truth is at the basis of dialogue as it is at the foundation of freedom. Religious freedom is the first of the fundamental rights: it is connected more than any other to the Truth" (37).

Inconsistency and Cohesion of *Dignitatis Humanae*

The last pages summarized the historical perspective from which André-Vincent looks at the right to religious freedom. Out of his preoccupation with the consequences of nineteenth-century laicist liberalism, and other offshoots of eighteenth-century rationalism, he stresses the importance of the question of ultimate foundation beyond the mere social and civil plan. Religious freedom has a spiritual quality and divine foundation, which can never be ignored. The demands of dialogue make it necessary to situate religious freedom at the temporal level, the level of the declarations of human rights. However, André-Vincent alerts, it would be to deprive it of its nature if religious freedom were reduced to this civil dimension only (35).

He positions himself, thus, in direct opposition to the methodological options championed by John Courtney Murray, which eventually predominated in the approach taken by *Dignitatis Humanae.* Analyzing the process of the genesis of the declaration, he acknowledges the pragmatic considerations that led the council to restrict the focus to the civil right, concerned only with external activity and limited to the juridical order. But this entailed the risk of misrepresenting religious freedom as merely an individualistic immunity in the modern perspective, without sufficiently denouncing all the negative attitudes toward religion associated with that viewpoint. The logic of modern freedom, he considers, goes directly and naturally from the exaltation of freedom to the affirmation of the absolute autonomy of reason, with no connection to objective truth. That, in turn, engenders religious indifferentism, the repudiation of any transcendence and, ultimately, the negation of God. This philosophical indifferentism then translates itself into a political indifferentism, an ideology determined to exclude all religion from public life (see 80–81). Such are the risks involved in the cooptation of modern formulations not sufficiently qualified.

In his opinion, even within the restricted social and civic ambit to which *Dignitatis Humanae* limited itself, reference had to be made to a general doctrine of Christian liberty, especially whenever what is at stake is the option between the gospel of Jesus, which says that "the truth will make you free" and another 'gospel' proposing that "freedom will make you true" (see 44). It is in the relation of the person to the truth that André-Vincent sees the crucial indispensable center of the whole issue of religious freedom (45). He questions, thus, the possibility of separating the two orders, the moral and the juridical (see 82). The taking into account of the situations of pluralism is not in question, but, in his view, only a strong, active dynamism of searching for the truth can, in a context of pluralism, preserve the promotion of freedom from decaying into indifferentism. Only within a clear movement of people toward the truth can pluralism be a regime of freedom (54).

The basic problem with the final text of *Dignitatis Humanae* for André-Vincent is, then, an inconsistency between, on the one hand, the traditional doctrine of natural rights, which provides the foundation for the right to religious freedom and, on the other, the language of a subjectivistic conception of the right, which provides for the definition of its object.[85] Taking its starting point from the liberal individualistic point of view, the declaration defines the right as negative and individual—an immunity of the individual against the state. However, the foundation for this right that *Dignitatis Humanae* proposes is not the will of the individual but the dignity of the human person, according to the traditional doctrine of natural rights, which includes activities positively defined and also a communitarian dimension. The conflicting result, in the interpretation of the French Dominican, is a modern definition of the object of the right set upon a traditional foundation for that right. Through the text of the conciliar declaration, runs, thus, in his opinion, "a hesitation or a kind of 'dialectical tension' between the point of view of the object (negative and individualistic) and that of the foundation (positive and communitarian)" (156).

Curiously, he shares with Murray the split feelings about, on one hand the definition of the right and, on the other, the foundations proposed to ground it. The positive/negative marks of the evaluation are, however, reversed. While Murray focused on the substance of the right and disagreed with most of the arguments for it, André-Vincent tries to remedy the dangerous ambiguities of the definition by accentuating what he sees as the central principle in the foundation. The only satisfactory way to overcome this conflict, André-Vincent immediately proposes, will demand the casting off of subjectivism and the stressing of the point "where the object and the foundation of the right come together: the ontological connection of the person to God-Truth."[86]

This ontological connection becomes the linchpin of his interpretation of the declaration, uniting object and foundation and harmonizing the first and the second parts, the natural law arguments and the rationale based on revelation. He recognizes, though, that the unifying role of this idea is more implied than clearly stated in the structure of the text. Moreover, as a matter of fact, the notion on which the declaration bases the unity of the two parts does not belong to the foundations but to the object—namely, the idea of noncoercion. However, in André-Vincent's perspective, in spite of the weak support from the actual text itself, the bond between person and truth is still the "mother-idea" *(l'idée-mère)* of *Dignitatis Humanae:*

> In the Declaration, the mother-idea appears with the foundation of the right to religious freedom: the ontological connection of the person to the truth, a natural connection grounding a natural obligation to search for the truth and to adhere to it, grounding at the same time a right to the freedom

> necessary to realize that obligation. The ontological connection of freedom to truth is the mother-idea of the Declaration. (203–04)

André-Vincent finds textual support for this bias in the first number of the declaration, the introduction. There, he highlights the references to the ontological foundation of freedom in the truth, something that is ignored or rejected in the atheistic liberal and existentialist conceptions of freedom typical of modernity.[87] On this basis, he objects to those who, because they defend a stricter differentiation between the civil right to religious freedom and the problem of objective truth, define, consequently, the right independently of any reference to religious truth, grounding it, instead, on a human nature without reference to God. In André-Vincent's judgment, "By separating thus freedom from religious truth, they intend to ground it on a reality more indisputable and easier to recognize by all: that of the natural dignity of man. But they empty this natural dignity of its content by depriving human nature of its existential relation to the Truth" (161).

Greater Role for Revelation

Another criticism of André-Vincent to *Dignitatis Humanae* refers to the sources for the arguments. The council, in his opinion, should have made explicit use of the data of revelation, especially the reference of every human being to Jesus Christ in whom the truth searched by all subsists (162). Stressing the importance of the reference in *Dignitatis Humanae,* number 1, to the "traditional catholic teaching on the moral obligation of individuals and societies towards the true religion and the one church of Christ," he argues that the council should have formulated a full theology of religious freedom based on the duties toward the truth that are part of the revelation in Jesus Christ. This would have reinforced the foundation of the civil right, for "freedom is grounded on the Truth" (163). Even the right to religious freedom, which belongs to the social and civil level, has its foundation in the relation of the human person to God.[88]

He joins, therefore, the choir of those who were disappointed with the secondary and subordinated role given to Scripture. In the arrangement of the document, the revelation-centered second part provides no more than an "extrinsic confirmation of natural law" (204).

At the end of the book, he sketches a theology of religious freedom in which he attempts to harmonize in a better way the contributions of reason and revelation, on the basis of a necessary connection between the natural human duties toward the truth and the redemptive role of Jesus Christ. The discussion is set in the context of the relations between nature and grace. He argues that if the declaration is read from the point of view of the foundation, from the duty present in human nature itself to search for the truth—an obligation that can only be discharged in freedom—then we see in it the necessity for Christ's role. Natural law and the gospel are connected, and only by taking them together, both nature and grace, can religious freedom be ultimately grounded in redeemed human nature, upon the grace of Christian liberty.

Religious freedom is rooted in the natural inclination of every human being to the truth, the ontological connection of the person with primordial Truth. This natural ordering founds, first, a moral obligation and, second, a requirement of freedom from coercion—so that the fulfillment of the obligation will not be impeded. Such is the natural level of the grounding of religious freedom. There is, however, the reality of sin, which destroys the natural orientation of the person to God, the natural grounds for religious freedom. Only grace, after that, can restore the dynamism of that inclination. If the right to religious freedom is grounded on human nature (in its ontological inclination to God), it is the redemptive grace of Christ that restores in human nature this foundation, this natural ordering.[89] This way, André-Vincent explains a harmony between reason and revelation, between natural law and the gospel, deeper than the mere superposition of the two parts of *Dignitatis Humanae*.

Nevertheless, in spite of the protestations against the lessening of the role of Scripture, his theology is far from giving a clear priority to biblical argumentation, as most in the French school preferred. What he looks to establish is a harmony between natural law and revelation, or, more concretely, he tries to provide a theological support for his essentially philosophical argument based on the ontological bond of human nature with absolute truth. Above everything, he wants to secure an absolute ground for the right to religious freedom that is not subjectivistic, pulling it unequivocally away from the modern concepts of freedom of conscience equated with absolute autonomy of the individual and sheer privatization of religion. To counter any connotations with this idea of absolute freedom, he asserts repeatedly the priority of truth over freedom. Freedom is not the absolute starting point, but it is rooted in the truth; it is through the discovery and actualization of her ordering to the truth that the person encounters his or her freedom. In order to support this opposition to modern subjectivism, he quotes John 8 as a proof that the gospel, contrary to modern thought, roots freedom in truth: "If you are my disciples, you will remain in my word; and you will know the Truth; and the Truth will set you free" (see 213).

FREEDOM AS SPONTANEITY, NOT IMMUNITY

The foundation of religious freedom in the truth makes the respective right essentially an empowerment. It does not subsist in the enclosed dominion of the individual but springs from the determination of the person before the Truth. A positive definition is necessary, for the concept of immunity does not sufficiently account for it.

> Freedom cannot be defined negatively: more than a non-coercion, it is a spontaneity; more precisely, a spiritual spontaneity; spontaneity of a nature which is finally and absolutely determined by the Absolute being only, of a will which beyond all goods and through them tends to the Sovereign Good; of an intelligence which through all truth and beyond all truth adheres to the Primordial Truth. (214)

It is in this spontaneity, empowered and anchored in the relationship (recognized or implicit) of the person with God, that André-Vincent finds the unassailable ground to protect religious freedom (especially in its social communitarian dimension). He defends it, thus, from the traps of an illusory, individualistic, subjectivistic foundation, of which state laicism disguised as neutrality in matters religious is the inevitable ideological counterpart. Through the exploration of the basic foundation implied in *Dignitatis Humanae,* he looks to overcome the limitations and pitfalls of what he sees as an inadequate definition of the object of the right by the declaration. From a focus on the ontological foundation he moves to an emphasis on the transcendent foundation and finally on the transcendence of the foundation.[90]

It is already plainly patent how this whole interpretation of André-Vincent is opposed, almost point by point, to the approach of Murray. Murray opted for a narrow delimitation of the issue and circumscribed the object to the juridical realm, giving more importance to the affirmation of the civil right than to its fundamental grounding. André-Vincent, in turn, was not satisfied with the definition of the object of the right, and he enlarges the question to include all its dimensions and puts the emphasis precisely on the foundational ontological and theological levels. Murray stays almost exclusively in the terrain of political philosophy. André-Vincent ventures deep in the realm of theology and revelation. For the former, it is primarily a matter of a civil freedom. For the latter, the question is centered on truth all the way. The two interpretations show clearly the lines of division between the so-called French and American schools engaged in *Dignitatis Humanae.* We have already seen how Murray pointed out the difference of historical experiences as the main reason for the basic disagreement. The contrast between immunity and spontaneity as the preferred way to define what kind of freedom is religious freedom serves to illustrate the difference of basic approaches in the context of Murray's assertion.

A positive definition of freedom inverts the direction of the basic argument of Murray to ground the right—the incompetence of the state. For Murray's perspective of freedom as immunity, the right is secured by a self-restraint on the part of the state, a self-recognition that the limits to its power do not allow it to intervene in the sphere of religious expression, a sphere that should be left entirely to persons and communities in society. For André-Vincent, the protective boundaries are not determined by the state's self-restraint but are imposed upon the state by the religious faculties of persons and communities, a power superior to the power of the state:

> In the religious domain the limit of the intervention of the State is not defined by its incompetence but by the competence of the persons and the religious communities: superior competence, competence present at the heart of a common good understood as the good of the persons, traversed by the religious *relationship* of the persons to God-Sovereign Good. Government officials must be cognizant of that *relationship* in order to recognize that limit. (189)

For André-Vincent, religious freedom is a right to be affirmed in opposition to the state (see 204), rather than to be acknowledged and respected by a constitutional government conscious of its own limits, as it would be for Murray. Behind looms clearly the difference of historical references to the role of the state regarding the church.

DISTRUST IN THE NEUTRAL STATE

André-Vincent shows a permanent suspicion of the religious neutrality of the state. He underlines the sentence of number 6 of *Dignitatis Humanae,* which obliges the state "to give effective protection to the religious liberty of all citizens by just laws and other suitable means, and to ensure favorable conditions for fostering religious life." Calling attention to the fact that this affirmation "goes beyond the pure and simple immunity, the individual right of non-coercion (wholly negative)," he states clearly, immediately after, the determining reason for his rejection of the negative definition of the object of religious freedom: "The mere abstention does not satisfy the requirements of religious freedom: strict neutrality is a myth unless it is not a mask for sectarianism" (177).

The whole preoccupation with setting the foundation upon the personal relationship with God is explained, then, by the fact that only in this transcendent ground can a power superior to the state be attained (179). Only through the recognition of this relationship will the state truly grant religious freedom (228).

And this recognition has to include an appreciation of religious truth,[91] even to the point of recognition of a particular religion, which, in his opinion, is not incompatible with religious freedom for all.[92]

On this basis, André-Vincent gives especial importance to the clauses in the number 6 of *Dignitatis Humanae* just quoted, together with the other one in number 1 about the traditional doctrine on the duties of public powers toward religion and the church in particular. He questions the postconciliar generalized rejection of the model of the traditional confessional state in exclusive favor of the American model of "benevolent neutrality" or the French *État laïque* (225). Profound doubts about the possibility of a lay state without laicism guide his resistance. Legitimate autonomy is certainly due to the political realm, but he cannot forget that "historically 'laïcité' signifies a quite different thing" (226). It has meant the exclusion of the church from any presence in society (denying the communitarian dimension of religion), under the claim of absolute autonomy for the state and for the individual against the church (227). For him, the lay state still means the nineteenth-century anticlerical liberalism.

If the preference for the definition of religious freedom as spontaneity imposed upon the state is prompted by a historically conditioned suspicion of the political power—and in as much as the whole construct of the ontological grounding of the natural right to religious freedom in the order of truth is intrinsically connected with its definition as a spiritual spontaneity with transcendent roots—then, the whole construct of a theology of religious freedom and of the relations between freedom and truth proposed by André-Vincent is still very much determined by a basic distrust provoked by the traumas of the encounter with Continental liberalism. It seems that, for him, the liberation in church-state relations effected by the first moment of *Dignitatis Humanae* was not as definitive as someone such as Murray thought it had been. And, thus, the optimistic views and openness to new explorations of the relation of the Catholic Church with democratic pluralistic societies inaugurated with Vatican II will tend also to be looked upon very cautiously by this line of interpretation of *Dignitatis Humanae*.

When describing the pastoral challenges confronting the council in its discussion of religious freedom, André-Vincent distinguishes the alternatives of favor versus disfavor of a more liberal concept of religious freedom in terms of a choice between two perils impending upon the practice of faith. The decision rests with which one is, in the end, feared most as the general attitude of the masses regarding the faith: infantilism or indifferentism (see 53)? To avoid the first above all, individual freedom and personalized commitment of faith are bolstered. If it is indifferentism that is the most feared peril for the faith, objective fidelity to the truth is stressed and the support of social institutionalization of religion is regarded more positively. Against infantilism, the price paid for a personalized, mature faith in a pluralist regime is a Christianity of the elite, the luxury of a minority (56). For André-Vincent, its associated consequence, generalized indifferentism, the apostasy of the masses, is a greater evil than the weaknesses of a "sociological" religion. Thus, his emphasis on the truth and on the need for a sense of the truth to inform the social structures. Between the two opposite risks personal freedom has to face, communal suffocation by society, on one hand, or hypertrophy on the side of the individual, on the other, he prefers to guard against the latter above all (see 190).

All the alternatives are framed in terms of a competition of freedom versus truth. More than concurrent, André-Vincent sees them as inclined to become rivals in societies dominated by liberal ideologies. The predominant approach of *Dignitatis Humanae* started from freedom, and intended to affirm freedom. He, nevertheless, argues for an interpretation of the declaration that reverses this tendency. An overcoming of the antinomy between the two is settled at the level of the ultimate foundations of religious freedom, in a way that reestablishes the balance in favor of the truth: Truth is the source of freedom.[93] The question that insinuates itself is whether this interpretation does not come dangerously close to reinstating the submission of freedom to the truth, even at the level which *Dignitatis Humanae* set out precisely and definitely to overturn, the level of the civil right to religious freedom recognized as an inalienable and universal demand of human dignity.

Pietro Pavan: *Dignitatis Humanae* as a Unified Totality

Both John Courtney Murray and Philippe André-Vincent start their interpretations of *Dignitatis Humanae* by highlighting one specific statement of the declaration. Each stresses the importance of a particular argument, uniquely decisive, in their perspectives, for solidly grounding the right. And, in either case, it is an argument that the conciliar text itself actually puts in a relatively secondary position. They explain the full reach and broader implications of this particular statement, claim for it a normative hermeneutical value, and then use it as the ultimate standard to evaluate the whole of the document. As a result, they both tend to give more importance to what the text should be, than to a consideration of the text as it is in its entirety, although Murray defends the declaration more, and, it could be argued, his study is more incomplete than biased.

In his commentaries on the declaration, Pietro Pavan, another of the influential participants in the redaction of *Dignitatis Humanae,* deliberately followed a different approach. Instead of focusing on a particular assertion or a specific argument, he defended the unity of the document and based all its interpretation on the central explicit emphasis of the text: the dignity of the human person.

DEFENDING THE UNITY OF THE WHOLE TEXT

For Pavan, the long and contrasted conciliar discussions constituted in fact "a process of clarification and exploration,"[94] which eventually allowed the council to reach a convergence of thinking. So, what is written in the declaration, in his view, is not the product of a halfhearted compromise but rather the result of a generally agreed consensus, which must be assumed as the categorical basis for any further discussion of the issues.[95]

In the declaration Pavan identifies four essential elements constitutive of the right to religious freedom; namely, its universality, its object or content (an immunity), its foundation (the dignity of the human person), and its nature (a natural, not a positive, right).[96] He then alerts against separating any of these elements from the unified and harmonious whole, forgetting their essential interconnectedness. The formulations through which these elements are defined in the text must be taken as explicitly stated, for they were the result of a deliberate and carefully discussed choice of terms by the conciliar fathers.

> The elements . . . which make up the content of the right to freedom in religious matters as defined and proclaimed in Vatican II should be considered simultaneously, as a whole, and should be understood in the sense given to them, as that sense *explicitly* emerges from the terms used to make it precise. . . . Because of the intimate relationship among the elements making up the document, by which they are closely linked and explain and justify one another, the document appears internally well structured and doctrinally valid only if this relationship be borne in mind. Otherwise it is impossible to grasp the interconnection among its parts and the document risks seeming unclear or even doctrinally inconsistent.[97]

Pavan underscored this point in later commentaries, precisely to counteract what he was seeing as revisionist attempts to interpret *Dignitatis Humanae* in ways contrary to the intention of the council,[98] or even to recover preconciliar doctrinal positions.[99] These tend to grant unwarranted, decisive interpretative weight to marginal affirmations in the text, then isolated from the general context and turned against the fundamental direction of the whole declaration. Against such contentions, Pavan reaffirms the need to interpret the declaration in its unity without manipulating its words,[100] and stresses again the real novelty brought into the Catholic tradition by *Dignitatis Humanae:* the right proclaimed

> was welcomed by the whole world and in all cultural environments . . . not as a reaffirmation by the Council of the Church's traditional, preconciliar position but as a new stance in regard to individuals, to other religious bodies, and to the civil authorities themselves. Thus every attempt to find grounds in the document for returning to preconciliar positions is useless.[101]

Although this defense of the declaration in its unity and consistence may seem to distance him from Murray, Pavan was one of the strongest supporters of the approach of the American Jesuit to the formulation and justification of the right to religious freedom, both during the council and after. Two aspects of his interpretation, in particular, put him squarely on the side of Murray: the epistemological accent on a historical starting point as against an essentialist discussion,[102] and the stark defense of the necessity of defining the right as an immunity. In what regards the justification of the right, Pavan was not as much interested in continuing to discuss the merits and efficacy of competing arguments. More than striving for a betterment of the form in which the doctrine was stated by the council, he wanted to assert what *Dignitatis Humanae* affirmed anew in the tradition of the church and, thus, promote it beyond any doubt as a novel but irreversible basis in Catholic social teaching.[103]

HISTORICAL DISCLOSURE OF A FUNDAMENTAL RIGHT

Pavan underlines what *Dignitatis Humanae* avows in its opening paragraph: The declaration constitutes a response by the church to historical facts that developed, for the most part, outside of, and sometimes even against, the church itself. And this applies both to the affirmation of the right as such and to its basic grounding. The fact is that the civil right to religious freedom had already been asserted in the constitutions of most civil societies. *Dignitatis Humanae* does not invent it; it is simply the way by which the Catholic hierarchy declares itself in favor of that right.[104] Similarly, a "characteristic phenomenon of modern times," "a much keener consciousness of the dignity of the person, seen as exigency of freedom in the exercise of responsibility,"[105] gave rise, in the conscience of people, to a general "demand to be considered and treated not as *things or instruments* but as *persons* conscious, free and responsible for their own actions."[106] As a consequence, a development of political structures allowing for a fuller expression of personal freedom was set in motion. The recent character of the whole process explains why the civil right to religious freedom only in modern times found its juridical enactment.[107] Such blatant historical reality finally both compelled the church to take a position, and inspired the church to find in its own tradition the grounds to approve, embrace, and develop the implications of such dignity, adopted by *Dignitatis Humanae* as the foundation of the right.

The proclamation of the right to religious freedom by the Catholic Church is, therefore, associated with a particular historical sociopolitical development, namely, the rise of the constitutional democratic state. That, however, does not make it contingent upon a particular conjuncture that may well change again in the future. It is a right discovered and affirmed but not invented. Rather, it is an attestation of a fundamental human right, a natural right. Although its proclamation was swayed by historical facts, its basis is to be found in the perennial demands of the dignity of the human person.[108]

In the course of human history, the civil right to religious freedom marked an irreversible progress of civilization.[109] In the church, the same irrevocability is stressed by the finally acquired realization that this right is fully in harmony with revelation and implicitly demanded by the gospel message,[110] a right immanent to the Christian conception of life, even if that requirement could only be translated in the institutions of political communities after human civilization had reached a sufficient degree of human maturity.[111] That certainly explains why this civil right was born historically in a civilization deeply penetrated by the ferment of the gospel.[112]

For Pavan, it is precisely the character of the right to religious freedom as a right natural to every human person that demands it be understood as an immunity. On this, he sides with Murray in defending *Dignitatis Humanae* against the frequent criticism of the negative form of defining the object of the right. He argues that only this concept of immunity can define a right belonging to every human being independently of his or her convictions in religious matters, avoiding unmistakably any idea that the object of the right is connected with the content of religious faith, in which case it would end up not sufficiently preserving the right for those not professing the Catholic faith.[113] Any attempt to use a positive definition, electing as the object of the right a faculty of everyone's conscience, sets also that protection on unacceptable bases, for, in the case that faculty is used to spread a false religion, the right would have as its object a bad thing.[114]

THE CENTRAL MOTIVE OF THE DIGNITY OF THE HUMAN PERSON

The focal point of Pavan's determined effort to promote a correct and integral understanding of the declaration of Vatican II on religious freedom is the exploration, development, and explanation in its elements and implications of what *Dignitatis Humanae* repeatedly and in a way that leaves no ambiguity proclaims as the foundation of the right, "the motive that marks and unifies the whole document":[115] the concept of the dignity of the human person.

The first thing he wants to make clear is that this dignity is inherent to every human person, in any circumstance, just by the fact of existing as a human person. He insists that *Dignitatis Humanae*

> is concerned not with the *moral* dignity that belongs to a person because of the uprightness of his or her conscience, but with the very *nature* of person. This dignity is grounded on the human reality which a person is, that is, on elements rooted in his or her being as endowed with intelligence and freedom. It is a dignity that every human person possesses always and everywhere simply by being a person, and not by behaving rightly in the moral field. It is the dignity that flows from the being of the person and inheres in the being of the person and does not depend on the deeds of the person—whether these be right or wrong, whether these be right because they correspond to objective truth, or right because of invincible ignorance.[116]

Pavan sometimes qualifies this dignity as "existential" or "ontological" to make an unmistakable demarcation from any moral undertone.[117] It is not a dignity dependent in any way on the rightness (objective or subjective) of one's conscience. By this clarification, the pitfalls of the discussion of the rights of the erroneous conscience are avoided. Once again by the same basic reasons, Pavan defends the only acceptable content of the right to be an immunity; he wants to make it absolutely clear that nothing in the foundation of the right may make it less than unconditionally universal.

The next step consists of explaining what are the "elements that penetrate and qualify" everyone's personal being to make up human dignity. He points out that in numbers 2 and 3 of the declaration,

> three elements are explicitly considered that constitute the dignity, ontologically understood, of the human person: (1) the inescapable responsibility of every person to fix his or her own relationship with God, (2) the nature and immediacy of the relationship between person and truth, and (3) identity—or the need for a person to be himself or herself.[118]

Responsibility means that, by nature, each person has to decide his or her relationship with God and cannot be substituted in that by anyone. Moreover—

here the implication for religious freedom—"this responsibility cannot be exercised other than freely, and this implies the exclusion of means of coercion, especially in the domain of religion."[119]

The second element, immediacy, regards the relationship between person and truth. Adherence to the truth cannot be forced. Nothing can come between person and truth; any coercive interference can only harm. In the sequence of knowing, loving, and acting through which the person, intelligent and free, discharges his or her duty to seek the truth, and to conform his or her life to it,

> truth cannot be known except in the light of truth. In the process of knowing, force from outside cannot take the place of evidence from within. Full adherence to the truth demands an act of love that can only emerge in freedom. Harmony between the truth known and life in all its expressions has no human value unless it is achieved not through pressures and impulses from without but by personal decisions.[120]

Finally, the third element, identity, addresses the domain of the external expression of one's beliefs. It means that "being always oneself in thought, will, and action, is an objective requirement for one's dignity." This indivisible unity and necessary succession of thinking, willing, and acting as stages of a person's development and expression of herself, implies, once again, an immunity from any undue external interruption: "to break this continuity in any sphere of life, but above all in the religious, by forcing a person to act in opposition to his own mind and will, or by hindering him from acting in harmony with either, is to harm deeply his dignity, to violate a fundamental right."[121]

Freedom as Possibility to Decide Responsibly. Pavan's views emphasize a preserve of irreducible sovereignty in each person's religious calling, an area of self-actualization that must be protected from invasion, in which only what emerges within itself has value. Freedom in this dominion is thus primarily immunity, and so it is described mainly in negative, defensive, or protective terms that assert the autonomy and independence of the person. There is in every human being a sanctuary that needs to be guarded against intrusion in order for his or her dignity not to be harmed. Pavan uses a series of spatial metaphors to describe it: "a reserved area,"[122] "a sphere of autonomy,"[123] or "a security zone," granting the inviolability of a personal realm within the confines of which the person may conduct his or herself on his or her own initiative and responsibility without the coercive interference of civil authorities or any other powers in society.[124] Freedom means first securing the possibility to exert self-determination. It is a freedom "regarded as an exercise of responsibility,"[125] but responsibility now primarily means independent unconstrained free decision not obligation toward a moral duty.[126]

Pavan makes this important distinction when explaining the meaning of the content of the right as stated in number 2 of the declaration: "[T]hat no one should be forced to act against his conscience in religious matters, nor prevented from acting according to his conscience."

> It must first be stated—he says—that here the term "conscience" means above all responsibility, so that the statement must be understood thus: In the religious sphere no one may be compelled to act in a way different from that in which he himself has ***decided*** to act, and no man may be prevented from acting according to this way.[127]

This statement is the operative meaning of conscience as responsibility in *Dignitatis Humanae,* different from the sense of conscience as "moral rectitude." In the latter case, the statement would mean to not be compelled to act or prevented from acting "in a way different from that in which he knows himself ***obliged*** to act." But this statement concerns already the problems of the true or the erroneous conscience, which are not touched by the declaration because "they are moral, not legal . . . [and] belong directly and formally to the relation between person and truth, not to the relation between person and person,"[128] a realm in which the true or erroneous character of the conscience does not condition the right.

For the judgment of the dignity of the human person upon freedom in matters religious, what is at stake is not the satisfaction of moral ***obligation*** but the conditions to exercise personal free ***decision***. The first requirement of human dignity in what concerns religious conviction is that every individual must be given the possibility to decide, even if it can be seen clearly that the way the person is deciding is objectively wrong. Human dignity exists in each person at the prior level of the conditions of possibility for the discharge of any moral obligation. It was the newly acquired historical awareness of this dignity that led people to demand that any external forces safeguard scrupulously the conditions for each person to assume with full maturity his or her religious option. That is the origin and the ground for the claim of a civil right to religious freedom.

Consequently, the right stands absolutely independent from any judgment on the truth of the belief in religious matters professed by the person. "Men's right to religious freedom, understood as freedom from coercion, is not based on the real or supposed truth of their religion, but on the indestructible responsibility of the individual to solve the religious problem by a personal decision."[129] It is a right founded on the person not on the truth, on the responsibility for one's self-determination in history not on a moral duty toward a transcendental truth. From the attentive consideration of human dignity followed a new ordering of human value, one in which primacy is imparted to subjective freedom over formal compliance with the truth: "Though all expressions of life may conform to the truth that has been grasped, they are not humanly valid if they are produced not through personal decision but under pressure from the surrounding world."[130]

Neither Indifferentism Nor Individualism. The sole focus of *Dignitatis Humanae* is the securing of a universal immunity from coercion in matters religious that is truly universal, hence, independent of individual moral uprightness or the objective truth of the particular religious conviction embraced. The emphasis on autonomous decision does not imply, however, any devaluation of the natural human obligation toward God and the moral duty before the truth. In no way does the immunity intend to open a realm for unencumbered subjectivism or religious indifferentism: "[R]eligious freedom as a right exists also in function of freedom as a duty in the religious field; and in that field it tends to unfold and expand in freedom as love."[131] Because neither being in truth or in error, nor having or not having discharged one's obligation toward the truth perceived conditions the fruition of the right to religious freedom, that "does not exclude—Pavan notes—that one of the most profound reasons for such a right is that men may be able faithfully and without hindrance to follow the light of truth, according to its presence in their minds."[132] At another time—responding to "those who have expressed and still express disappointment about the right to religious freedom as proclaimed by the Council, on the ground that a right with a merely negative content has very little impact on religious life"—he sets the immunity in its larger context: the "right with a negative content . . . is based on a presupposition . . . that with this right goes the recognition that human beings as persons are entitled to a reserved area within which they are called by nature and bound by duty to act on their own initiative and responsibility."[133] The immunity secures the reserved area so that the person may, then, properly respond to the call and fulfill the duty. In this larger picture, the triad responsibility, immediacy, and identity constitutive of the human dignity upon which the immunity from external coercion is grounded corresponds, in each person, to the duties of religious quest, of faithfulness toward the truth encountered, and of religious sincerity. This correspondence is what distinguishes the concept of religious freedom proclaimed at Vatican II from the religious freedom promoted by eighteenth- and nineteenth-centuries ideologies, which conspicuously rejected any duty toward an order of objective truth.

> Vatican II presupposes the existence of an order of truth objective, universal, absolute, valid for all; order of truth of which the dignity of the human person is an essential element: dignity understood in an existential sense . . .; order which everyone must strive to get to know, to which one must adhere in the measure one has already discovered it, and according to which one ought to live: *freedom as right is affirmed in order that there may be no obstacles to act and celebrate freedom as duty,* and as love for the good, above all for the supreme Good which is God.[134]

Nonetheless, the primary statement continues to be the assertion of the immunity. That immunity is what specifically concerned *Dignitatis Humanae,* because it was the new aspect in the social teaching of the church that needed to be affirmed and justified with all the emphasis a novelty requires. The traditionally established duties of the person toward religion and the truth, however, are not revoked or downgraded by the affirmation of the new right. They are actually explicitly recalled in the first and third numbers of *Dignitatis Humanae.*[135] Only now they have to be understood in the context that includes also the right to religious freedom as an imperative of human dignity.

In the end, however, even within an enlarged context, the corollary is the same:

> Whatever the level in which we consider the relationship between the human being and the truth, be it between the human being and the truth as value, or between the human being and the living truth which is God, or between the human being and the truth revealed manifested above all in Jesus Christ, divine Word made human, we arrive always at the same conclusion: human beings cannot organize and live this relationship in a manner adequate to their dignity of persons and to their nature, that is *consciously, freely,* and in a *responsible* manner, if they do not enjoy in their social relations the right to freedom in the religious domain. This right then must be understood as a fundamental right of the person, or in other terms, a natural right.[136]

In spite of the emphasis on a personal "reserved area," this immunity does not promote any kind of disconnected individualism. Freedom for personal decision does not mean isolation.[137] Commenting on number 3 of *Dignitatis Humanae,* Pavan notes that "the knowledge of the divine law results from personal inquiry into truth, carried on with the aid of instruction and dialogue." The formation of one's responsible decision takes place in social interchange, which cannot be regulated by force, but, instead, works through the method of rational persuasion and profits from the largest participation possible of all in a committed search for the common good.[138]

For that dialogue to be really fruitful, there must be honesty in intersubjective relations regarding the truth, both the truth encountered in one's conscience and the truth met in the thought of others. A sort of environment in which personal inquiry, sincerity, and honesty are encouraged "presupposes an atmosphere of freedom in society and the absence of any coercion that would force men into particular lines of thought. For such compulsion would inevitably lead to lies, double talk, and in the religious sphere especially to mere formalism."[139]

The fulfillment of the right to religious freedom certainly *presupposes* those conditions. At the same time, the more the principle of noncoercion is respected, the more it helps to *generate* them. "It is indeed a right that cannot fail to contribute to creating a social setting in which human beings, far from finding obstacles, are attracted toward satisfying two of their deepest exigencies which are at the same time two precise duties," namely, "that of professing one's religion sincerely" and that of following faithfully one's inner knowledge of the truth.[140]

There can be, thus, a virtuous circularity. To put it in motion, though, especially in a society in which there are many factors that make it increasingly difficult to act responsibly, there is a great "necessity to educate men to the right use of freedom in all spheres."[141] This is how Pavan interprets the aim of number 8 of *Dignitatis Humanae.*

The strictest respect for noncoercion, therefore, does not in any way imply passivity. Education for a better self-knowledge of human reality and for moral maturity, particularly for the exercise of responsibility and the respect for the rights of others, will help to develop a social atmosphere of free interaction, confidence, esteem for one another, and benevolent cooperation. There, Pietro Pavan believes, "those who are in the truth can confess it openly, and those who are in error can find the truth. This is true in every sphere, hence also in religion."[142]

The church's shared responsibility for this atmosphere of fertile freedom does not limit its apostolic commitment to proclaim the word of Christ, Pavan stresses. The mandate is not softened, only the method for carrying out this mission is conditioned, *Dignitatis Humanae* 14 states. This method has to retain the highest esteem for the freedom of any person, to work as invitation and never as coercion, so that the one addressed may come to accept the Spirit's invitation knowingly and freely.[143]

It is obvious, then, that Pavan sees no support in *Dignitatis Humanae* for the tendencies to privatize religion. The ambit of the immune personal space and the scope of the activities protected in the text of the declaration include religious cult, private but also public, free communication of one's religious convictions, and particularly the right to try to influence all temporal activities by one's faith. This last point the declaration attributes explicitly only to religious communities, in its number 4, but, Pavan argues, applies also to personal rights.[144]

Equally denied is any suggestion that the rejection of the traditional confessional state means a capitulation to the laicist or neutralist conception of the state.[145] Pavan considers the doctrine of *Dignitatis Humanae* to be an endorsement of the "democratic-social state founded on law," a state which certainly is "unqualified to decide the merits and contents of religious systems" (as of any concrete expressions of all spiritual values) but which acknowledges its duty to defend juridically the right of citizens to religious freedom and to politically "ensure that the citizens do not lack means to exercise their religious rights and fulfill their religious duties." Just because such a state acknowledges its religious incompetence, "it does not follow that it should be regarded as neutral or skeptical in matters of religion, or hostile to religion and hence as openly at odds with the gospel message and with the Church's sociopolitical teachings."[146]

Act of Trust in the Power of the Truth. *Dignitatis Humanae* states a commitment of the church to the defense of religious freedom as a fundamental right of the person. It does it through a shift of emphasis from the rights of the truth as an abstract value, in favor of the promotion of the dignity of concrete human beings in their historical context. The defense of the right becomes a claim that the church should uphold on behalf of any human being without exception, even against the claims of a state that calls itself Catholic, to the point that "the Church would be standing up for the atheist's right to remain an atheist." Pietro Pavan feels the need to state that expressly. Even if to some this interpretation "might give the impression that *Dignitatis Humanae* shows small esteem for the truth," that is a misperception. In reality, he contends, "truth is constantly the unifying and vitalizing principle in the Declaration—so much so that the document might be called a homage to truth."[147] First, the argument of the declaration is founded on an objective truth ("known from the revealed word of God and from reason itself" says *Dignitatis Humanae,* 2): the dignity of the human person understood in the existential sense.

Second, the emphasis on noncoercion and scrupulous respect for each person's stage of knowing and adhering to the truth is also done in the service of the truth. It is a service, however, that focuses overridingly on the process by which the concrete human person may arrive at the knowledge of the truth and gives lesser consideration to the relationship of each person individually with objective truth.[148] The untouchable dignity of the person requires, as a necessity, that the only truly ennobling and humanly acceptable way for the person to fulfill the conditions to commit herself to the truth is a process utterly personal, based on responsibility, immediacy to the truth, and sincerity, carried out in communion with others in society in a context of free and honest interchange and mutual assistance as it is described in the second paragraph of number 3 of the declaration. Each one of these aspects, and all together, demand immunity from any external coercion.

This inviolable principle of freedom concerns, thus, first and foremost, in *Dignitatis Humanae,* the removing of all obstacles to a personal encounter with the truth in which the person is free to respond, compelled solely by the power of the truth itself. It does not apply in the same way to the personal duty toward objective truth once this has been properly recognized. Failure to keep these distinctions in mind may well lead to the misperception, which Pavan speaks about, that *Dignitatis Humanae* shows "small esteem for the truth," and may lead to consequent attempts to force upon it interpretations that give less recognition than is due to the rules the declaration defines for the process of arriving at the truth, its principal and fundamental statement.

Third, Pavan sees also in the declaration a reconfirmation by the church of its trust in the power of the truth, a confidence sometimes in the past displaced by excessive accommodation to the protection of earthly powers and situations of privilege,[149] but which the church now tries to restore to its original purity.[150] More sensitive to the example of Christ and the Apostles, *Dignitatis Humanae* urges, in the church's evangelizing mission, an attitude of greater reliance on the appeal upon people of the "human-divine ideal of Christ" and on the direct action of the Holy Spirit in them, resisting thus the ever lurking temptations to resort to some sort of coercion, always contrary to the spirit of the gospel.[151] Under this renewed faith in the power of the truth, the social environment created by the regime of religious freedom is seen both as the best possible situation for those who are in error to find the truth,[152] and as "an advantage for the Church, since, in the long run at least, truth always ends by dissolving error."[153]

This can easily be labeled as one more instance of overconfident exhilaration in the aftermath of the council. However, in the end, even if the predicted success of the truth was being overblown by easy optimism, that does not change the fundamental character of the utterances of *Dignitatis Humanae.* The imposition upon the activity of the church of a framework that gives primacy to the respect for personal self-determination and the promotion of the conditions of possibility for the fulfillment of human dignity is irrevocable. Meanwhile, it may have proved harder than expected for truth to impose itself by its force only; mature personal responsibility may still animate the exercise of individual freedom in a much lesser degree than would be desirable. Yet, none of these apparent setbacks will justify any rolling back of the demands protecting the immunity of every person set by *Dignitatis Humanae.* The right to religious freedom, and the corresponding duties it imposes upon all social bodies, the church included, translate a fundamental claim of the nature of human beings. It cannot be subordinated thus to any other external interests, not those of organized religion, nor even those of the advancement of the truth. If the fruition of the right is not dependent on whether the obligation to seek the truth is carried out or not, as number 2 explicitly declares, neither can the priority to the promotion of freedom and personal responsibility be questioned just because apparently the voice of the church keeps losing power of persuasion in society.

A final note helps to explain Pavan's confidence that the power of the truth always prevails in freedom. He does not attribute the diversity of personal responses to God and the truth primarily to an opacity to the truth that sin has caused in human freedom. From this perspective, only Christ's redemption can restore true religious freedom, because only he can cure this defect in the fallen human condition.[154] Pavan underlines, instead, that what makes personal surrender to the truth a problem is a certain penumbra or mystery that involves the relationship between self and God, a condition that leaves the person free to adhere or not, and so calls for an exercise of responsibility.[155] Not so much defect in people, but excess of mystery on the part of God is what he invokes to explain the lack of uniformity in human responses in the religious domain, even among people sharing the same cultural traditions.

This suggestion shows how the theological place of religious freedom in Catholic doctrine has changed with *Dignitatis Humanae* in the way Pavan interprets it. Before, while still seen more properly as religious toleration—a constrained toleration for an evil that was better not to fight—the issue of religious freedom inhabited the area of moral casuistry as a particular instance of an option for a lesser evil. Now, when it has been fully recognized as an inalienable requisite of human dignity for the religious searching of every person, religious freedom touches theological roots deeply embedded in the dimension of mystery that always permeates the relation between God and humanity.

Fundamental Assertions of *Dignitatis Humanae* as Parameters for the Service of the Church to the Human Search for the Truth

The analysis of the works of John Courtney Murray, Philippe André-Vincent, and Pietro Pavan has revealed three quite different takes on the same Vatican II document. What can explain such dissimilarities in the interpretation of the same text? Ultimately, behind the opposite mindsets, there will be differences of fundamental theological views on the present human condition and on the relationship of the divine with human reality. These, though, may be both cause and consequence of the kind of apprehension of historical reality that determines in great part the type of approach to *Dignitatis Humanae.*

More immediately, then, each of the distinct constructions responds certainly to a particular perception of the situation of the church and of the world, and of the role of the church in the world. As we have seen in the comparison between Murray and the French-speaking theologians, their differences were in good part supported and driven by a diversity of past historical experiences, namely, the quite unlike memories and predispositions regarding the encounter between Catholicism and liberalism. But the present and the future of the life and mission of the church seemed to be even more determinant in their interpretative choices. The commentaries show also a kind of defensive bias. Each one seems to sense the danger of what would be, in his view, a particular less-careful reading of some aspects of the declaration and preemptively reacts against it. For Murray and Pavan, that would be everything that curtailed the impulse given by Vatican II to the promotion of freedom, personal responsibility, and dialogue in church-society relationships, a menace present in any revisionist tendency to read *Dignitatis Humanae.* For André-Vincent, it would be those elements that could serve to encourage indifferentism and individualism and so he emphasizes everything that puts the accent on the primacy of the truth. Each one has, thus, accentuated in the text of the declaration what would more effectively counter his most feared interpretative deviation and, consequently, would better prevent the anticipated detrimental consequences of that deviation for the presence of the church in the contemporary world.

We see again how there continues to be a reciprocal influence between fundamental options regarding the relationship of the church with pluralistic societies, on one side, and basic approaches to the interpretation of *Dignitatis Humanae,* on the other. The declaration settled a long and difficult conflict, gathered the lessons of many different attempts to deal with the challenges of liberalism, and became emblematic of what looked, at the time at least, like a new promising attitude of the church before modernity. The confrontation with the fundamental assertions of the declaration can still serve, thus, to clarify and evaluate those competing theologies and practices of the social mission of the church. Those assertions will work as parameters that will expose the risks and dangers of the basic position assumed, and, hopefully, will help avoid the repetition of past errors or dead-end paths. This is of an even greater importance in the context of the third moment, in which much of what is newly challenging the church is also still closely related to the trials of the past more or less directly connected to the issue of religious freedom.

In the survey of typical interpretations, what was most obvious was great disagreement. Nevertheless, in spite of all the differences, all the interpretations were still dealing with the same text. Even when they stretched out to subjects not expressly present there, each one credibly claimed to be developing aspects present in the text. They all interpreted the same document, even if some acknowledged that they were giving central importance to what is less than nuclear in the structure of the declaration. In a comparative evaluation of these interpretations, there is certainly place for value judgments on how well each one deals with the integrity and balance of the text, and whether any emphasis on the partial threatened to undermine the essential. However, if, before that, we assume the absence of a blatant lack of cohesion in the conciliar declaration, this diversity of interpretations recommends an effort to find in them levels of complementarity by gathering from each one the relevant contributions for a more comprehensive explanation of the text of *Dignitatis Humanae.* Furthermore, it encourages an attempt at a systematic account of the entire content of the declaration, as faithful to the proportion of its different elements as possible. It seems to be viable, at least, to offer a summary of the fundamental assertions of *Dignitatis Humanae,* in which all the emphases of these interpretations will find their place. Against the background of the whole, the particularity of each will come out more visibly, and the fitting degree of pertinence of each one will also be easier to evaluate.

That same systematic set of assertions and parameters will serve, then, as a basis to explore the continued relevance of *Dignitatis Humanae* for the challenges of the third moment.

THE ESSENTIAL PROCLAMATION

"This Vatican synod declares that the human person has a right to religious freedom." Such is the opening sentence of the first paragraph of number 2, the central segment of *Dignitatis Humanae*,[156] proclaiming solemnly the primary and substantial goal of the declaration. This statement, in itself, is not subject to interpretative controversy, here all agree. The text continues by describing in what that freedom consists (a point of contention already): a double immunity from coercion against one's conscience in religious matters, in individual or communitarian expression, private or public activity. Then, it identifies on what the right is based: the dignity of the human person. Finally, it prescribes that such human right should become a civil right expressly guaranteed in the juridical order of every state.

This formal declaration, by itself only, changed the official position of the Catholic Church, putting to rest the thesis/hypothesis formulation, and signified the acceptance by official Catholicism of a constitutional practice that the church had opposed for centuries. In terms of doctrine, it established a fundamentally different starting point for the consideration of the role of governments regarding religion. Essentially, it is a statement about a civil right, about a particular area of the legal relations between the state and individuals and groups in society, namely the domain of religious belief and religious expression. This is where Murray kept the focus of his interpretations. At this level, *Dignitatis Humanae* is clear and there is not much room for creative disagreement. It is on the justifications advanced to ground this proclamation, and also on the implications of supporting statements framing it in the text, that interpreters disagree most.

UNWAVERING ASSERTION OF THE MORAL DUTIES TOWARD THE TRUTH

Dignitatis Humanae was finally recognizing the fundamental assertion of the liberal individual right to religious freedom. For that reason, the text is very careful in distancing itself from all unacceptable principles and practices that had been historically associated with ideological liberalism. It does that not just by a careful definition of the contents of the right newly espoused, but also by explicitly restating once again those principles in the name of which the church had rejected the liberal religious freedom of the eighteenth and nineteenth centuries. The council wants to leave no doubts at all that the recognition, newly awarded, of this right involved no compromise whatsoever with any of the modern assaults on religion and the church. Scattered throughout the declaration are categorical statements and careful qualifications, which constantly recall these traditionally asserted bases of the church's moral and social teaching.

First, to dismiss up front any possible doubts, the declaration reasserts the traditional self-understanding of the church and of its mission: "[S]ince people's demand for religious liberty in carrying out their duty to worship God concerns freedom from compulsion in civil society, it leaves intact the traditional catholic teaching on the moral obligation of individuals and societies towards the true religion and the one church of Christ." And so the council states unapologetically the belief that "this one and only true religion subsists in the catholic and apostolic church," and that from Christ it has received the commission to announce it to all (*DH,* no. 1). Later, the declaration reasserts that "the catholic church is by the will of Christ the teacher of truth. Its charge is to announce and authentically teach that truth which is Christ, and at the same time to give authoritative statement and confirmation of the principles of the moral order which derive from human nature itself." As it proclaims the right to religious freedom, the Catholic Church reaffirms also its commitment to evangelization, to the spreading of the word in obedience to the command of Christ, and encourages all Christians to engage in that task "with the confidence and boldness of apostles, even to the shedding of their blood" (*DH,* no. 14).

Second, religious indifferentism is also explicitly rejected. The declaration reasserts that "all people are bound to seek for the truth, especially about God and his church, and when they have found it to embrace and keep it," obligations that "touch and bind the human conscience."[157]

Third, *Dignitatis Humanae* leaves no space for relativism either, as it recalls the existence of a "supreme rule of life," "the divine law itself, objective and universal." God enables all people to share in the knowledge of that law, and thus all are capacitated to "recognize the unchanging truth" (*DH,* no. 3).

Fourth, it does not condone a religion purely individualistic. The inclusion in the definition of the right of the immunity from being prevented to act according to one's conscience already implied it (*DH,* no. 2). Number 3 makes it explicit: "The social nature of human beings, however, requires that they should express these interior religious acts externally, share their religion with others, and witness to it communally." Number 4 fleshes out the implications of all this, in terms of the freedom to be granted to religious communities for organizing themselves internally, setting up institutional structures, and giving public witness to their beliefs. People cannot be "denied the free and corporate practice of their religion within the limits set by due public order" (*DH,* no. 3).

Fifth, neither does the doctrine of *Dignitatis Humanae* settle for a view of a religion privatized, kept outside of the public sphere. The declaration recognizes as part of the right to religious freedom the freedom to erect and support religiously inspired associations for all sorts of lawful social purposes. Moreover, it recognizes also as "a further component of religious liberty that religious communities should not be prevented from freely expounding the special value of their teaching for the right ordering of society and for the revitalizing of all human activity" (*DH,* no. 4).

Sixth, there is not even endorsement of a neutralist view of the role of the state regarding religion. *Dignitatis Humanae* revoked the support for the confessional Catholic state as the sociopolitical ideal. (Although, in a controversial paragraph in number 6, it continues to allow for a special constitutional status of one particular religion; such an opening is stated in conditional form and emphasizes the duty of that state to uphold equally the freedom of every person and religious community, something confirmed by the principle stated further down in the same number that "the state must ensure the equality of citizens before the law.") But it does not defend a stance of absolute indifference of the state toward religion. The end of number 3 tries to strike this balance in a sequence of two sentences to be kept in counterpoint to one another: "So the state, whose proper purpose it is to provide for the temporal common good, should certainly recognize and promote the religious life of its citizens. With equal certainty it exceeds the limits of its authority, if it takes upon itself to direct or to prevent religious activity." The second sentence is a new basic principle in the argument for religious freedom; the fundamental thrust of the document stresses its direction. However, the qualification offered by the first sentence serves as a reminder that the council is not pushing for the extreme position of a total rejection of any role for the state.

During the redaction of *Dignitatis Humanae,* these statements worked as a series of reassurances against the anxieties and concerns that, within the church, fueled much of the resistance to the new doctrine on religious freedom. Stating the permanence of the traditionally affirmed fundamental principles of the social doctrine of the church regarding freedom, they define, in the framework of the declaration, the external boundaries within which the distinct proposition, the real breakthrough, of *Dignitatis Humanae* was going to be stated. They are, thus, indispensable to situate the new teaching, but they are not the center of it. Afterwards, they serve also to dismiss any misunderstandings of the intention of the council caused by hasty or superficial consideration of the declaration in a too liberalistic reading.

These examples, and others that will come into view in the continuation of the analysis, show that the kind of development of the theology of religious freedom André-Vincent wants to prevent is already clearly counteracted by the declaration itself. The degree to which it is done, however, did not appease the fears and suspicions of the French theologian. He tried to strengthen considerably the weight of these elements, to the point of putting also upon them the whole burden of the justification for religious freedom. Consequently, he was less successful in securing a credible basis for the new element *Dignitatis Humanae* wanted to include in the church's social doctrine.

NEW EMPHASIS ON PERSONAL FREEDOM

The council made once again explicit the centuries-old rejection of the errors of laicist liberalism. That cannot be used to mask, however, that *Dignitatis Humanae* signified the culmination of a momentous development in Catholic social teaching. The main point of the declaration consisted precisely of the espousing of the central tenet of liberal modernity: the exaltation of the freedom of the human person. The duties associated with the traditional principles are not diminished, but now the declaration affirms, with new emphasis and broader recognition of implications, another principle which, in spite of its relative novelty, is no less fundamental: the respect for the dignity of the human person, translated in an exigency of responsibility and freedom for the personal discharge of everyone's duties toward the truth and God.

The second paragraph of number 2 is the place in which the requirement of non-coercion as absolute condition for the search and embracing of the truth in religious matters is made more starkly. In its entirety, it summarizes the essential teaching of the declaration, and the succession of its sentences carries the argument to its sharpest formulation in the whole document. It begins with another reaffirmation of moral obligation, expanding slightly on what had already been said before: "In accordance with their dignity as persons, equipped with reason and free will and endowed with personal responsibility, all are impelled by their own nature and are bound by moral obligation to seek truth, above all religious truth. They are further bound to hold to the truth once it is known, and to regulate their whole lives by its demands." This is what was taken for granted, the basis from which the council would advance and what it in no way wanted to undermine. The novelty brought about by *Dignitatis Humanae* is stated in the ensuing sentence: "But people are only able to meet this obligation in ways that accord with their own nature, if they enjoy both psychological freedom and freedom from external coercion" (*DH*, no. 2). The recognition of this exclusive condition is the big doctrinal turn, which needs to be made manifest in all its incisiveness.

So the declaration goes further, to make clear that it means a radical change on the grounding for the right to freedom, refusing any dependency on any moral prerequisite and definitively steering it away from the old reasoning that "only truth has rights": "Thus the right to religious freedom is based on human nature itself, not on any merely personal attitude of mind." And, in order that no doubts may remain about the scope of the principle, it spells out a crucial consequence: "Therefore this right to non-interference persists even in those who do not carry out their obligation of seeking the truth and standing by it; and the exercise of the right should not be curtailed, as long as due public order is preserved" (*DH,* no. 2). This proposition, more than any other one in the declaration, establishes unequivocally that, in the historical reality of people, the value personal freedom always prevails over any intent of externally enforced objective conformance with truth. Even if a person ignores or rejects truth, still that person's right to immunity from coercion stands undiminished; freedom is upheld even when invoked against truth. Therefore, the aim of compliance with the truth can never justify the bracketing of one's personal right to immunity; no material upholding of truth ever justifies its perfunctory realization at the expense of personal freedom.

Number 2 is the central article of *Dignitatis Humanae.* It states the essential substance of the document, defining the right proclaimed, the basic ground to support it, and the range of its application. There we find the affirmations that, in the whole declaration, most obviously make a difference, that is, introduce progress and new insight in the continuity of the church's official teaching. The way it is interpreted, or even just quoted, is thus an immediate clue as to what kind of bias may be guiding the reader.

What makes *Dignitatis Humanae* stand out is its unequivocal placing of freedom first regarding religious duties, both for the moral development of the person and in the social order. The declaration deepened the twentieth-century centering of Catholic social doctrine on the person and the requisites of human dignity. In the domain of religious freedom, this new doctrine displaced the old reasoning of rights based directly on spiritual values. The person, free and responsible, repossessed the precedence; human dignity and its requirements has to be the starting point and the purpose of any urging of religious duties. This ordering of values implied the avowal by the church that its action in the world should and would be primarily about the exaltation of the dignity of every person, not about the preservation or advancement of a disincarnate truth. Freedom is the necessary path to the attaining of the truth. In this the church follows the example of God in God's dealings with humanity: "God calls people to serve him in spirit and in truth, so that they are bound to him by personal decision and not by external force. For he looks to the dignity of the human person, whom he has created and who needs to be guided by his own judgment and enjoy his freedom" (*DH,* no. 11). No real service of the truth can circumvent careful reverence for personal freedom. This is the aspect that Pavan privileged in his analysis of the conciliar document.

Dignitatis Humanae also changed Catholic doctrine on the duties of the state regarding religion, as Murray stressed, almost exclusively, in his commentaries. Correlated to the resurgence of the values of the person and the affirmation of religious freedom was the demise of a conception of the common good that regarded social compliance with religious truth an essential factor for political unity and public morality. Associated with a paternalistic understanding of the political function, it included the formal acknowledgment, protection, and favor of the true religion, even if it had to be imposed by the state, among the attributions of the political power.

The new basis of the social order proposed by *Dignitatis Humanae* states that a "principle of full freedom is to be preserved in society according to which people are given the maximum of liberty, and only restrained when and in so far as is necessary" (*DH,* no. 7). Presently, as article 6 declares, "The common good of society . . . consists chiefly in the safeguarding of the rights and duties of the human person." Therefore, among the attributions of government in the service of the common good, preservation of freedom and protection of human rights takes the place of promotion of the truth as the first task of the state in what concerns religion. Religion continues to be recognized as a valuable resource for social life and the declaration attributes a role to the state in making that positive influence effective. However, in the regime of religious freedom, the state does not care for religion directly. Its function is merely to protect the indiscriminate religious freedom of every person, "to give effective protection to the religious liberty of all citizens by just laws and other suitable means, and to ensure favourable conditions for fostering religious life." Under these conditions alone, "citizens will have the real opportunity to exercise their religious rights and fulfil their duties," and this is the way through which "society will itself benefit from the fruits of justice and peace which result from people's fidelity to God and his holy will" (*DH,* no. 6). In the scale of values to protect and promote in society, likewise, the declaration puts personal religious freedom as first and foremost.

Moral duties toward the truth and the personal right to freedom, as described in the last two sections, constitute two sets of principles that coexist always in some tension. In the area of religious freedom, the duty toward truth had had considerable prominence in the teaching of the church for many centuries, while the right to freedom was a recent retrieval. *Dignitatis Humanae* puts them together, the new and the old, and gives priority to freedom. The immediate challenge, after such a substantial reconfiguration, is to find the new balance, an equilibrium between the binding force of the moral obligation and the fundamental primacy of freedom. It does not do to be so zealous with the duty to truth, be it by inertia or by fear of it being in jeopardy, that no due space is allowed for personal freedom. Nor can imprudent enthusiasm for personal freedom lead to the throwing away of the duties regarding truth.

Certainly the declaration puts more emphasis on the affirmation of the right to freedom, because that was precisely its objective, the new thing that it wanted to establish. Nevertheless, as it has been shown, frequent qualifications leave no doubt that this right is to subsist within the horizon and the framework of the traditional duties toward objective truth. Nothing of them is denied when respect for personal immunity from coercion is asserted anew as a precondition for the actualization of those duties.

Similarly, the claim to inner personal freedom, because it is a fundamental element of natural human dignity, recognized as such by the church after having become part of the modern self-awareness of humanity, must continue to be primary and inviolable, even as historical social contexts evolve. No urgency to stress the duties may lead to ignoring or weakening the right. The church cannot dispense with the right in favor of the duty, not even when confronted with cultural challenges that make maximalist claims for individual freedom, but forget almost completely the associated duties regarding truth.

These two commitments are to be held together, not one against the other, but the two upholding each other mutually, in a way that neither is ever sacrificed to the other. *Dignitatis Humanae* affirms both concurrently, sometimes by putting them closely together in a unique formulation. Number 3 offers a proposition with this confluence of claims: "[A]ll have both the right and the duty to search for religious truth, so that they may by the prudent use of appropriate means form for themselves right and true moral judgments." The side of the obligation toward an objective truth is affirmed by the recalling of the duty and in the qualifications attributed to the judgments: not just any kind of judgment (there is no conceding to subjectivism or relativism) but "right and true" moral judgments. However, it is people who have to "form for themselves" those judgments. Because they are free and responsible by nature, and thus their autonomy of sovereign decision making in religious matters cannot be betrayed, religious truth cannot be imposed on them.

The remaining clause concerns "the prudent use of appropriate means." That refers already to another set of propositions of *Dignitatis Humanae,* the ones that try to offer a concrete way for people to fulfill these two demands of their nature, the right and the duty, and also a practical direction for the church to help and not hinder people in that task and still discharge the gospel mission to bring all to the knowledge of the truth.

ENCOUNTERING THE TRUTH IN FREE DIALOGUE

How can a real, personal religious quest take place, one that breaks with indolent propensity to subjectivism, brings the person to an honest confrontation with rightness and truth, and still scrupulously respects everyone's inner freedom for a conscientious autonomous decision? The way pointed out by *Dignitatis Humanae* follows through the social and communicational natural dimensions of the human person. The second paragraph of number 3 enumerates the "appropriate means" to provide each person in his or her personal journey with the conditions propitious to encounter the truth and decide for the truth: "Truth, however, *Dignitatis Humanae* says, is to be sought in a manner befitting the dignity and the social nature of the human person, namely by free inquiry assisted by teaching and instruction, and by exchange and discussion in which people explain to each other the truth as they have discovered it or as they see it, so as to assist each other in their search." Freedom is essential, but with it comes an obligation to inquire and a need for help from teaching and instruction, all in a context of dialogue and mutual help, and all making it possible, thus, for the truth to be known and "embraced by a personal act of assent" (*DH,* no. 3).

On the part of the church, coercion upon people is rejected and mere formal compliance devalued. However, respect for personal immunity does not mean leaving each person alone to decide, enclosed in his or her individualistic absolute independence. It does not imply that the church sets itself aside, inhibited into indifference or presumed impotence. On the contrary, respect for the dignity of the person requires active involvement in the human process of searching for the truth. The church does not abdicate from engaging people.

Freedom of conscience is unassailable but there is space and need for the formation of one's conscience in freedom. *Dignitatis Humanae* recalls the important role of the magisterium for that: "In forming their consciences the christian faithful should give careful attention to the sacred and certain teaching of the church" (*DH,* no. 14). It also stresses the crucial importance of religious education, both in the family and at school (*DH,* no. 5), and in the public mission of the church: "[R]eligious communities are entitled to teach and give witness to their faith publicly in speech and writing without hindrance" (*DH,* no. 4). The divine command binding the church to "teach all nations" is not watered down, as all of number 14 powerfully reminds us. The disciple owes to Christ the obligation of announcing loyally the truth learned from him, but "at the same time the love of Christ presses the disciple to deal lovingly, prudently and patiently with those who are ignorant or mistaken about the faith" (*DH*, no. 14).

So, once again, there is a tension between obligation and right, truth and freedom, tension now between an obligation of every Christian faithful and the right and dignity of his or her neighbors. The closing of this article summarizes it: "[A]ccount must be taken of one's obligations to the proclamation of Christ the life-giving Word, of the rights of the human person, and of the measure of the grace of Christ given to each by God to summon him to the free acceptance and profession of the faith" (*DH*, no. 14). This is no more than the explicit appropriation by the church of what the declaration had already ascertained for all religious communities: "[I]n propagating their religious belief they must always abstain from any kind of action that savours of undue pressure or improper enticement, particularly in regard to the poor or uneducated" (*DH*, no. 4).

Dignitatis Humanae sets a new immediate priority for the mission of the church in the service of the truth. First and foremost in the rank of its preoccupations no longer is the defense of objective truth, but the promotion of persons in their dignity. The new ideal is not so much that the same truth be formally recognized by all without exception, but rather that every person may find a social environment of unobstructed communication in which each one will have the real possibility of encountering enlightenment about one's own experience of the truth and learn with the experience of others, and, finally, choose the truth in full awareness of it and in full possession of oneself. The church cannot impose the truth, directly or by the agency of the state, so it concentrates on creating the conditions in which the truth will impose itself by its own power only. For that, it does not just have to continue to propose the truth it knows, but it must also apply its efforts of persuasion in a way that fosters the development of free interchange, true dialogue, and fruitful interaction, in an atmosphere of universal good will, openness, attention to the other, and mutual trust.

This is the new parameter for the church's mission of spreading the faith—neither the vindication of objective truth in every instance and at any cost, nor the extolling of freedom with no regard for truth. Rather, it is the promotion of responsible freedom as the way to serve the truth, directly (the dignity of the person is a fundamental truth) and mediately (in freedom, truth will triumph on its own). Dialogue and invitation, instead of paternalistic social pressure, is the way to foment personal maturity and responsibility. It cannot dispense with freedom, but it will only be successful with the help of an unrelenting determination to educate consciences.

The declaration does not overlook the difficulties before such a strategy in the contemporary context of the crisis of freedom. Number 8 describes the dangers for freedom as coming from two sides, defect and excess: restrictions that put people "in danger of being robbed of their power of free decision" and exaggerated claims of absolute autonomy that "in the name of freedom . . . reject all control and discount every duty of obedience." In response, "this Vatican synod exhorts all, and particularly those who have the charge of educating others, to apply themselves to bringing up people who will respect the moral law, obey legitimate authority and have a love for genuine freedom." The focus, however, is not on the moral law or authority, but on fully developed persons, for the text continues: "[T]hat is, people who will use their own judgment to make decisions in the light of the truth, plan their activities with a sense of responsibility, and freely combine their efforts with others to achieve all that is just and true" (*DH,* no. 8). The answer to the crisis of freedom is not a reinforcement of heteronomous ordinances, but a reaffirmation and empowerment of personal judgment, responsibility, freedom, and collaboration. More and better freedom and responsibility, not less, will yield the remedies for the crisis of freedom.

The decentering of the church's primary attention from transcendental truth in favor of the concrete person forced the church to decenter itself too. In *Dignitatis Humanae* the traditional claim for freedom of the church is not called for by itself, but is included and subsumed in the demand of general recognition for a universal right of the person. The declaration continues to defend the right of the church to full freedom of action for its ministry: "This freedom of the church is a fundamental principle in all relations between the church and both the state and the whole social order." It even reaffirms the divine origin of this institutional right, a liberty given to the church by Christ: "[T]he church claims freedom for itself as a spiritual authority, established by Christ the lord." Therefore, to go against it is to act against the will of God. However, "if the principle of religious freedom prevails as one not merely set forth in words, but genuinely put into practice," those demands are found to be completely fulfilled. In a situation like that, "the church truly has the solid basis in law and in fact for that independence which is necessary for the fulfilment of its divine mission." The declaration attends to the universal human right first, and only derivatively to the freedom of the church, in as much as, in the approach of *Dignitatis Humanae,* they can be separated: "There is therefore a harmony between the freedom of the church and that religious liberty which should be accorded as a right to all individuals and communities, and should be sanctioned by legal enactment" (*DH,* no. 13). It is this universal regime that the church works for, not its own privilege. What the declaration does is to promote this polity. Actually, more than making any special claims for a distinct freedom for itself, the declaration holds the church as one equally responsible for the protection of the right to religious freedom, together with individuals and social groups, civil authorities, and other religious communities.[158]

The doctrine of *Dignitatis Humanae* signifies a complete turnabout in the attitude of the church in the face of social pluralism in religious matters. The old position settled for toleration as a lesser evil. Now, religious freedom is seen as positive in itself. It is good for the individual person, for the church, and for the living of the faith, in all its dimensions: "[T]he ideal of religious freedom greatly helps to produce the conditions in which people can be openly invited to christian faith, and can embrace it of their own accord and witness to it in action in their whole manner of life" (*DH,* no. 10). It is even an indirect source of social improvement: "[R]eligious freedom should serve this further purpose, that people should act with greater responsibility in fulfilling their social functions in life" (*DH,* no. 8). All is advantageous with religious freedom. It is not an inevitable inconvenience, complicating things, to be confined as much as possible. Instead, the council establishes this respect for personal freedom demanded by human dignity as a necessary condition, and a means and way for personal and social accomplishment. This freedom, with all its requirements, has thus been constituted a truly fundamental basis for the mission of the church to persons and societies.

Learning from History and Human Experience

The distinct content of the teaching of *Dignitatis Humanae* is of remarkable consequence. But the methodological process by which, according to the declaration's own description, the church arrived at the recognition and justification of the right to religious freedom has great significance too.

The declaration begins by paying attention to what is happening in the world. Its opening paragraph notices that "the dignity of the human person is a concern of which people of our time are becoming increasingly more aware" (*DH,* no. 1). This shows in growing demands for "the use of their own responsible judgment and freedom . . . without external pressure or coercion" and claims "that bounds be set to government by law" in order that reasonable freedom for persons and social groups will not be stifled. The council takes notice of this "demand in human society for freedom," and, "keenly aware of these aspirations," wishes "to assert their consonance with truth and justice."

Moved by this external stimulus, then, it turns inside and "examines the sacred tradition and teaching of the church" (*DH,* no. 1) to find there new insights with which to endorse and buttress the human yearnings it finds in the world. The last article of the declaration returns to "the signs of our times," namely, the claims for freedom of the people of today,[159] and observes also how "clearly all nations are daily becoming more united, people of different culture and religious belief are bound together by closer ties, and there is a growing awareness of the responsibility of each." After it had already proclaimed, promoted, and justified this right, the council "urges Catholics and begs all people to reflect deeply on the degree to which religious freedom is a paramount necessity in the present situation of the human family," especially to the end "that relations of peace and harmony may be established and deepened in the human race" (*DH,* no. 15). Concrete historical human reality is, thus, a crucial element at both the beginning and the end of the declaration, framing the starting motivation and the further goal of *Dignitatis Humanae.*

It was human experience, discerned and formulated far in advance outside the church, that alerted the teaching church to a deeper exploration of its own tradition, and prompted it to the awareness of newly unveiled implications of the word of God. The church was a latecomer. The reasoning of *Dignitatis Humanae* does not mask the fact that, in this case, it did not lead but was led, and not even without initial resistance.

The second article of the declaration sets two concurring sources inspiring the new doctrine: the basis of the right is "the dignity of the human person as this is known from the revealed word of God and from reason itself" (*DH,* no. 2). Number 9, though, makes clearer how the two interacted. First, it affirms that the demands of human dignity "have come to be more fully known to human reason from the experience of centuries." Then it accounts for the part of revelation, but in a formulation that clearly stresses its after-the-fact supportive and confirming role: "[T]his teaching on freedom also has roots in divine revelation, and is for that reason to be held all the more sacred by Christians" (*DH,* no. 9). Such a subsidiary role was determined by two reasons: the absence of any explicit command in revelation; and the long inability of the church to develop a reading of Scripture more alert to attitudes, and less focused on the literal, which would have allowed it to draw the lesson.

What *Dignitatis Humanae* can say, in its number 9, is that, "although revelation does not affirm the right of immunity from external coercion in religious affairs in so many words, it nevertheless makes plain the whole scope of the dignity of the human person." This is achieved primarily in the contemplation of the attitude of Christ, which works as an exemplar: revelation "manifests the respect Christ showed for the freedom of people in fulfilling their duty in believing in the word of God; and it instills in us the spirit that the followers of such a master should always have as their ideal and model." Number 10 develops the regard for freedom in the act of faith, something invariably upheld in the tradition of the church, into encouragement, by expansive analogy, for religious freedom. Number 11, in a long sequence of passages from the Gospels, gives word and action illustrations of Christ's reverence for personal decision and respectful invitation without pressure; and also, with another series of references from other writings of the New Testament, of the practice of the apostles as they followed the example of their master. Nevertheless, the declaration recognizes that all these illustrations are just ways in which "light is thrown on the general principles on which the teaching of this declaration on religious freedom is based" (*DH,* no. 9). In the end, the recourse to revelation succeeds to grant approbation, albeit somewhat external, to the claim of the right and to the legitimacy of the church's promotion of it. The conclusion of the foray of the declaration into Scripture reads: "Hence the church is being faithful to the truth of the gospel and is following the way of Christ and the apostles, when it sees the principle of religious freedom as in accord with human dignity and the revelation of God, and when it promotes it" (*DH,* no. 12).

The urgent necessity to solve the issue of religious freedom pulled the council into the use of a methodology for moral reasoning that gives a vital role to inspirations received from human experience in history, and, for once, without a doubt, positioned the church in the learning side of the lauded process of dialogue with the world. Its humbling effect shows also in the refreshingly candid admission by the declaration that the church itself has acted against principles it now recognizes most in harmony with the gospel and clearly embodied in the way of Christ: "[A]t times in the life of the people of God, as it has pursued its pilgrimage through the twists and turns of human history, there have been ways of acting hardly in tune with the spirit of the gospel, indeed contrary to it" (*DH,* no. 12).

Nevertheless, in an effort to refer the good of the present self-consciousness of humanity back to the positive influence of the Christian tradition, and thus to allow the church still to claim some credit for it, *Dignitatis Humanae* continues: "Thus the leaven of the gospel has long been at work in the minds of people and has played a great part in the course of time in the growing recognition of the dignity of the human person, and in the maturing of the conviction that in religious matters this dignity must be preserved intact in society from any kind of human coercion" (*DH,* no. 12). The unquestionable fact that the church was late in adopting this conviction implies that, in this area of religious freedom, the power of the gospel leaven broke through with its fruits first outside the church rather than within it. In this particular matter, the leaven of the gospel seems to have needed the help of the secular world to move the teaching and action of the church. So much is tacitly admitted by the conciliar text.

This process of learning from historical human experience, if consistently continued, configures a new element of great importance in a renewed attitude of the church in its dialogue with the world. Gómez Mier[160] has claimed that this methodology amounted to a true paradigm shift in the epistemology of Catholic moral theology as this addresses concrete issues in the world. It allowed breaking open the dead end of the old exclusive reliance on "literal authorities" of written documents (be it proof-texts from Scripture or, more often, papal decrees), to recognize the new authority for today of significant human experiences. While the old methodology served to maintain a church unified in doctrine around a strong papacy, it also made it very difficult for the church to adapt to modernity, the regime of freedoms and pluralism, and made it incapable of dialoguing with secularity.[161] The new paradigm, in turn, starting from radical experiences of human life, opened the church to respond to the signs of the times, and made it able to interact with particular cultures.

Gómez Mier sees the contest of paradigms continuing after the council and still in contemporary theology. In interpretations of *Dignitatis Humanae,* the application by some to the text of mental schemes typical of the old paradigm results in readings of the text neighboring the conclusions of the preconciliar doctrine.[162] Now, the crucial thesis defended by Gómez Mier is precisely that the change of doctrine that provided a solution for the practical issue of religious freedom would not have been possible without a revolutionary change of methodology in moral reasoning. The reason is that "different paradigms generate different 'doctrines,' that is, different 'norms' in social morality."[163] Even if such a strict dependence of the doctrinal conclusion of *Dignitatis Humanae* on a particular methodological process as Gómez Mier claims may be a bit exaggerated, it still calls attention to a very important reciprocity between result and process, and the method of moral reasoning and propositional content, in what regards the object and the argument of the conciliar declaration on religious freedom.

From this point of view, if the quarrel of paradigms is still going on at the level of the reception and appropriation of *Dignitatis Humanae*—and the survey of interpretations proposed in this chapter leaves no doubt that it is—it becomes very important to analyze the methodological affiliation of every interpretation and of any attempted development of its doctrine, to test whether it is concordant with the paradigm that generated its doctrines and norms, or against it. As the affirmation of the right to religious freedom could not have come to be without a new paradigm, attempts to return to methodologies characteristic of the old paradigm in the interpretation of this right—even if claiming no intention of challenging what *Dignitatis Humanae* formally declared, but just the way it justified it—cannot but, at least, affect the full effectiveness and range of the original doctrine. The logical rule here is that the more intricately connected product and process are, the more difficult it becomes to keep the same actual dynamism of the formal outcome, with all its implications, when the methodology that produced it is reversed. Therefore, a revisionist methodological turn in the reading of the text of the declaration would bring its doctrine to a confused status, and would deprive the church, once again, of means already tested, which promise the continuation of a more fruitful encounter with the modern world.

Conclusion

I have attempted to articulate a comprehensive purview of the totality of *Dignitatis Humanae,* of its object and arguments, content and method, centered on the constructive tension between a clear assertion of priority to personal freedom and an equally careful attention to not lessening any individual obligations toward the truth. The importance of such comprehensive reading is manifold. It elucidates with detail the precise scope of the right to religious freedom, what kind of change it accomplished in official Catholic social teaching, and the traditional elements of it, which it was careful not to counter. It also exposes better the fundamental principles upon which this immunity is justified and those within which its exercise and ultimate end are framed. And, by making manifest what is granted, but also equally what is not compromised, it automatically denounces incomplete tendentious readings and may also help to appease the fears of misinterpretations that keep driving overly defensive interpretations of the text and approaches to its doctrine.

Besides being more equitable with the text, revealing its exact purpose and respecting the balance of substantial affirmations and stated qualifications, such systematic exposition, in addition, brings to a clearer focus the whole resonance of the declaration in the life of the church. *Dignitatis Humanae* did not only unequivocally change the official Catholic position on the strict issue of the acceptance by the church of the constitutionally guaranteed right to religious freedom, but it also has suggested, particularly in the arguments invoked to provide justifications and limits for that right, methodologies and set directions for the church's engagement with modern societies that have implications beyond the limited field of civil religious freedom. That was proved immediately by the fruits of the first moment of *Dignitatis Humanae* as it was translated into a positive impulse to renew the mission of the church to society, and contributed greatly to a much-improved receptivity to it on the part of the secular world.

Meanwhile, partial or one-sided interpretations have distracted the church from attending to the full implications of the basis upon which the consensus of the council was built. Those parameters highlighted in the comprehensive interpretation of the declaration, however, in as much as conciliar authority has affirmed them as essential requirements of human nature, form now a set of acquired principles in Catholic social doctrine. Consequently, they ought to continue to guide the church in a whole range of applications to which they are relevant, in particular in the historical context of the third moment, the challenges related to the role of the church in contemporary pluralistic societies. These are still very much defined by a confrontation of Catholicism with evolved forms of the same liberalism that originally raised the problems the council addressed in *Dignitatis Humanae*. Today, the engagement takes place in a context with a degree of pluralism in society that is more widespread and much deeper that the one of the second third of the twentieth century. But the way the conciliar church justified, then, its response to the particular problem of religious freedom continues to offer now the most elaborate set of fundamental principles, and also the most promising practical guide the Catholic Church has available to face these new or just renewed challenges.

Before testing these principles and methods on particular issues of the third moment, it is necessary to look in detail to the teaching of John Paul II regarding the themes of *Dignitatis Humanae*. His personal use, interpretation, and development of the doctrine of the declaration on religious freedom have been, indisputably, the most determinant contributions to fashioning the position in which the Catholic Church finds itself now before the challenges of the third moment and the kind of attitude it has been adopting to respond to them.

The analysis of the teaching of John Paul II will also identify the issues that are now more contentious in the relation of the church with pluralistic liberal societies. Those will be precisely the most apt test to the claimed continuous relevance of the articulated system of parameters set by *Dignitatis Humanae* for church-society relations.

NOTES

Bibliographic information for *Dignitatis Humanae*, cited in this and subsequent chapters, can be found in the references under Vatican II 1990.

1. See, for an account of the process of the drafting of *Dignitatis Humanae*, Regan 1967. A developed analysis of the evolution of Murray's thought can be found in Hooper 1986.
2. Murray 1993a, 230.
3. Murray 1966d, 570. He suggests here two reasons for this necessity: to make clear that it was a matter of principle not of expediency; and to prove that the argument can be made in terms of rational and authentically Christian principle, distinguishing

thus the church's claim from the arguments of others based on skepticism, relativism, indifferentism, or laicism.

4. Murray 1965b, 135.
5. Murray 1993a, 233. For a detailed analysis of the problems with the arguments of the first two drafts, see Murray 1966e, 16–27.
6. Murray 1993a, 234.
7. Murray 1966d, 571.
8. Ibid.
9. Murray 1993a, 237.
10. Ibid.
11. See, for his own account of this process, Murray 1966e, 15–42.
12. Murray 1993c, 206.
13. Murray 1993a, 237.
14. Murray 1993c, 206
15. See especially Murray 1993a, 1966d.
16. Murray 1993a, 240.
17. Murray 1966d, 572.
18. Ibid., 573.
19. Ibid. See also Murray 1966e, 31–32.
20. Murray 1966d, 574.
21. Murray 1993a, 231: "To clarify this point, let us suppose that there does exist in human society a power that possesses the right to prohibit religious practice. Such a power could only be the public power (the state)." See also Murray 1966e, 41: "If there be an authority that might possibly enter a counterclaim to the claim of the human person to immunity from coercion in matters religious, this authority could only be government, which is responsible for the establishment and maintenance of the juridical order of society." And, for a more complete explanation and summary of his argumentation, Murray 1966d, 569: "If an authority exists that is empowered to restrain men from public action in accordance with their religious beliefs, this authority can reside only in government, which presides over the juridical and social order. Therefore, in order to prove the validity of the moral claim of the human person to immunity from such restraint, it is necessary to show that government can enter no valid counterclaim. Here the political issue in the question of religious freedom appears. It is the crucial issue. It concerns functions and the limits of government in the order of religion. It may perhaps be doubted whether the declaration manifests sufficient awareness that this political issue is the crucial issue. Fortunately, however, it states the two principles which avail for the solution of the issue." He is referring here to the principles of the free society and of equality before the law.
22. Murray 1993a, 232.
23. He considered that the one true objection against the declaration consisted of the rejection, supported on nineteenth-century papal teaching, of its political affirma-

tion that the functions of the civil power do not include the protection of the true religion as part of the duties of the government toward the common good. See Murray 1967d, 117.

24. See ibid., 116.
25. Murray 1966d, 568: "It is proper to a juridical formula . . . that it should define the outside limits of a sphere of human activity and guarantee the integrity of this sphere against coercive intrusion from without, but that it should not enter, as it were, into the sphere itself, there to pass moral or theological judgments on the beliefs expressed, or on the actions performed, within the sphere. Such judgments are 'unconstitutional,' beyond the competence of purely juridical authority."
26. A few times, in his formulations, he enumerates the juridical power of the state as only one (although with special importance) among several possible agents of coercion in religious matters. See Murray 1966e, 40: "The right to immunity from coercion . . . is asserted against all 'the others'—other individuals, others organized in social groups, and especially that impersonal 'other' that is the state, the institutionalized agencies of law and government." Commenting on the third draft of the declaration, he had already written that what this text had "primarily in view was legal coercion exercised by government; also in view were other forms of compulsion, direct or indirect, brought to bear by institutions or forces within society." Murray 1965c, 40. See also Murray 1966e, 28–29; 1966d, 568; 1965a, 538.
27. Murray 1966e, 29 (emphasis added).
28. Yves Congar agrees with the wisdom of this strategy of avoiding dispersion with other complex and very problematic questions. See Congar 1967, 13–14.
29. See Murray 1994b, 188–90.
30. See Murray 1966a, 694–95, n. 58: *Dignitatis Humanae* was careful not to touch freedom within the church, but it is a stimulus for reflection on those issues. He took up that reflection in Murray 1966b, 734–41. See also Murray 1965c, 42: "The Declaration dealt with religious freedom as a constitutional issue, a problem in the juridical order of civil society. But in the minds of some, this issue was confused with another—the presently sensitive question of freedom and authority within the Church. This confusion gave rise to a vague fear that a conciliar declaration in favor of religious freedom would somehow be misinterpreted by the faithful and either cause trouble of conscience or possibly even undermine the authority of the Church. This confusion of two altogether separate issues was lamentable, and the ensuing fear was irrational."
31. Murray 1993a, 232. See also Murray 1966d, 565–66.
32. Murray 1994b, 189.
33. See Murray 1993a, 241–42.
34. The results of this work are documented in Murray 1960.
35. In an interview right after the council he could say: "I think that essentially what you find in the document is what I would call the essence of the liberal tradition of the West. It is the tradition of a free man in a free society. It is the theory of what we would call 'constitutional government.' . . . Thus the political tradition

that the Declaration affirms is the political tradition within which the American commonwealth came into being and in which our Constitution and the First Amendment took shape." Murray 1967c, 281.

36. Murray 1967a, 668.
37. Murray 1966e, 27–28. He had already said this, still during the council, when presenting the contents of the third draft in Murray 1965c, 40.
38. Murray 1967a, 668.
39. Ibid., 671
40. Ibid. See also Murray 1966d, 568.
41. See the following recognition by Murray of how this was an important factor at the council: "The long shadow of the Church's nineteenth-century struggle with Continental laicism and its deceptive conception of the religious neutrality of the State hung heavily over the whole conciliar argument about religious freedom. This is why the final text, at the instance of many Fathers, was amended to include this statement: 'Civil government, whose proper purpose is to care for the common temporal good, ought indeed to recognize the religious life of the citizenry and to show it favor . . .' (n. 3). This is also why the final text includes the further statement that government is bound not only to protect religious freedom but also 'to provide conditions favorable to furtherance of religious life' (n. 6)." Murray 1994a, 256. These statements intended to qualify the definition of religious freedom as immunity, which for Murray was necessary and sufficient.
42. Ibid., 257.
43. Hamer 1967, 104–05.
44. Delhaye 1969, x. For an analysis of Delhaye's preferred approach, characterized by an insistence on the primacy of the argument from revelation, see Wallace 1987, 196–244.
45. Murray 1965b, 139.
46. Coste 1969, 8.
47. See ibid., 487.
48. Ibid., 25–27.
49. Ibid., 10–11.
50. Ibid., 13.
51. Ibid., 14.
52. Coste adds an overview of the Old Testament to the sequence of themes of the second part of *Dignitatis Humanae,* whose outline he follows closely for the New Testament.
53. See ibid., 47.
54. Here, he follows the lead of Benoît 1967, 205–13, quotes of which he uses to state his conclusions.
55. See Coste 1969, 9.
56. Ibid., 79.
57. Ibid., 82. For a similar criticism of his lack of exegetical study and much weight

laid on a theological interpretation of Scripture, see Wallace 1987, 264–66 and also the conclusion at 317–18: "What he gives is more properly a theological reflection supported by scriptural references. There are some strong theological claims, for example that liberty of conscience is directly implied in the redemptive act itself. . . . More specific arguments are drawn from the behavior of Jesus Christ as presented in the Scriptures. Such considerations provide the elements of what might be called a theology of liberty, but these must be understood along with other theological considerations . . . they can scarcely be considered as 'foundations' of the teaching on the right to religious liberty except in a rather general sense."

58. Coste seems to be adopting a distinction between two levels of the right that another French theologian, Broglie 1964, 1965, proposed during the council. For a description and analysis of Broglie's contribution see Wallace 1987, 52–143.

59. Coste 1969, 83: "Revelation does not explicitly affirm the first [the civil right to religious freedom], that is clear, . . . but it implies it though. Nevertheless we claim that it affirms explicitly the second—which is the essential—that is, the fundamental human right to religious freedom and that it affirms it precisely as immunity from all external constraint in the religious domain. With roots that go as deep as the Old Testament, it is the meaning of the behavior and the orientations of Jesus Christ, as Lord of the Church and of the world: respecting it fully himself, and willing the total freedom of faith, prescribing the distinction between the political and the religious domains and renouncing completely to the means of pressure that his compatriots had integrated in their messianic hope."

60. See ibid., 86: "Our previous faith approach was essential and primordial. But it is not sufficient. Or, moreover, it is our faith approach itself that claims a subsequent rational approach. . . . Our rational approach will act upon our faith approach and will allow it a new deepening in the unity of a personal reflection permeated by the evangelical spirit."

61. See Murray 1994b, 194–95. Historical consciousness and the secularity of society and state are described in this essay as the two great movements of the nineteenth century, both initially opposed by the church.

62. Murray 1965c, 41.

63. Ibid., 42.

64. Ibid. See also Murray 1965b, 136–37.

65. Murray 1965c, 42.

66. Murray 1967a, 672–73.

67. Murray 1966d, 570–71.

68. Murray 1993c, 215.

69. "The American constitutional principle of the equality before the law, in its application to freedom of religion, carries no connotations of this theological error [religious indifferentism]. This fact was never attended to, or understood, by the apostolic hierarchy of the nineteenth-century Church in Europe. It may be doubted whether a general understanding of the fact prevailed at Vatican II." Murray 1967a, 673. See also Murray 1966d, 568: "In our [American] case the juridical formula, 'the free exercise of religion,' contains no positive evaluation of the religious phe-

nomenon in any of its manifestations. It simply defines the immunity of these manifestations from interference, as long as they remain within the outside limits of lawful freedom."

70. Murray 1967a, 669.

71. Ibid.: "The criticism, however, seemed to reveal a reluctance or a failure on the part of some of the Fathers to grasp the true theoretical, as well as practical, position of the problem."

72. Murray 1966e, 37.

73. Murray 1966d, 568–69.

74. Murray 1967a, 673. In another essay, however, Murray concedes a little more to this objection. Describing the twofold foundation of the church's right to freedom given by *Dignitatis Humanae* (the theological foundation on the mandate of Christ and, in social and political terms, the foundation on the dignity of the human person and her consequent necessary freedom in the practice of religion), Murray writes that "if the unique theological title [to freedom by the church] is not asserted, the way is opened to indifferentism." However this title cannot be invoked against secular powers in society and state, because that would violate the differentiation of the secular and sacral orders. "Hence the autonomy of the secular order requires that, within this order and in the face of its constituted organs of government, the Church should present her claim to freedom on these secular grounds—in the name of the human person, who is the foundation, the end, and the bearer of the whole social process." The best argument to support this kind of claim is, then, the political argument of the limitation of civil power. The same differentiation of orders requires that the right to religious freedom be defined primarily as immunity. The entitlement to freedom from the mandate of Christ is a freedom "for," but this is a discourse "in the transtemporal order of the history of salvation," the order of the relationship of the person with God, while "the technical issue of religious freedom rises in the juridical order, which is the order of horizontal interpersonal relations among men, between a man and organized society, and especially between the people—as individuals and as associated in communities, including religious communities—and the powers of government." Asserted in this order, the freedom of the church can only be freedom "from," an immunity. Otherwise, if the freedom of the church in the juridical order makes claims beyond the "self-denying ordinance on the power of government," that "claim can only be that government should use its power in furtherance of the Church's divine mission," and the differentiation of the two orders would not be respected. Murray 1993c, 210–12.

75. Murray 1965c, 43.

76. Murray 1967a, 672.

77. Ibid., 673.

78. Murray 1994b, 187.

79. Ibid., 190.

80. Murray, 1966c, 674. See also Murray 1966f, 592.

81. Murray 1966d, 565. See also Murray 1994a, 258; 1965c, 43; 1966c, 673.

82. André-Vincent, 1976.

83. For the distinction of these two conceptions of rights see especially ibid., 105–08 and 147–52. As a summary/conclusion of the possible equivoques associated with the use of the language of rights, see ibid., 151: "Such is the doctrine of fundamental rights, which is at the crossroad of three orders: ontological, moral, and juridical. It supposes the realist (classical) notion of natural right. But it makes use of the language of modern natural right. There is a great risk of seeing in fundamental rights mere "subjective rights," powers given to an absolute subject, and not goals of right, foundations for the search, the determination of the right. The language of modern natural right tends to confuse the juridical and ontological orders."

84. For the transcendent foundation, see especially ibid., 118–24.

85. Ibid., 155–56: "The Declaration formulates an objective requirement of natural law as it founds religious freedom in human nature; but it does in the optic of modern natural right. The last redaction confirms the double affiliation to the traditional theological doctrine and to a conception of right dominated by subjectivism."

86. Ibid. See also ibid., 218: "[I]t is in the duty to honor God that we find the right to religious freedom in its foundation. Non-coercion in the exercise of this fundamental obligation proceeds from the nature of the religious bond itself: the One who is the Truth (and who is Love) cannot attract to Himself but freely."

87. Ibid., 159: "Freedom flows from the nature of the Truth: it is required by the personal relationship of man with the Truth. This rational evidence is stated since this first moment of the declaration: it will develop itself throughout the text." In this same page, other sentences repeat this idea: "In the Declaration, the problem of foundation is first. . . . The problem of foundation is the problem of the Truth. . . . the true "freedom of conscience": it is grounded on the essential (ontological) relation of all judgment to the Truth. . . . it is this obligation of the conscience regarding the Truth that grounds its freedom."

88. Ibid., 191: "The right to religious freedom locates itself in the social and civic domain. But its foundation transcends this domain; and it was necessary to go to the foundation. We have seen it, religious freedom grounds itself on the personal relationship of the spirit to the truth, of man to God." See also ibid., 215–16: "Every man finds in the religious act the meaning of his life. He is so ordered by his nature, whatever his religion or irreligion. 'Ontological obligation', it has been said: religious obligation written in the nature of the human being, in his ontological structure. That structure founds religious freedom."

89. Ibid., 208: "The foundation of religious freedom is in the natural ordering of the spirit to God, Primary Truth, and Sovereign Good. Now this ordering lost by 'the sin of nature' re-emerges in the soul through the grace of Jesus Christ."

90. A sequence of three quotes illustrates this process. First, the idea more often repeated throughout the book, the basis of the whole thesis: "Religious freedom roots itself in the natural foundation of freedom: the ontological relation of man to Primordial Truth." Ibid., 207. A second step is described by a sentence in a footnote at the beginning of the book: "[T]his individual right is founded more

on the nature of the religious act which requires a free relation with God, than on the nature of the human person and its individual dignity." Ibid., 13, n. 7. Finally, he puts such an accent on the divine pole of the relationship that it almost ceases to be a human right: "[T]he fundamental right to religion [le droit fondamental de religion] contains in itself the foundation of all rights, of all powers, of all freedom: it emerges in the human person facing society, facing the universe: it manifests in her something that transcends the whole society and the whole universe: a relationship to God: it is in every man the demand of what is due to God by all men: more than a right of man, a right of God." Ibid., 215. Here he does not speak of a "right to religious freedom" but of a fundamental right to religion, "droit fondamental de religion," which constitutes an ultimate empowerment, stronger than any other created power.

91. Ibid., 230: "The State that would as a good sociologist concentrate on the social utility of religion would be prepared to enslave it. To recognize the religious fact means approaching religious truth. . . . The recognition of the religious fact must go just there in order to ground religious freedom on its natural base, religious truth."

92. Ibid., 229: "The particular recognition of a given religion will in no way be contrary to religious freedom, it will rather confirm it if it starts from the truth that is its principle. For religious truth even without the light of Revelation contains the demand of religious freedom. The recognition by the State of the religious fact under the sign of its truth implies necessarily the affirmation of religious freedom." See also ibid., 231: "Does a 'saine laicity' oppose itself to the State confessing the truth of a given religion? We do not think so. Even more: the contrary will appear evident to anyone who knows clearly religious truth and has seen in it the foundation of true laicity as well as of true religion. A 'saine laicity' is the one that recognizes religious in all its truth. This recognition is implicit in a non-confessing State, it is explicit in the State that confesses the true religion. In both cases it is a State aware of its duties towards God and towards men." In a footnote to this paragraph, he concludes that in this perspective there is a drastic reduction of the distance between the lay and the confessional state. This laicity is demanded by the gospel as a consequence of the distinction of powers declared by Christ. This way, even "the confessional State, if it is Christian, cannot but make its own that 'saine laicity', as well as the other elements of religious freedom." As an illustration, André-Vincent refers to the postconciliar evolution of the status of the Catholic Church in Spain.

93. This is the final judgment of André-Vincent on *Dignitatis Humanae,* ending with a proposal to go theologically beyond it: "The Declaration in spite of its weaknesses has overcome the antinomy [of truth and freedom] and opened a way to the synthesis by going to the foundation. Its major intuition surpasses the conflict of freedom and law as it discovers in the truth the source of freedom as well as of the first obligation of man. To reassess this intuition of the natural order in the light of the gospel, that is the task for a theology of religious freedom today." Ibid., 232–33.

94. Pavan 1989b, 344.

95. Pavan 1976, 19.

96. Ibid., 13. Regarding the last element, the nature of the right, for an account of how the alternative positive/natural right separated the minority and majority groups at the council, and the reasons invoked by both, see Pavan 1989a, 65. Also Pavan 1967, 149–52; 176–80.
97. Pavan 1976, 19.
98. In the commentary published fifteen years after the council, he denounces two of these wrong interpretations. The first, that the conciliar fathers had adopted, at least implicitly, the position of those who claim that freedom, whatever the direction of its exercise, is always well exercised, that any arbitrary use of freedom is justified by freedom itself. This interpretation, he denounces, is radically opposed to the certain and incontestable content of the declaration. The second, the claim by some "who are or declare themselves Catholic" that the document would have only a contingent pastoral value, and that when the contemporary culture overcomes this phase the church will return to its traditional pre–Vatican II position. Pavan, 1989b, 345–47.
99. See Pavan 1976, 32. He refers here to three positions: that only the one who is in the truth (a Catholic, therefore) has a natural right to religious freedom, while others may have only a positive or legal right conditioned to the historical situation; the claiming of a preeminent juridical position for the Catholic Church in civil societies; and that the state cannot be anything but Catholic. In all these, there is a return to the position that only the truth has rights.
100. Ibid., 33: "The document is what it is, and it can only be understood by giving its words the meaning they have in common usage and in the context of the document itself."
101. Ibid.
102. "We take here as a starting point not the relationship between God and human beings, but, as we have seen, the acknowledgment of a fact: the growing awareness that human beings of the modern era have acquired of their proper dignity as persons. We have chosen that way of formulating the problem because it has a universal value; but also because it responds better to the psychology of men of today, and, therefore, is more accessible to them." Pavan 1967, 164.
103. See Pavan 1976, 13–14: The right "in all its essential elements . . . represents a new position in the tradition of the Catholic Church, but a new position that reveals itself as an intrinsic development in the sociopolitical teaching of the Catholic Church. It is a new step forward in that teaching, but a step forward that is not reversible—for two reasons: (1) It is a right not entirely linked with the historical situation—even though it was because of the historical situation that the conciliar fathers decided to examine it and to take a clear position on it. (2) It is a right founded in the dignity of the human person."
104. Ibid., 21.
105. Pavan 1967, 201.
106. Pavan 1989b, 352.
107. Pavan 1967, 179.
108. Commenting on number 15, which describes the features of the present historical

situation used by a group of conciliar fathers as the conjuntural basis to ground a positive right, Pavan makes clear that "these historical facts have certainly contributed to the decision of the Council fathers to proclaim religious freedom as a right of the person today; but this right is based, as has been said before, not on historical facts but on the claim due to the dignity of the human person." Pavan 1989a, 86. For later reaffirmations of the same point, see Pavan 1989b, 416; 1986, 28.

109. Pavan 1967, 179–80.

110. In Pavan 1989b, 353–54, commenting on the second paragraph of number 1 of the declaration, he writes: "The conciliar Fathers in fact, while presenting the Church in clear and unequivocal terms, with its true face as it really is, at the same time define and proclaim religious freedom a fundamental right of the person: *not because they were moved by an excessive spirit of adaptation to the times, but because it is a right that responds to the objective demands of the Catholic religion itself;* it is therefore a right included in seed in the gospel message" (emphasis added).

111. Pavan 1967, 193.

112. Ibid., 180.

113. Pavan 1989a, 66: "[T]hose fathers who continued to base the content of the right to religious freedom on the elements of religious faith could not but express their opinion that such a right belongs only to those who professed the true faith."

114. Pavan 1976, 20.

115. Pavan 1989a, 67.

116. Pavan 1976, 15.

117. In Pavan 1976, he speaks of "dignity understood 'ontologically,' " but in later commentaries he prefers the qualifier "existential." See Pavan 1986, 31 ("dignità della persona intesa in senso esistenziale") and passim; and also, Pavan 1989b, 351 and passim.

118. Pavan 1976, 15; see also 20–21.

119. Ibid., 16.

120. Ibid., 17.

121. Ibid., 18.

122. Pavan 1967, 166, 168.

123. Ibid., 171, 172.

124. Ibid., 154.

125. Pavan 1989a, 63.

126. "The freedom of the person is approached from the point of view of man's duty to assume responsibility for his relation to God in personal decisions. When the person has reached the point at which he can distinguish between true and false, between good and evil, he shares in deciding his own eternal destiny. True, this remains always a gift of God, but it is at the same time the result of a personal decision; therein lies its highest dignity." Ibid., 67.

127. Ibid., 66.

128. Ibid., 66–67.

129. Ibid., 75.
130. Ibid., 68. See also Pavan 1989b, 368.
131. Pavan 1976, 22.
132. Pavan 1989a, 67.
133. Pavan 1976, 21.
134. Pavan 1989b, 387.
135. Pavan notes that these clarifications were intended to appease the fears of some that the declaration might lead to religious indifferentism. See Pavan 1989a, 63.
136. Pavan 1967, 163.
137. Pavan 1976, 37: "[T]he process by which truth is known . . . is an intimately personal and unrepeatable process, yet one which is carried out not in isolation but in communion with others."
138. Pavan 1986, 29.
139. Pavan 1989a, 69. See also Pavan 1967, 162.
140. Pavan 1976, 22.
141. Pavan 1989a, 75.
142. Ibid., 77.
143. See Pavan 1976, 28.
144. See Pavan 1967, 154–56, 157. And also, for the argument that the pursuing of social public influence is a right of all religious believers, Pavan 1986, 39, 43.
145. In Pavan 1989b, 383, he describes the model adopted as that of a "Stato di diritto democratico sociale laico pluralista," as opposed to a state "anticlericale o laicista o neutro."
146. Pavan 1976, 30–31. See also Pavan 1967, 187.
147. Pavan 1976, 36.
148. See ibid., 37: "The document calls attention to some characteristic features of the process by which truth is known." Although, he adds, "the Declaration also reverts frequently to the relation between human beings and objective truth." Pavan recalls, then, examples from numbers 1, 11, and 14.
149. "I think, then, that we can legitimately conclude that the Second Vatican Council, proclaiming the right to religious freedom in an age like ours ridden with skepticism and materialism, an age in which totalitarian regimes and tendencies still play a large part, paid homage to truth by reconfirming its own trust in truth. If the Catholic Church in the course of her life through centuries of history has emerged from countless crises with renewed vital energy, this is not so much because of the favor and support of earthly powers which she has from time to time enjoyed, not because of the privileged legal positions which states have sometimes conferred on her, but rather, primarily if not exclusively, because of a confidence always robust and undiminished in the divine efficacy of the message of salvation of which she is the bearer." Pavan 1976, 38.
150. In Pavan 1986, 58–59, he suggests a parallel between the present times and the historical context of the beginnings of the church. Today, in a situation of

secularization and in many places secularism, like in the first centuries within the Roman Empire, the church, trusting only the force of its message, once again calls the many who live in a purely horizontal dimension to let themselves be touched by the message and the person of Christ.

151. See Pavan 1967, 203.
152. Ibid., 188.
153. Pavan 1976, 26–27. He explains how the safeguarding of the right benefits the truth in the long run: "[T]hose who belong to the true religion are thus enabled to profess it and propagate it, and those who are in error have the chance to discover that true religion, but in a way that corresponds to their dignity and to the nature of the relationship between person and truth." Ibid., 31.
154. This is the position of André-Vincent, as seen above.
155. Pavan 1967, 196–97.
156. I will use here the English translation of *Dignitatis Humanae* offered in Vatican II 1990, 1001–11. Unless cited as a note, subsequent citations of *Dignitatis Humanae* will appear parenthetically in the text with the abbreviation *DH*.
157. *Dignitatis Humanae,* no. 1. Restatements of this duty appear frequently in the first part of the declaration: see especially numbers 2 and 3.
158. See *Dignitatis Humanae,* no. 6: "Hence protection of the right to religious freedom lies with individual citizens and with social groups, with the civil authorities, with the church and other religious communities, each in their own way in view of their obligation towards the common good."
159. The beginning of number 15 states: "There is general recognition that people today want to be able to give free expression to their religion in public and in private, and that religious freedom is stated as a civil right in many constitutions and given solemn recognition in international documents."
160. Gómez Mier 1997.
161. See ibid., 82.
162. Ibid., 198.
163. Ibid., 89.

Three ❧

Dignitatis Humanae in the Pontificate of John Paul II

John Paul II has been a significant actor in each one of the three moments of *Dignitatis Humanae*. Obviously, after he was elected pope in 1978, he became the determinant voice of the church on the issues of the historical phases both of the second and the third moment.[1] Before, though, he had already had a noticeable role in the first moment, as he took active part, as a bishop, in the conciliar discussions on religious freedom and also on the elaboration of *Gaudium et Spes*. His interest on issues of religious freedom goes back, thus, to long before he became pope. In his own native context, he had all the incentive to develop his own thinking on these issues, and, at the time of the council, he had the opportunity to become familiar with related questions and perspectives larger than those operative in Poland.

Through the unfolding of the chronological phases, it will be important to notice how much of what have become characteristic approaches to religious freedom and correlated topics by Pope John Paul II had already been shaped and ascertained before his becoming the bishop of Rome. Has the papacy substantially developed or even significantly changed his thinking, or has he essentially been applying his own long-held personal views in his ministry to the universal church? Or, in terms of the conceptual framework of this book, how exactly has the quality of his personal exposition to the realities of the first moment, and his experience of the initial historical context of the second, influenced the kinds of developments he, as pope, has proposed until the end of the second moment and his basic posture before the challenges of the third?

Karol Wojtyla at Vatican II

Monsignor Wojtyla—auxiliary bishop of Cracow in the first and second sessions and titular archbishop from the third session on—had, for his circumstance, a particularly high number of interventions at Vatican II.[2] The *Acta* of the council register twenty-four contributions, starting with an eight-page letter of December 30, 1959 to the Ante-Preparatory Commission, in which he suggested nine points for the council's consideration. Of the twenty-three interventions in the four sessions of the council, eight were oral addresses to the *Aula,* and the rest written statements submitted to the commissions. Three topics concentrated most of his attention: the document on the church, with especial emphasis on the section on Mary (six interventions); religious freedom (five interventions); and *schema XIII* on the relation of the church with the contemporary world (six interventions).[3]

SUGGESTIONS FOR THE COUNCIL

What did the young Polish bishop expect from the council? Among the nine points he suggested the council should consider, we do not find any direct reference to the issue of religious freedom. However, the first of these points singled out the contemporary problem of growing materialism (or materialisms) as a challenge the church could not ignore. The adequate answer to this challenge, Monsignor Wojtyla suggests, would consist of a doctrinal clarification and forceful affirmation of a Christian personalism, based on truths partly accessible to rational light but fully known only through supernatural revelation. This Christian personalism is, thus, to be clearly distinguished from other forms of personalism still tainted with individualistic and materialistic residues. This was the word, in the perception of the Polish bishop, that contemporaries, even nonbelievers, were expecting from the council in order to address the problems being faced by the human person in the world, problems driving many to an "excessivam 'fidem humanisticam' " and, more often even, to desperation about human existence.[4]

This first part of the letter to the Ante-Preparatory Commission of the council, sketches, in a very synthetic way, a general theological outlook on the modern world, the condition of the human person in it, the way God relates to the world and to humanity, and the role of the church at the service of revealed religion. In Monsignor Wojtyla's perception, the world is drifting away from God, threatened by ideologies that put obstacles to the development of, or even deny, the spiritual dimension of the human person. Only with supernatural resources can this tendency be reversed. He puts great emphasis on the centrality of the human person, but not without a cautious attitude toward secular humanisms and overly confident views of human nature and of the possibilities of reason. Human beings cannot dispense with the help of revelation, both for an integral anthropology (to understand themselves) and a competent ethic (to find guidance for their action in the world). The role of the church is to defend and promote the practice of religion, to allow and help each person to develop his or her relationship with a personal God.

With this theological framework, the bishop from Cracow came to the council. There, he certainly had opportunity to develop, and probably even change, some of his perspectives. Nevertheless, it is worth noting that he started with ideas of his own on the relationship of the church with the world. It was from and against this background that he would speak in, and listen to, the conciliar discussions.

Third-Session Debate on Religious Freedom

In the fall of 1964, during the third session, the issue of religious freedom, now in the process of becoming a document independent of the decree on ecumenism, was discussed in the *Aula*. Archbishop Wojtyla made a speech about the project of declaration, after having already submitted two written observations on the same topic to the competent commission earlier that same year.

In the oral intervention of September 25, 1964, he begins by identifying in the present form of the document two ends that he considers should be more clearly distinguished, maybe even remitted to different documents: the first, the goal of promoting ecumenism; the second, the defense of the freedom of the human person in modern society and state.[5]

For ecumenism, it is of crucial importance to understand correctly the connection between freedom and truth: "If freedom, on one hand, is for the sake of truth, on the other, it is impossible to be fully accomplished without the help of the truth. . . . There is no freedom without truth." In support, he quotes John 8:32: "The truth will make you free." The goal of the ecumenical action is the freeing of Christianity from divisions, but that is possible only when the unity in truth is accomplished. He, therefore, rejects the principle of religious freedom toward our "separated brethren" as a mere principle of tolerance, not because it is unsatisfactory in terms of respect for their freedom, but because it means too much resignation with the "status quo" and does nothing to lessen the division. The objective of the ecumenical effort cannot be just greater toleration of differences, but, it should rather be, through greater incentive to the efforts to reach the truth, more progress in the acceptance of the truth by all, "for nothing else but the truth will free us from separations of many kinds."[6]

The emphasis on truth is here supported on a kind of utilitarian reasoning, but, in one of the written observations on this same draft of the schema, he develops an ethical argument to question the limitation of religious freedom to the ambit of tolerance. After highlighting the distinction between the ethical and the juridical aspects, addressed together in the proposed draft, he continues by saying that, although these two aspects are intimately connected, they should not be confused, as he thinks the authors of the schema do when they define religious freedom merely as "immunity from external coercion." Without questioning the principle of respect for the invincibly erroneous conscience (which should be considered just as a principle of religious tolerance), he suggests that, over against that principle, preference should be given to another, namely, that we ought to follow the sincere conscience formed in the truth. Therefore, the definition and concept of freedom in the document ought to be corrected by stressing the importance for freedom of objective, not just subjective, truth.[7]

Concluding, he sees the need to relate better the rights of the person with the right to the truth itself, because the human person attains perfection in the truth, truth that constitutes the foundation of true freedom.[8] In these written observations too, he seems to be still reasoning from the principle that freedom, in its fullness (more than mere tolerance), belongs by right exclusively to the truth. This line of argument, however, with the prevalence of truth over freedom stated in such a way, had difficulty in providing unequivocally a sure foundation for a universal right to religious freedom.

The second of the two ends of the draft he identified in the speech to the *Aula* was the civic dimension of religious freedom. Archbishop Wojtyla states that, here yes, what is at stake is the principle of tolerance, constitutive of "a fundamental right of the religious man in society, that must be strictly respected by all, especially by those who govern public affairs." It is necessary, however, to take into consideration how differently the laws of the many different states compare to the divine law, revealed and natural. Especially, it cannot be forgotten that "atheists desire to see nothing else in any religion but the alienation of the human mind, from which they want to liberate man, even through those means proper to the state." To defend religious freedom against this state-supported atheistic attack, the human person has to be presented in all the sublimity of his or her rational nature, of which religion—the free, personal, and conscientious adhesion of the human mind to God, born of the yearning for the truth—is precisely the culmination. The man that looks sincerely for the truth in his relationship with God requires freedom, and no secular arm should interfere with this relationship, "because religion by its own nature transcends all things secular."[9]

It is clear how much Archbishop Wojtyla's own historical context influenced his views on the issue of religious freedom. Speaking from his personal experience in Poland, he wants the council to promote religious freedom primarily as a way to denounce governments dominated by militant atheistic ideologies. He then grounds the fundamental nature of such a right on the privileges of the truth, and the duties to search for it in relationship with God and other people; and also on the preeminence of the transcendent dimension of the human person over any power in society or state. In the political dimension of religious freedom too, there is an inseparable link between freedom and truth. With this foundation, the right is a fundamental right of the "*religious* man."[10] Therefore, his considerations, at this time, focus almost exclusively on the rights of the church to freedom and not so much on a general human right to religious freedom. He does not elaborate here if, and how, the argument can be extended equally to the rights of those who do not search for that truth with the same resolve. In a final paragraph, he makes even more explicit the connection with the truth:

> The right to the exercise of religious freedom is tied with those rights of the human person that refer to the truth—that is, the right to know it, to pass it on to others and to communicate it with others. . . . Moreover—the right to a life, not only personal and private, but also communitarian and public, lived, in different dominions, in the light of the truth which we profess.[11]

The emphasis on freedom's conjunction with truth is fundamental and, therefore, extends also to the juridical dimension of religious freedom. Although this was just one intervention at an early stage of the debate, when the whole discussion was still very much taking place in the framework of the old doctrine, it is certainly sound to infer that the topics singled out here were of critical importance for the Polish archbishop.

At the beginning of this speech in the *Aula,* he had suggested that it would be better to deal with the two aspects of religious freedom, as he described them, in two different documents, and that the second one could be part of the document on the church in the modern world. It happens that a month later Monsignor Wojtyla, during the discussions on *schema XIII,* submitted to the council, in the name of the Polish bishops, a complete alternative schema, which a group, under his direction, had put together in Poland.[12] In examining this document, which intends to be a complete treatment of the topic of the relation of the church with the contemporary world, it will be possible to identify with less tentativeness the great lines of his thinking on the issue of religious freedom at this stage of the council.

Alternative Schema on the Church in the Contemporary World

We find references to issues of religious freedom in three places in this document. The first is the opening chapter, which deals with the foundations of the presence of the church in the world. After grounding the presence of the church to the world in God's will, a presence which is described as a continuation of the mystery of Incarnation in which the church, under the guidance of the Holy Spirit, strives to unite the whole human family in the Mystical Body of Christ; and after asserting from the mysteries of creation and redemption the particular dignity of human beings, especially their spiritual dimension; the next paragraph is titled "right of man to religion." This human right to profess religion is presented as the counterpart of the duty to render cult to God. Because man is wholly dependent on God and with his intellect can know God through things created, he has the duty to worship God. Moreover, this "relation of man to God is deeply personal and intrinsic but also extrinsic and social." Therefore, the religious truth encountered has to be communicated to others—not just fellow believers but strangers too. This way "the right to profess religion establishes the right to know religion, and finally the right to teach religion." The conclusion, thus, can follow: "The existence of the church in the world is as closely as possible connected with these fundamental rights of every human person. These rights are violated every time man is deprived of the possibility of professing religion by word and action, or the church itself is persecuted."[13]

The central issue here clearly is the freedom of the church. The human right to religion (here no "right to religious freedom" is referred; only right "ad religionem," or "ad religionem profitendam," or "ad vitam religiosam") is evoked mainly as support for a claim of freedom for the activity of the church. Both the rights formulated and the justifications for them have in mind the case of believers, practicing believers, for that matter. The basis of the argument is the duty of human beings, created and redeemed by God, to acknowledge through worship this dependence, and to develop their spiritual vocation in an active relationship with God, privately and publicly, individually and communally expressed. The weight of this divinely and humanly imposed duty is invoked to secure the counterpart right of immunity: No power of this world can interfere with the profession, expression, and spreading of religious truth.

The next paragraph expands on the connection of the human right to religion with the freedom of the church to do its apostolate. The church's mission is to preach revealed truth, and, by doing that, the church responds "to that right of the human person which is among the highest rights, the right to know the truth" (301). The apostolic activity of the church, therefore, cannot be restricted, because that would deny people the possibility to come in contact with religious truth, evaluate it, and freely convert to it.

The final paragraph of this chapter invokes the concept of freedom of conscience, also in support of the claim of freedom for the church: "Adherence to the church is a free act of the person, which ought to be respected by others, especially by public authorities" (302). And again it is the duty of conscience of the believers in Christ to worship God, and of the pastors and other ministers of the church to evangelize, that grounds this immunity.

The right to unobstructed freedom for the apostolate of the church, established in the context of the foundations of the presence of the church in the world, is the central goal of this whole chapter. The reasons that cause the church to be present to the world ground also its right not to be restricted in the internal activity of its members and in its reaching out beyond the group of the faithful. The primary addressees are state authorities and the argumentation is theological, explaining how the natures of the church and of its mission require immunity from external interference in its apostolate.

The second instance of a discussion of issues directly related to religious freedom appears in chapter 3 of the proposed schema. Recalling the principal rights and goods of the human family that need to be defended, the schema elaborates on the good of freedom. Part of the mission of the church is, together with all people of good will, to search for the conditions of true freedom. Here, of special importance, is freedom of conscience, which must be respected by all, especially by public authorities. The matter of freedom of conscience consists of "the right to govern oneself according to one's conscience formed in good faith." The qualification is important, so much so that the same idea is immediately repeated, but now with the requirement of right formation of the conscience in first place: "The dignity of the person demands that man form his conscience in the truth and that he act from the persuasion of his conscience." Obligation to the truth and right to freedom are put in parallel as demands of the dignity of the person. This dignity is threatened every time "it is impossible for man to follow his right persuasions and he is coerced to actions contrary to his conscience." The emphasis on the commitment to the truth notwithstanding, it is explicitly affirmed that the respect for the conscience extends also to the conscience invincibly erroneous (309). Nonetheless, although physical pressure or coercion of any other type are excluded, this principle of tolerance does not forbid the church to continue to encourage people to form their consciences in the truth and to try to persuade people of the truth by means of compelling arguments, the text concludes.

Two points are worth underscoring in this section. First, the argument is again directed primarily against antireligious political authorities from where the great menace to freedom of conscience is perceived to come. Freedom of Christian believers to practice their religion is what continues to be chiefly in the mind of the proponents of this text when they defend freedom of conscience.

Second, although in no way restricting the claims of freedom, there is a clear intent not to let the prerogatives of the truth remain unmentioned. Maybe in an effort to counterbalance what was being seen as a too unilateral emphasis on freedom, this alternative schema does not miss an opportunity to stress the importance of searching, respecting, and promoting the truth.

The third reference to issues of religious freedom appears right at the end of the schema, in a paragraph about the relationship of Christians to non-Christians and to secular society. The argument here starts from the demands of human rights universally recognized, not from theological axioms or the privileges of revealed truth. As the church respects these rights, so it demands that its members, and the institution itself, be respected on the same basis. Persecution of the church, or any limitation of its activity, causes believers to suffer vexations and discriminations, which contradict the commonly accepted rights of the human person. These natural rights are to be also the foundation of the relationship between public authorities and the church (313).

This section gives a more extended notice to the rights of non-believers. It reinforces the previous references to the rights of the erroneous conscience, leaving no doubts that the accent on the rights of practicing religion and the obligations to the truth is a matter of emphasis, not of exclusivity. The mention is, nevertheless, still instrumental. The focus continues to be the defense of the right of Christians to live their religion, as the formulation clearly shows:

> Just as coercion exercised over non-Catholics, so that they come to profess the Catholic religion, would contradict the rights of the person and the principles of the church, so too it contradicts human rights if Catholics are by physical force, or extreme pressure, separated from Christ and from the church and forced to accept another religion or to profess atheism itself. (313–314)

The point is further developed. Although the church preaches the truth revealed by God, and desires greatly to bring all to the faith, it does not force anybody to accept it, but rather, out of respect for the person, leaves that to the responsibility of human conscience. If the church reaffirms this attitude it ought, therefore, also to declare solemnly, through the council, that "the systematic combat against religion and the church, and the introduction of atheism in political life in such a way that it becomes the goal of the state, deeply contradicts all human order and the objective good of contemporary society" (314). The affirmation of religious freedom—here explicitly including the freedom not to be coerced to believe—continues, understandably, to be set in the context of a plea for freedom of the church.

The topics related to religious freedom accounted for in this schema of the Polish bishops, which pretended to be a comprehensive treatment of the relationship of the church with the contemporary world, do not differ, neither in emphasis, nor in extension, from the points of the previous (and I may advance, also of the future) interventions of Monsignor Wojtyla in the conciliar discussions about the doctrine on the right to religious freedom. He continues to single out political authorities as the bearers of the burdens of the right; the preoccupation centers almost exclusively on the freedom of the church; and the obligations toward the truth continue to be the ultimate basis of the arguments for the right.

Fourth-Session Discussion of *Dignitatis Humanae*

In the fall of 1964, Monsignor Wojtyla raised again his voice in the debate on religious freedom, when the now independent conciliar declaration was close to its final form. His intervention asks, generally, for greater clarity of the whole document and touches three particular points. The first demands that the declaration not just repeat what had already been established in civil legislation of many countries and international conventions, but that it give the foundations of the position on the doctrine of the church,[14] that is, on revelation, as he further clarifies in the written observations submitted at the same time.[15] He questions also the appearance of too great a separation between reason and revelation created by the titles of the two chapters. He does not want to leave any doubt that the source of the doctrine on religious freedom is revelation itself.[16] Human reason may have reached the same conclusions, but it was just a recognition of what had already been revealed.

The second point stresses responsibility as the personal-ethical counterpart to the ethical-social significance of religious freedom. In as much as it is an immunity, it is a duty to be discharged primarily by civil authorities. However, how each one will use this right personally is of the greatest importance for the individual person before God and also for the social order. The binding force of the conciliar declaration obliges every person to assert not only his or her freedom but also his or her responsibility in matters religious. The preoccupation to balance freedom with responsibility reaches the point of giving preeminence to the latter over the former: "Responsibility is as it were the summit and necessary complement of freedom."[17] After this ordering of the two concepts, it is, thus, conceivable to try to ground the duty of civil powers to respect personal and communitarian religious freedom on the impositions of this responsibility, with which nobody can interfere.

The affirmation of the objective value of religion is stressed primarily to counter those who attack it, but also to warn those who may be tempted to misinterpret the doctrine of the right to religious freedom as an excuse to relax their human religious duty to search for the truth and adhere to it. They ought not to look at religion as a matter of an entirely subjective choice. That is why Monsignor Wojtyla wants to stress the great responsibility correlative to freedom, the grave obligation adjoined to the right. The reason for this observation against unqualified promotions of freedom is insinuated in one sentence: "These things must be stressed so that our declaration appears deeply personalistic in a Christian sense, and by no means suspect of liberalism or indifferentism."[18]

His opposition to communism, and the intent to expose how much it is a threat to the church, has been constantly in the background of Monsignor Wojtyla's conciliar statements on religious freedom, obviously because of the particular situation of the church in Poland. Here, he alludes to his own suspicions regarding other modern ideologies, which were more typical, at the time, of the West than of Eastern Europe. All in all, he tries to prevent the council from unwillingly giving any kind of comfort to philosophies that, in the contemporary world and through the instrumentality of the state or through more subtle cultural influences, threaten the full development of the religious vocation of the human person.

The third point of this speech is about the setting of legitimate limitations to religious freedom.[19] He questions the opportunity of stating that such limitations could be imposed " 'according to juridical norms, determined by the needs of public order,' therefore in simple conformity to positive law,"[20] as the draft of the document read, because that, in many places, "could give occasion to abuses against true religious freedom."[21] Obviously, he had his own historical and geographical context in mind.[22] The only limitations to religious freedom, in as much as it is a natural right (founded in the law of nature, "ergo divina"), can only come from the moral law itself; positive law cannot impose limits, except if they directly and strictly derive from the moral law.[23]

THE RELATED PROBLEM OF ATHEISM

After his last intervention on the debate on *Dignitatis Humanae,* the discussions around what would become *Gaudium et Spes* would get the best of his attention. In this context, he made still another reference to the issue of religious freedom in a new speech to the *Aula,* half of it dedicated to the problem of atheism.

He distinguishes between the atheism born of personal conviction and the one that results from the pressure of atheistic propaganda. Although he understands the desire of persuaded atheists to persuade others, he wants to reaffirm that any violation of the personal and communitarian right to religion gravely acts against the moral law of nature. And this happens whenever "it is rendered almost impossible to profess the faith officially and in public, while the profession of atheism is almost required."[24] Again there is a forceful affirmation of the human right of believers to practice their religion unhindered by any interference of antireligious public authorities, a right based on the natural moral law.

In the next paragraph he makes the case for an approach to dialogue with atheism less metaphysical (centered on the question of the existence of God) and more anthropological. His point seems to be that it is necessary to go to the anthropological roots of atheism to be able to address its present political challenges. Again, he sets the issues on an anthropological framework, focuses on the person, but without ever forgetting to stress that only through faith and revelation can full understanding of the human person be achieved and the solution for humanity's problems encountered. Concluding, he avows that the dialogue is very difficult, "especially when atheism is attached to relativism and ethical utilitarianism,"[25] a passing reference upon which he does not elaborate, but which, again, insinuates criticism of ideological tendencies detrimental to religion, other than communism.

Conclusions

The first impression we get from reading through Monsignor Wojtyla's pronouncements at the council is that he intervened often and energetically. He had ideas of his own and was not afraid of defending them. Jan Grootaers locates the core of the whole of his interventions in a permanent preoccupation with the church-world relationship.[26] It is no surprise, then, that the issues regarding religious freedom were very much in the center of his contributions to the work of the council. There is no doubt that he was always in favor of the doctrine of the declaration; time and again he would start his critical observations with a general proclamation of support for what was being proposed. His interventions, understandably, did not so much repeat that with which he was in agreement, but highlighted, rather, points that needed, in his view, clarification or recognition.

Nevertheless, in spite of the ready and resolute assent to the essential proclamation, it seems clear that he kept some reservations about the structure of justifications offered for the right. He defended a greater role for revealed sources, and repeatedly stressed the prominence of truth over freedom. These emphases put him on the side of conceptual frameworks not totally squared with the full theological balance of the new doctrine of *Dignitatis Humanae* and the new thrust of all its implications, especially its repercussions for the church itself and its attitude toward the world. Any ethical arguments for religious freedom had the problem of a too exclusive focus on the discharge of the human religious obligation. Such arguments certainly supported the rights of those who practice religion, but it was not so clear how it would defend the immunity of those who do not take their religious responsibility seriously. Again, it put almost all the emphasis on the church's right to freedom and showed less sensibility to the larger scope of questions involved in the issue of religious freedom. The risk of this strategy was that it might appear that the individual right to religious freedom was being stressed mainly as an opportune instrument to strengthen the case of an embattled church against its enemies.

Certainly the duress under which the Polish church was finding itself explains and justifies Monsignor Wojtyla's tenacious accentuation, almost to the point of exclusivity, of the freedom of the church as the crucial point at stake and the denunciation of the anti-religious ideology of communism. These are precisely the central issues and the fundamental church attitude characteristic of the second moment of *Dignitatis Humanae.* The challenges to the church typical of the first moment were primarily a concern of the bishops of Western Europe and the United States. The historical circumstances were different to the point that words and concepts used in the West could, in the actual context of the East, mean slightly different things, and might have, if used unqualifiedly, unintended consequences for the life of Catholics there.[27] At the same time, the archbishop of Cracow may have also lacked a full sense of the great differences between the communist project of absolute secularization of society, and the processes of liberal secularization taking place in the West.[28] This may help to explain why Monsignor Wojtyla did not make any reference to issues of the first moment, and seemed even to have little sensitivity to the significance and consequence for the church of a successful resolution of those doctrinal and political quandaries, something possible only through both a radical development in the church's traditional doctrine and a conversion of its attitude toward modernity. For him, it seems, the problem of religious freedom did not call for any change on the part of the church; it was clearly a mere matter of the church "ad extra," as he declared in his first oral intervention on the topic.[29]

Some themes recur through all the pronouncements we have analyzed. They suggest the general lines of a personal theological anthropology that has worked as a unifying background for his critical reading of the successive drafts and his suggestions of corrections or developments.[30] First of all, there is the attempt to develop a consistent personalist approach, looking at the problems from the perspective of their impact on the experience of human beings, and taking the person as both the end of, and way to, the solutions being sought. However, in his concept of person, the transcendent dimension of openness to God and the radical dependence on revelation for the full truth about our condition and destiny cannot in any way be overlooked, or even just presupposed; they always have to be clearly in the forefront of this personalism, if it is to be truly a "Christian personalism," free of humanistic excesses. Already in 1959, at the beginning of his letter to the Ante-Preparatory Commission, he called for a resolute exposition of the "transcendental spiritual order."[31] Six years later, almost at the closing of the council, intervening in the debate on *schema XIII*—after underlining that this schema is assumedly pastoral, therefore attending firstly to the human person[32]—he still finds the need to call the council to stress, much more than the draft of the pastoral constitution was doing, the transcendent soteriological dimension of the work of the church. He also defends the constitutive importance of the theological concept of redemption, vis-à-vis creation, for the understanding of the Christian signification of the world and the relationship of the church with it.[33] Generally, he criticizes the schema for a certain idealized view of the world—describing more how it should be than taking it as it really is—which, then, takes the presence of the church in a way not sufficiently realistic. The document is wanting, he concludes, in the "sense of Christian realism."[34]

To the accent on the transcendent corresponds, thus, a certain ambivalence toward the world, a cautious suspicion regarding the capacities of reason and a certain anxiety about the effects of a human freedom entrusted to itself without external restraints. As an answer to these misgivings, then, he highlights the significance of redemption, the indispensability of revelation, and the duties toward objective truth. In terms of the big, simplistic partisan divisions of the council, Monsignor Wojtyla sided with those who feared too much "horizontalism" in *Gaudium et Spes*;[35] and his views on the way the church should deal with the modern world clearly aligned him more with the forlorn "Augustinian" side of the conciliar majority, than with the "Thomists."[36]

In his participation at the council, at least in what the *Acta* registers, the future Pope John Paul II passed over the questions of the first moment of *Dignitatis Humanae* as they would affect typical cases such as Spain and the United States, but, in turn, he energetically assumed the challenges and the attitudes of the second moment. His general theological conception, just sketched, suggests already proclivities that are particularly relevant in the shaping of contemporary, alternative basic attitudes of the church before the challenges of the third moment. The scattered allusions to secularist threats other than communism (e.g., secular humanism, materialism, indifferentism, individualism, relativism, utilitarianism) list a good number of the designated "big enemies" of the church at the end of the millennium. There is, thus, promise of relevant continuities. But it is the way all these announced inclinations will play out in the interpretation and application of *Dignitatis Humanae* during his papacy that will ultimately decide the lasting import of the ideas defended by the archbishop of Cracow in the debates of Vatican II about the right to religious freedom.

Implementation of the Council in Cracow

In 1972, Archbishop Wojtyla wrote an extended introduction to Vatican II to guide the diocesan synod of Cracow in the study of the council.[37] The book is basically a presentation of the great themes of the council, organized in an alignment of quotations from all the documents, interspersed with short commentaries.[38]

Four times is *Dignitatis Humanae* quoted with prominence: at the beginning, when he explains faith as a human response in freedom to the initiative of God; then, when speaking of the sense of responsibility of the Christian; later, in the chapter on the ecumenical attitude; and, finally, in the last section of the book, when he deals with the rights of religious communities to religious freedom. A look at these passages, noting especially the sentences and clauses favored by frequent quotation and those that are passed over, will give us an idea of Archbishop Wojtyla's valuation of *Dignitatis Humanae,* his favorite reading of it, and, thus, the thrust of his initial interpretation of the conciliar declaration.

The second chapter of the first part describes faith as an encounter between God and the human person, a gift always originating in God's self-revelation but also demanding human response. It is in order to explain what the council says about this human participation that *Dignitatis Humanae* is recalled. First, Archbishop Wojtyla quotes sentences from numbers 10 and 11, which stress the scrupulous respect for human freedom in God's invitation, confirmed in the practice of Jesus (quotes from numbers 11 and 9). Then he turns to numbers 2 and 3 to establish the fully personal character of the act of faith. In number 2, he singles out the first two sentences of the second paragraph, which talk of the "moral obligation to seek the truth" and "to adhere to the truth." In number 3—concluding that faith is a problem of conscience—he quotes the last sentence of the first paragraph: "[E]verybody has the duty and consequently the right to seek the truth in religious matters" (22–23).

In this section, thus, *Dignitatis Humanae* is used to stress the individual responsibility and obligation toward the truth on the part of believers. Archbishop Wojtyla explicitly concludes that the council's affirmation of the right to religious freedom in relation to the secular public order does not in any way diminish the "postulate of conscious faith"—the duty of conscience to enrich one's faith, responding responsibly to God's revelation—as the selected quotes of *Dignitatis Humanae* have shown (23). This response has to be both individual and private and social and public.

The emphasis on passages in *Dignitatis Humanae* that talk about the truth continues in the following chapter about faith and dialogue. Here, the three quotes from numbers 3 and 1 of the declaration refer to dialogue as a necessary means to search for the truth and a fruit of its sharing. Readiness to participate in dialogue, however, cannot be separated from responsibility to the truth; it cannot signify, therefore, any kind of indifferentism (26–29).

The three other extended references to *Dignitatis Humanae* all appear in part III. In the section on the attitude of Christian responsibility, the general thesis is that "only the responsible man derives true profit from inner freedom," because there is close "interdependence and mutual influence between responsibility and liberty." This "fundamental postulate of responsibility," which emphasizes the dignity and vocation of the human person, is established by the council "particularly in the conception of man's relationship with God that is presented by the Constitution on Divine Revelation and the Declaration on Religious Liberty" (292–93). Then, to support his thesis, he searches *Dignitatis Humanae* for instances in which freedom and responsibility are paired together: number 1, "men should exercise fully their own judgment and a responsible freedom"; number 7, "in availing themselves of any freedom men must respect the moral principle of personal and social responsibility"; and number 8, "try to form men . . . who will form their own judgments in the light of truth, direct their activities with a sense of responsibility".

The next instance is the chapter on the ecumenical attitude, which is defined as an expression of faith in God and Christ, and also an "expression of a profound love for man and respect for his inner liberty—that 'responsible liberty' which corresponds to an inward conviction concerning truth, 'especially in the religious sphere', as the Council states in its Declaration on Religious Liberty."[39] Worth noting in the sequence of five consecutive quotations from *Dignitatis Humanae* that follow in the text is the repeated referring of the right to religious freedom to a grounding in revelation and in the demands of faith. Accentuating the objective anchoring of the right, he quotes the clause from number 2 that founds the right not on any subjective attitude of the individual person, but on human nature itself, but the following sentence—which grants the continued fruition of the right even to those who do not serve their obligation to seek the truth and adhere to it—is not quoted.[40]

So far, the selections of *Dignitatis Humanae* have been applied to the personal, individual aspect of the religious relationship, a somewhat indirect use of the declaration. It is right at the end of the study that Archbishop Wojtyla deals with the communitarian and civil secular dimensions of the right to religious freedom, the primary object of the conciliar document. The basic point here is to show that "this fundamental right of the human person also belongs to religious communities,"[41] as it is based on human nature, which is, itself, social. The quotes begin with those passages that stress the communitarian dimensions of the right, mainly from number 4, and continue with the exposition of the consequent duties of public authorities regarding religious communities (quotes from number 6 and also number 5). After acknowledging the council's recognition that civil legislation had preceded the church in the declaration of the right, he claims for the church a different grounding of the right—"as regards the Church, its attitude towards religious freedom is based above all on the very nature of faith"[42]—and cites excerpts from the second part of the document stating the permanent doctrine of the church that no one is to be coerced to believe. He then concludes with words from the first number of *Dignitatis Humanae* that this doctrine upholds the traditional Catholic teaching on the moral duty of individuals and societies toward the true religion and the Catholic church. Thus, "the conviction of the legitimacy of the principle of religious freedom, based on the very nature of faith, is linked in the Christian's mind with his profound conviction concerning its truth."[43] This certitude establishes an obligation to grow in the knowledge of, and to announce and defend, that truth, while respecting others according to the spirit of the gospel (quote from number 14). This sense of mission, in order to be carried out, necessitates religious freedom. The last quotation from *Dignitatis Humanae*, number 13, directly grounds the claim of freedom for the church on the duty imposed on it by the divine command to preach the gospel to all.[44]

Taking into consideration the historical context from which and to which he writes, it is fitting that the point of arrival of this work is the defense of the freedom of the church to serve the demands of the truth. Archbishop Wojtyla's reasoning here shows a preference for the theological argumentation of the second part of the declaration, consistent with his preoccupation with an objective grounding of religious freedom in revealed truth, and in continuity with what had already been the emphases in the application of *Dignitatis Humanae* to the personal dimension of faith.

This study, in what concerns the interpretation of *Dignitatis Humanae*, reasserts the main ideas and the general direction of Monsignor Wojtyla's participation at Vatican II. The set of references shows a careful study of the document, a good assimilation of its important points and, certainly, unquestioned agreement with the essence of its doctrine. There are also clear signs of a consistent pattern of accentuation and omission. First, there is, understandably, an exclusive focus on a second-moment kind of reading and use of the declaration. In spite of this, his particular way of reading *Dignitatis Humanae* established a characteristically personal apprehension of the issues of religious freedom with little or no explicit recognition of the problems of the first moment. The consistency of concerns, conceptual emphases, and methodological preferences in both his participation in the process of redaction and the initial interpretation of the conciliar declaration demonstrates the deep-rooted character of the views of Karol Wojtyla on issues directly and indirectly related to *Dignitatis Humanae*.

John Paul II and the Second Moment: Opposition to Atheistic Totalitarianism

The great expectation created in the fall of 1978 by the election of Karol Wojtyla as bishop of Rome not only had to do with him being a non-Italian (the first time that happened in more than 450 years),[45] but even more with the fact that he was coming from Poland, one of the more Catholic of the countries in Eastern Europe, and a part of the world in which totalitarian communist regimes had, for some decades, severely limited the church in its ministry and in the free organization of its internal life.

The geographical and historical context from which John Paul II came, and the mood of the church at the time he entered the world scene, were both being dominated by the ideological and political contest between Catholicism and atheistic communism. Although the duties of his new office required him to attend now to many other issues of the universal church, it was to be expected that the new pope would dedicate particular attention and bring renewed energy to this confrontation. Since the right to religious freedom was the most visible focus of conflict, the use, interpretation, and development of the doctrine of *Dignitatis Humanae* would certainly have a central place in this papacy. And so it was. As bishop of Rome, Karol Wojtyla did not just immediately engage the issues at the pastoral and doctrinal level, but played also a decisive personal role in the unfolding of political events that would culminate with the collapse of communism in Eastern Europe and the Soviet Union.[46]

At once, in the first message of his papacy, the day after his election, John Paul II professed his particular solicitude for all "those who are oppressed by whatever injustices or discrimination whether it has to do with economy, life in society, political life or the freedom of conscience and just religious freedom."[47]

This statement indicates already two very significant traits of John Paul II's promotion of the right to religious freedom. On the one hand, it is the pastoral concern for concrete Christian persons being persecuted or discriminated against because of their religious convictions that will constitute the motivation, the starting point, and the constant focus of his speaking up for religious freedom all through his pontificate.[48] John Paul II will not promote religious freedom in abstract, or simply as a general principle. His advocacy is clearly focused on historical and geographical concrete situations, and it will have, therefore, a distinct political character.

On the other hand, the second trait, he places this political advocacy for freedom of the church, focused on the concrete and particular, in the context of a comprehensive and deeper picture of the fundamental and more universal values at stake. He will not uphold the right to practice one's religion as an isolated right, but will rather set religious freedom (or the lack thereof) as a particular consequence of a general policy of respect (or disrespect) for human rights, and even, as we will see, as a special test or foundation for the honoring by political powers of all the other human rights. The claim at the juridical and political level is also accompanied by a critique of the ideologies and philosophies driving and supporting the totalitarian practices. The safeguarding of religious freedom is intimately connected with the pope's commitment to promoting a culture fully respectful of human dignity and supportive of the complete development of the whole person, individually and socially. The establishment of this unbreakable linkage between the right to religious freedom and the other fundamental human rights immediately places John Paul II's teaching on religious freedom in continuity and dialogue not just with *Dignitatis Humanae* but also with the broader recent Catholic tradition on human rights.

The most significant documents of Catholic doctrine on human rights, especially the right to religious freedom, are John XIII's encyclical *Pacem in Terris* and Vatican II's declaration *Dignitatis Humanae. Pacem in Terris* is also the culmination of the development that, through an ethical approach relying almost exclusively on reason and natural law, put the concept of human dignity in the center of Catholic social teaching. In Vatican II, *Gaudium et Spes* maintained the foundational role of the dignity of the human person, but approached it from a radically theological perspective, with abundant use of religious language and biblical symbols. *Dignitatis Humanae,* in turn, in its essential argument, continued to rely on natural law and common human reason, although it attempted to provide also, in the second part of its text, scriptural and theological support and confirmation for the general principle of religious freedom.[49]

These two methodologies of approaching the promotion of the dignity of the human person—represented by *Pacem in Terris* and *Gaudium et Spes*—

coexist in tension in recent Catholic social teaching on human rights. The natural law approach, in spite of the significance of the conciliar constitution, continued to be prevalent. John Paul II, however, has shifted the balance. He prefers the approach of the conciliar text,[50] "his style . . . enhances the strain in contemporary Catholic thought which stresses a biblical and theological explicitness in the Church's social message."[51] This methodological preference is at the source of the most distinctive traits of his development of the Catholic Church's teaching on the right to religious freedom.

From the Traditional Natural Law Approach to Favored Theological Arguments

Since the beginning of his pontificate, John Paul II shows to be very much aware of the coexistence in the tradition of the two methodologies to ground the right to religious freedom. In his first encyclical, describing *Dignitatis Humanae,* he writes that in it "is expressed not only the theological concept of the question but also the concept reached from the point of view of natural law, that is to say from the 'purely human' position, on the basis of the premises given by man's own experience, his reason and his sense of human dignity."[52] The simple fact that he switches the order of these two conceptions relative to the text of *Dignitatis Humanae* gives an immediate clue about his preferences. It seems that, from the start, he was particularly interested in recovering to the foreground the teaching of the second part.

Although he preferred the theological approach, as it is usual in papal teaching, John Paul II began his initial pronouncements on religious freedom by restating the most recent church documents on the topic.

His first extended treatment of the issues of religious freedom took place less than two months after his election, in the form of a letter to the Secretary General of the United Nations, on the occasion of the thirtieth anniversary of the Universal Declaration of Human Rights.[53] The first part of this letter keeps the language within the limits of a strictly natural-law argument and draws extensively on the teaching of John XXIII. John Paul II reaffirms the church's promotion of human rights and fundamental liberties. The criterion to guarantee them is the dignity of the human person—a dignity inherent to the nature of the person recognized universally by the commonly shared capacities of human reason from which directly flows rights and duties universal, inviolable, and inalienable—a dignity, therefore never forfeited, even when the person errs (the last clause in a direct reference to *Pacem in Terris*).[54]

This human dignity sustains an intrinsic human freedom, proper to each person, that can never be revoked because it is not conditioned to any kind of use each individual may make of it. The same conclusion—a very important one in view of past attitudes of the Catholic Church—is restated by John Paul II, almost two years later, in a letter on freedom of conscience and of religion addressed to the heads of state signatory to the 1975 Final Act of the Helsinki Conference on Security and Cooperation in Europe, on the occasion of a summit in Madrid. The pope's more elaborate argument rests on the same basis: "[T]he starting point for acknowledging and respecting that freedom is the dignity of the human person, who experiences the inner and indestructible exigency of acting freely 'according to the imperatives of his own conscience.' "[55] Explaining further what the respect for this "inner exigency" implies, he immediately proceeds to describe it in terms that include both a religious and a nonreligious personal option, either one to be equally reverenced by others:

> On the basis of his personal convictions, man is led to recognize and follow a religious or metaphysical concept involving his whole life with regard to fundamental choices and attitudes. This inner reflection, even if it does not result in an explicit and positive assertion of faith in God, cannot but be respected in the name of the dignity of each one's conscience, whose hidden searching may not be judged by others.[56]

The following paragraph of the letter summarizes and consummates the argument with a direct reference to one of the most significant sentences of *Dignitatis Humanae:*

> This concrete liberty has its foundation in man's very nature, the characteristic of which is to be free, and it continues to exist—as stated in the Second Vatican Council's declaration—"even in those who do not live up to their obligation of seeking the truth and adhering to it; the exercise of this right is not to be impeded, provided that the just requirements of public order are observed."[57]

Only in one other of his major addresses on religious freedom will John Paul II again explicitly evoke this clause, the starkest affirmation of the implications of the dignity of the human person in what concerns religious freedom in the whole declaration. That is the case of a speech of 1984 to the V International Colloquium of Juridical Studies, meeting in Rome in celebration of the twentieth anniversary of *Pacem in Terris.* Here, he describes the dignity of the human person as the "meeting point for a profitable, rather necessary, dialogue between the church and the world in our time;"[58] and then makes references to the passages of *Pacem in Terris* and *Dignitatis Humanae* on the rights of the nonreligious person. The citation of John XXIII is a mere reiteration, but the evocation of the passage in *Dignitatis Humanae* number 2 makes an even clearer statement on the broad range of the right to religious freedom than the letter to the Madrid summit:

> Such right is a human right and therefore universal: because it does not derive from the upright acting of the persons or from their right conscience, but from the persons themselves, that is from their existential being, which, in its constitutive components, is substantially identical in every person. It is, therefore, a right that exists in every person and exists always, even in the case it is not exercised or may be violated by the same subject to whom it is inherent. In fact the violation of a right does not involve its destruction, but it demands that it be reinstated."[59]

In sum, three points stand out in these initial dealings with the right to religious freedom, which basically limited themselves to reiterating the content of previous teaching, relying still fundamentally on a natural-law kind of approach. First is the centrality of the concept of human dignity, defined as something inherent to human nature, recognizable in all people by all people simply through the use of reason, unconditional, and that can never be forfeited. This concept, defined in philosophical terms, constitutes a meeting point for dialogue with the world. Second, the right to religious freedom is carefully characterized as a universal human right, avoiding any description circumscribed to the practices of believers; the emphasis is on human freedom, not on freedom of the church. Third is the explicit affirmation that the freedom necessitated by this dignity is independent of the quality of the acting of any particular person. Therefore, it cannot be revoked and remains an active right even in those culpable of error or negligence. This last point is particularly significant because, in spite of its outstanding importance for the full meaning of *Dignitatis Humanae,* it will virtually disappear from the pronouncements of John Paul II on religious freedom based on a more theological approach.

Even after he entered more confidently into the development of his distinct perspective on the issue, John Paul II would continue to invoke notions of natural-law reasoning in defense of the right to religious freedom.[60] The dignity of the person has certainly continued to be "the fundamental concept for John Paul II's social and political thought."[61] He will, however, set these concepts and mold his teaching in a much more distinctly theological framework.

Already in the letter celebrating the thirtieth anniversary of the United Nations' human rights declaration, John Paul II's first pronouncement on religious freedom, there was a complementary treatment of similar, yet more strictly theological, issues. The opening of the paragraph immediately after the reference to the rights of the person in error ("For believers. . .") sharply switches the kind of argument and even the argument's style—from now on the pope puts great emphasis on the use of the first person. It is in this second part that he deals more specifically with the right to religious freedom. This final couple of pages, as a matter of fact, anticipates some of the most typical approaches and emphases of what will be the standard teaching of John Paul II on this topic.

The first thing to notice is that a special status among human rights is given to the right to religious freedom. Here John Paul II wants to speak of human rights, but "especially of one of them which undoubtedly occupies a central position"; and this "central position" is justified by the fact that "the problem of religious freedom . . . is at the basis of all other freedoms and is inseparably tied to them all."[62]

Second, he combines the affirmation of the right with the clear identification and strong political indictment of those who infringe it, but also with the rebuttal of the ideologies that guide and support them. He denounces "forms of government" that "deter citizens from the profession of religion" and, more generally, the type of state that "proclaims itself atheist" in a "kind of 'negative confessionalism.' " But his incrimination does not stop at the political level of totalitarian governments. The real culprits are the ideologies behind them, and so, setting the issues in a larger framework, he calls for the overcoming of "the baneful positions of secularism."[63]

Third, he reaffirms the dignity of the human person as the source and the basis of the right but adds a theological rooting for this dignity, anchoring it on the transcendent dimension of the person, on the person's connection with God: "[A]ll rights derive from the dignity of the person who is firmly rooted in God."[64]

Finally, there is the explicit qualification that, although the emphasis is on the vindication of human rights, it is important not to forget the moral responsibility of individuals in the exercise of their rights.[65]

This sequence of topics introduced at the beginning of his magisterium will serve now as a guide for a more systematic presentation of the distinctive lines of the teaching of John Paul II on the right to religious freedom.

Religious Freedom, the First Human Right

One of the distinctive emphases of the social teaching of John Paul II has been his persistence in attributing a special fundamental status to the right to religious freedom among all human rights.[66] He uses several different kinds of terminology to mark that distinction and usually follows immediately with suggestions of reasons, also numerous and of varied type, for why that is so.[67]

The right to religious freedom, he says, is "not merely one human right among many others,"[68] but "rather, (it) is the most fundamental, since the dignity of every person has its first source in his essential relationship with God the Creator and Father, in whose image and likeness he was created, since he is endowed with intelligence and freedom."[69] Since it is their "source and synthesis,"[70] "in any consideration of fundamental human rights, *a primary place must always be accorded to freedom of religion*."[71]

This setting apart is not just a placing of honor, but a real ascendancy that translates into a role and criterion of judgment for any society: "The civil and social right to religious freedom, inasmuch as it touches the most intimate sphere of the spirit, is a point of reference of the other fundamental rights and in some way becomes a measure of them,"[72] that is, "the respect for religious freedom acts as a valid test for the respect accorded to the other fundamental rights,"[73] and, indeed, for all authentic human progress.[74] The distinct standing of this right over other human rights is supported on the eminence of the human activity that it protects. The spiritual dimension is the measure of all human greatness and religious freedom the highest form of freedom induced by civilization and culture.[75] "Religious freedom thus becomes the basis of the other freedoms."[76]

Therefore, the scrupulous respect by the political power of the civil right to religious freedom in all its dimensions is the most eloquent recognition and acceptance by the state of the limitations of its power over its citizens,[77] which, in turn, is the indispensable condition for a free society.[78] "A state cannot define itself 'democratic' if it puts any obstacle whatsoever to religious liberties."[79]

These are powerful affirmations. They strengthen the foundation of the right to religious freedom theoretically, reinforce the public impact of the claim for its observance everywhere, and submit the offenders to increased pressure. The basic argument to justify this singular rank and fundamental character is of a theological nature. It consists of its direct connection to the spiritual transcendent dimension of the person. A certain hierarchy of inner functions in the human person translates into a similar hierarchy of fundamental human rights.

This is a kind of language and a line of reasoning deeply grounded on elements proper to revealed religion, which, on one hand, underline a greater intrinsic commitment of the church to the right to religious freedom and put its advocacy in the forefront of its social doctrine. On the other hand, in order to have real impact on the cause of religious freedom, there must be at least respectful goodwill toward religious faith on the part of the addressees. Theological argumentation will probably not impress the antireligious or even merely secularist governments responsible for offenses against religious freedom. John Paul II wants to engage societies and governments, so he advances other arguments of a basically consequential nature to try to prove the social and political importance and the general benefits of the respect for this freedom.

In this second kind of argument, the basic claim is that full respect for religious freedom is indispensable and of great benefit for the promotion of the common good, because it liberates individual citizens for a full-hearted commitment to the commonwealth. The import of religious freedom expands, then, from the sphere of individuals to the global well-being of whole societies.

> Religious freedom, an essential requirement of the dignity of every person, is a cornerstone of the structure of human rights, and for this reason an irreplaceable factor in the good of individuals and of the whole of society, as well as of the personal fulfillment of every individual. It . . . is an essential element for peaceful human coexistence.[80]

Now, noncomplying governments are not so much denounced, publicly shamed, and pressured to change as they are called to consider their own self-interest. Religious freedom strengthens people's moral integrity and sense of responsibility.[81] Effective respect for this right will contribute to the strengthening of international peace, as well as "help to ensure the order and common welfare of each nation, of each society, for, when individuals know that their fundamental rights are protected, they are better prepared to work for the common welfare."[82] History proves it, for experience shows that

> suppression, violation or restriction of religious freedom have caused suffering and bitterness, moral and material hardship. . . . By contrast, the recognition, guarantee and respect of religious freedom bring serenity to individuals and peace to the social community; they also represent an important factor in strengthening a nation's moral cohesion, in improving people's welfare, and in enriching the cooperation among nations in an atmosphere of mutual trust.[83]

There is very often, in these alignments of reasons, a subtle development that deserves notice. Frequently, John Paul II moves from the description of the good consequences for societies of the upholding by the state of every person's right to religious freedom, to the enumeration of the benefits brought to civil society by Christian believers who in full freedom express publicly their religious faith. The source of the social advantage shifts, thus, from the sense of personal reassurance induced by civil freedoms to the public contribution of the unique values of religious faith.

Already in the letter to the Secretary General of the United Nations in 1978, he says he is making a "solemn appeal" that religious freedom be respected because of his "profound conviction that, even aside from the desire to serve God, the common good of society itself 'may profit by the moral qualities of justice and peace which have their origin in man's faithfulness to God and to his holy will.' The free exercise of religion benefits both individuals and governments."[84] Now he stresses the point that not just religious freedom but, more specifically, "the free and effective exercise of religion contributes to the strengthening of security and cooperation between peoples."[85]

Therefore, the ultimate benefit for society of a scrupulous respect for the individual right to religious freedom is the freeing of Christian believers to provide society with means for social improvement nowhere else available but in religious faith. Their added contribution to the common good "is not just a matter of feeling better disposed to collaborating with others by reason of the fact that one's own rights are ensured and protected; it is rather a matter of drawing from the deepest resources of a right conscience higher incentives for the task of building a more just and more human society."[86]

This shift in accent—from the upholding of a civil-right protector of human freedom to the promotion of the social value of religion—gives priority to a conception of religious freedom centered on the idea of social empowerment of religion. This empowerment has to include not only the political and juridical protections of individual freedoms in matters of religion, but also a welcoming receptivity on the part of the powers regulating civic discourse, and the providing of concrete means for religious people and religious institutions to be able to propose the public implications of their faith. This way, they will be able to bring religiously inspired values to their participation in the shaping of society.

Such an emphasis gives a more substantial content to this freedom. It does not claim it simply as a "freedom from" but reaffirms it as a "freedom for"—for the social exercise of religion in benefit of the whole commonwealth. It also redresses somewhat the balance of the elements of the notion of religious freedom, remitting to the background the prima facie conception of *Dignitatis Humanae* that the right is first and foremost an immunity of the personal conscience from the powers of the state in order that every person may freely search for the truth, adhere to it without any sort of constraints, and practice it without any undue restrictions or discriminations. John Paul II, by stressing the dimension of empowerment over that of immunity, moves away from excessively liberalistic interpretations. But the bias also focuses the description of the right on entitlements of believers and religious institutions, running the risk of seeming to identify the promotion of the right to religious freedom with the narrower defense of the freedom of the church.

THE ROOTS OF THE OBSTACLES TO RELIGIOUS FREEDOM

John Paul II defends religious freedom before political authorities at the national and international level by taking the side of those who cannot reclaim their rights, providing them with the voice in the international scene that they do not have on their own.[87] He has not been shy in accompanying the general advocacy of the right and the expression of solidarity with the victims with firm indictments of those responsible for its systematic infringements—governments which, almost always against the letter of their own constitutional orders, are not just insufficiently defending this civil right of their citizens, but even often actively transgressing it themselves.[88]

The perception of where lies, in each period, the greatest obstacle to the mission of the church and, simultaneously, the main threat to the formation of the conscience and the practice of the faith of its members is the determining factor in shaping the pastoral advocacy and the doctrinal teaching on religious freedom in both the second and third moments of *Dignitatis Humanae.*

That is why the pope's denunciation of these regimes during the second moment is not just political, that is, limited to the level of the lack of effective juridical protection and the presence of practical infringement by the power of the state of basic human rights. John Paul II looks for the ultimate causes of these problems in "the ideologies that have dominated our century," so marked by a totalitarian attitude that some of them "have even become a sort of false secularist religion."[89] Thus, he sets his charge against communist regimes on the issue of religious freedom in the broader framework of a larger and more important battle between religion and irreligion. The conflict of the second moment is just the emblematic instance of "the confrontation between the religious view of the world and the agnostic or even atheistic view, which is one of the signs of the times of the present age."[90] It is the secularism and atheism that support and drive communist politics that he sees as the real enemies of what he wants to defend when he defends religious freedom.[91] The contest is cultural and ideological, and the way to engage it is through the affirmation of the spiritual transcendent dimension of the person as constitutive of what is "substantially human." It is crucial to counteract the accusation leveled against believers in modern times that religious faith is tantamount to human alienation. Only then the principle of religious freedom will be correctly understood and implemented.[92] The whole address to the UN at the beginning of his pontificate is structured around a call for a greater regard for the spiritual dimension of humankind. Modernity has impoverished humanity in this area.[93] He makes a sustained case for the urgency of its recovery in which the role of believers is indispensable and should not be restricted.

The confrontation of views of the world, in the context of which local constraints on religious freedom take place, is determined, finally, by conflicting views of the human person. The defense by the church of the right to religious freedom goes deeper than the active resistance to unjust juridical orders or even political ideologies. Ultimately, what is at stake is the operative idea of itself that humanity is developing. Here, John Paul II cannot but denounce erroneous or impoverishing conceptions and forcefully propose the full richness of the Christian alternative: "Before so many humanisms, often locked in a vision of man narrowly economic, biologic or psychic, the church has the right and the duty of proclaiming the truth about man, received from its own Master."[94] It is, thus, on a particular humanism, thoroughly informed by a theological view of the truth about the human person, that the specifying traits, and the particular approaches, of John Paul II's doctrine on religious freedom find their ultimate basis. The issues, in their whole depth, are not just political but reach the level of theological anthropology: understanding of the condition of humankind in this world, knowing the prudent amount of trust that can be placed in human nature and in our capacity to know its finalities through reason, and learning how our constant dependence on God relates with human autonomy.

Transcendent Grounding of Human Dignity

In the analysis of J. Bryan Hehir, all "the social teaching of Pope John Paul II is rooted in a theological argument concerning the human person as the foundation and basis of any social system,"[95] unfolding in a framework of four interrelated steps that start with a preference in theological anthropology and then, through Christology and ecclesiology, arrive at a social ethic.[96] This heuristic scheme is a particularly fitting guide for a deeper probe into the basis of his doctrine on the right to religious freedom. Most of his preferred emphases on the topic and also the general option for a thoroughly theological grounding of the right can be explained through this theological pattern. In *Redemptor Hominis,* the fundamental statement of John Paul's theological anthropology, we can already find a sketch of how the concatenation of these four steps works in the case of religious freedom.

The fundamental axiom and guiding principle of the whole anthropology of John Paul II is a sentence from *Gaudium et Spes* that he quotes very often: "The truth is that *only* in the mystery of the Incarnate Word does the mystery of man take light."[97] This affirmation immediately says that there is no authentic anthropology without the support of Christology, but it also suggests definite limits for any social ethic. Human beings cannot know, by themselves only, their own full truth. Therefore, when it is a matter of defining ultimate human meaning and finding guidance in life, they are not advised to put complete trust on whatever they, on their own, are able to find about their nature and destiny. Such principle lays the ground for a prudent amount of distrust on the capacities of human reason, for an allegation of substantial incompleteness, then, of any exclusive natural-law kind of ethical approach to fundamental human concerns, and, concurrently, for a strong assertion of the indispensability of the contribution of revelation:

> The man who wishes to understand himself thoroughly—and not just in accordance with immediate, partial, often superficial, and even illusory standards and measures of his being—he must with his unrest, uncertainty and even his weakness and sinfulness, with his life and death, draw near to Christ. He must, so to speak, enter into him with all his own self, he must "appropriate" and assimilate the whole of the reality of the Incarnation and Redemption in order to find himself. (no. 10)

No complete ethic is possible without a Christological step. A theological foundation is necessary even for such a fundamental notion as human dignity. Only through the mediation of Christ can each human person grasp the integral scope of his or her dignity, for it is "in the human dimension of the mystery of redemption . . . [that] man finds again the greatness, dignity and value that belong to his humanity."[98]

The church has been entrusted with a particular responsibility and obligation toward this exclusive truth, and so, "with a unique assistance of the Holy Spirit" (no. 12), its mission consists in providing to every person the continued possibility of a personal encounter with Jesus Christ, in which the depth of the truth about humanity will be revealed to him or her (nos. 10 and 13). The world cannot dispense with this assistance. The resources of human philosophies are insufficient and, moreover, contemporary culture has strayed a long way from this truth. It has been following distorted anthropological views, especially, in our times, conceptions of the person in which freedom is misunderstood as an end in itself separated from the truth.[99] The proclamation of the revealed truth about humankind is today a particularly urgent service to people's *true* freedom, the freedom that they can only achieve in the full knowledge of their dignity revealed in Christ. This function gives the church a particular status of unique guardian of true human freedom (no. 12). Thus the ecclesiological step. It is this status that primarily warrants the right of the church to full freedom in society. Between Christ, who entrusted the truth about humanity to the church, and the concrete people who desperately need that truth to bring them to true freedom, stands the ministry of the church connecting offering with need. Any obstacle put to the mission of the church is, thus, cause of great harm for all people. "Jesus Christ is the chief way for the Church . . . and is the way to each man. On this way leading from Christ to man, on this way on which Christ unites himself with each man, nobody can halt the Church. This is an exigency of man's temporal welfare and of his eternal welfare."[100]

The particular bias of the concrete teaching of John Paul II on the right to religious freedom rests, thus, on a typical outlook on the world and the human person associated with a logic integral to his personal theology. A theological anthropology postulating the need of Christology to substantiate human dignity fully, combined with a faultfinding reading of the situation of humanity in the contemporary world, justifies the overemphasizing of theological language and the recourse to the contents of revelation, as opposed to a philosophical approach to the right within the limits of human nature and common reason.

Moreover, John Paul II sees this kind of theological grounding as a particular service of the church to the cause of human rights, by complementing the manifest deficiency of the official declarations of human rights—a mere listing of rights without advancing any kind of foundation for them—with anthropological and moral bases.

> In this field, the Catholic Church—and perhaps other spiritual families—has a unique contribution to make, because it claims that human dignity and inviolable human rights have their roots in the transcendent dimension of each individual and nowhere else. . . . For its part, the church is convinced that it is serving the cause of human rights when, true to its faith and to its mission, it proclaims that the dignity of the individual is based on his being a creature made in the image and likeness of God. When our contemporaries cast around for something on which to base human rights, they ought to find those transcendent foundations in the beliefs of the faithful and in their moral sense, which are indispensable if these rights are to be kept safe from all attempts at manipulation on the part of human powers.[101]

Such a consistent proposing of a justification of the right to religious freedom based on the demands and privileges of a transcendent truth about the human condition entrusted to the church by divine revelation has effected a development of the doctrine of *Dignitatis Humanae*. On one hand, it grounds the church's commitment to the promotion of religious freedom more deeply in premises intrinsic to the most basic tenets of its received tradition and identity. Therefore, it surely reinforces the credibility of the claim that it is from the core of the gospel that the church draws the inspiration and the criteria to defend human rights; it does not do it out of opportunism.[102]

On the other hand, however, some of these theological emphases also give rise to some difficulties. First, the accentuation of the unique role of the church in announcing the truth about the dignity of the human person further highlights the partiality of a notion of religious freedom proposed primarily as freedom of the church. The language and formulas used, if not sufficiently qualified, may look too self-serving of the interests of the church.

Second, a too unilateral theological framing of the notion of human dignity may have some ambiguous consequences. In his consistent grounding of the right to religious freedom on human dignity, John Paul II is faithfully continuing the tradition of Catholic social teaching. However, he tries, through qualifications and developments of a theological character, to deepen and complement the traditional philosophical founding of human rights—and the right to religious freedom in particular—on human dignity. That is where some nuances raise difficulties. The question that some of his formulations evoke is whether the notion of human dignity as the bedrock of the right to religious freedom is something that can stand on its own or needs the support of some connection to the transcendent, needs to be literally upheld by a power and majesty superior to human nature.

In his pronouncements, many times the concept of human dignity is described as something intrinsic to being human, not to be made dependent on anything outside itself. However, more often, we find propositions that secure this inherent human attribute on an ultimate anchoring in the divine, be it an orientation or a dependent attachment of humanity to God. For instance: "The freedom of the individual finds its basis in man's transcendent dignity: a dignity given to him by God, his creator, and which directs him toward God."[103] Or: "[T]he dignity of every person has its first source in his essential relationship with God the Creator and Father, in whose image and likeness he was created, since he is endowed with intelligence and freedom."[104] Is the transcendent securing of human dignity supplementary or supererogatory in the establishment and defense of the human right, satisfying the preferences of a confessional framing of the question, or does it tend to become the exclusive factor under whose strength and command the right can subsist? For instance, what can be the real meaning and full implications of the statements already quoted that the roots of human dignity are "in the transcendent dimension of each individual *and nowhere else*," and that such "transcendent foundations . . . are *indispensable*"?[105]

These and other similar formulations seem to indicate that his preferred theological approach does more than just supplement the traditional natural-law appeal to an intrinsic character of human nature. It shifts the basis of the argument for religious freedom to an explicit sustaining of human dignity on the actual connection of the person with God. They convey the strong impression that John Paul II believes that without an anchor in God provided by revealed faith it is impossible to grant a firm holding to the notion of dignity of the human person, and, therefore, to the respect for basic human rights, especially religious freedom.

This conclusion, in itself, remains still within the boundaries of subtle distinctions between different theologies of the relationship between nature and grace. But, if John Paul II refers ultimately the notion of human dignity to some kind of connection with God, a further question follows: What kind of connection is that? Is any kind of explicit acknowledgment and living harmony with these transcendent roots necessary to justify and sustain effectively the claim of such rights at the civil level? Is there any implication, then, that would distinguish in terms of their status, passive and active, vis-à-vis the right to religious freedom, those who utterly reject or simply ignore this transcendent dimension and its claims from those who fully adhere to the demands of this theological vision? If there is, we would be again at the root of the old position that only truth has rights. In spite of a few ambiguous affirmations,[106] however, the kind of connection with God that John Paul II sees as indispensable to sustain the claims of human dignity refers to the ontological, not the moral, level. Even affirmations—like the one that "man cannot be genuinely free or foster true freedom unless he *recognizes and lives the transcendence of his being* over the world and his relationship with God; for freedom is always the freedom of man made in the image of his creator"[107]—refer to a dimension of freedom quite different from that concerning the civil right to religious freedom even in its broadest implications. There is not, therefore, any questioning of the universal and equally due human right to religious freedom.

The methodological preference for theologically emphatic conceptualizations and formulations, the way John Paul II does it, has relevant consequences for the impact of the doctrine of *Dignitatis Humanae*. Some significant statements on freedom of conscience and religion, because they lack clearly noted and precisely defined transitions and distinctions between one conceptual level of freedom and another, allow for a grain of ambiguity. We cannot forget that he was responding primarily to the urgent needs of the second moment, circumscribed to particular historical contexts, and such ambiguity is of more consequence for the perception of the church's attitude in historical contexts of the first and third moments. But many of this pronouncements addressed the universal church, or the whole world, and, therefore, they have consequences for historical circumstances other than the one first in his mind. For societies most deeply affected by the first moment, this more explicitly theological justification does not as effectively cancel suspicions about the church's intentions. This option for a new primary method to justify the right, even if it does not intend to invalidate the primary approach taken by *Dignitatis Humanae,* may weaken or depreciate, or, at least, give less visibility to, some of the values acquired for church-society relationships. It looks like this theological perspective tends to leave out some very positive traits of the doctrinal development that enabled the right to religious freedom to be finally recognized by the Catholic Church at Vatican II, a development made possible by a methodology of moral reflection that started from human experience, and not so much from the authority of revelation.

The explicitly theological justification appears together, in the theology of John Paul II on religious freedom, with claims that the church has the exclusive understanding of the only solid foundation of human dignity, and with frequent assertions of the uniqueness of the church's contribution, which, in view of the history of affirmation of the civil right to religious freedom, seem exaggerated. The converging sum of all these features does not convey, as clearly as it perhaps would be desirable, especially in typical statements defending primarily the freedom of the church and the rights of believers, that the doctrine of *Dignitatis Humanae* defends with equal determination a thorough protection of the broader right to religious freedom at the level of society, for believers and nonbelievers alike.

Establishing the starting point for the justification of the right to religious freedom on the claims of a truth adequately known only through revelation has its disadvantages too for the dialogue and cooperation with nonbelievers. It means that, for those who do not adequately acknowledge that truth in terms of religious faith, the main grounding of the right the church offers them is, in terms of their own outlook in life, somewhat extrinsic. If the basis of the justification tends to be exclusively theological, the security of the right of nonbelievers before any possible heaviness of religion upon them will be dependent on what, in their eyes, will be a concession outside their scope of argument. This is particularly relevant in contexts profoundly marked by the first moment, where it continues to be important to build mutual trust and find common ground for dialogue and cooperation. If revealed truth is presented ultimately as the only solid ground for the right recognized by the church, that language is not as effective in separating the current stand of the church from the old position of condescending toleration in the protection of the freedom of non-believers. A reinforcement of the theological character of the doctrine on the right to religious freedom, even maybe a certain strengthening of the role of the truth, certainly do not have to imply a return to the claims of privilege for the church in society, or any kind of reversal of doctrine, but it continues to be important to make that unequivocally clear, and the theological formulations preferred by John Paul II do not always achieve that.

The possible tendency for misleading understandings of these formulations on the grounding of the right is compounded by the views of John Paul II on what kind of demands such right exerts at the personal level of the individual conscience, on how that human dignity, whatever its ultimate justification, is primarily expressed existentially in the life of every person. This question is the topic of the pope's relentlessly repeated views on the relationship between freedom and truth.

A Right as a Function of a Duty: Truth above Freedom

The development of doctrine that culminated in *Dignitatis Humanae* was essentially a process of recognition of the primordial place of freedom of the individual conscience among the central and indispensable elements protective of the dignity of the person in society. The privileges of that freedom as an immunity from any external coercion in matters religious were finally recognized over absolutist claims made in name of the truth. This development did not deny the existence of an objectively true religion or the universal duty of people to search for it and embrace it when encountered, but it accredited freedom as the necessary, indispensable, and unique way fully respectful of human dignity to access to that truth. It thus reversed the emphasis on the exclusive rights of truth, if necessary even at the expense of the freedom of some individuals or groups, which had been the starting point of the old doctrinal formulations of the thesis/hypothesis theory. The new conception does not promote freedom at the expense of the truth, but it firmly establishes freedom as the first existential value of the human person, never to be externally constrained, not even in the service of objective religious truth. Such an evolution in the doctrine of the church accompanied, although belatedly, a momentous philosophical, political, and cultural paradigm shift in Western civilization, which, not without many an exorbitant claim and grave disarray in many societies, has put the freedom and the rights of the individual in the center of the whole social order.

The teaching of John Paul II on the person and society has insistently denounced the dangers of an excessively one-sided emphasis on individual freedom characteristic of contemporary culture. Concurrently, he has deliberately and forcefully promoted, also in the name of human dignity, a greater attention to the biding command of the prerogatives of the truth over human conscience. His frequent discussions of the dialectic between freedom and truth have a direct import on his teaching on the right to religious freedom and concern fundamental standpoints in the interpretation and development of the doctrine of *Dignitatis Humanae*. Through them we may more clearly identify in his anthropology the precise locus where, among the dimensions of each individual conscience, the dignity of each and every person is first and foremost expressed; and also through these frequent discussions, therefore, we may more clearly identify what exactly is the moral prerogative that the right to religious freedom ultimately is intended to protect and foster.

In his pronouncements we find many propositions extolling human freedom, but rarely without some kind of explicit or implicit qualification included or readily following. For instance in the 1988 World Day of Peace Message, he writes that "Freedom is man's most noble prerogative. . . . Without freedom, human acts are empty and valueless." This "freedom with which man has been endowed by the Creator" he describes immediately after as

> the capacity always given to him to seek what is true by using his intelligence and to embrace without reserve the good to which he naturally aspires, without being subject to undue pressures, constraints or violence of any kind. It belongs to the dignity of the person to be able to respond to the moral imperative of one's own conscience in the search for the truth.[108]

Freedom, thus, in as much as it is a capacity to fulfill this moral imperative, exists in function of the truth; it is affirmed in the measure it is ordered to the good and the truth. "Truth . . . is the root and rule of freedom," he says at another time.[109] It is the claim of the moral imperative, upheld by the excellence of its end—the truth—that supports the immunity of that freedom. In spite of the exalting initial affirmation of freedom, the more prominent role is actually assigned to the duty toward the truth.

In fact, truth is the center of gravity of John Paul II's defining of the human person in the dialectic between freedom and truth. For this discussion, his basic starting point is another of his favorite quotes, a line from the Gospel of John, which is evoked innumerable times all through his writings and addresses: "You will know the truth and the truth will make you free."[110] In *Redemptor Hominis* he interprets these words as

> containing both a fundamental requirement and a warning: the requirement of an honest relationship with regard to truth as a condition for authentic freedom, and the warning to avoid every kind of illusory freedom, every superficial unilateral freedom, every freedom that fails to enter into the whole truth about man and the world. Today also, even after two thousand years, we see Christ as the one who brings man freedom based on truth, frees man from what curtails, diminishes and as it were breaks off this freedom at its root, in man's soul, his heart and his conscience.[111]

The Message for the 1991 World Day of Peace, a lengthy exploration of the meaning and content of freedom of conscience, brings further light to the meaning of the "requirement" and "warning" that John Paul II finds in the Johannine axiom. First, let us consider the requirement for authentic freedom. How does it work and what does it imply? The message uses again a dialectic between capacity and duty, ability and obligation. John Paul II begins with an affirmation of the moral capacity of the human person,[112] not, however, as an exaltation of human autonomy, a profession of trust in people's natural moral insight and intuitiveness for the right. Rather it lays down the basis for the obligation to conform to objective truth. The whole emphasis is on each person's responsibility, invalidating, thus, excuses for overlooking what is indeed a clear call of the truth.

This constitutive aptitude to choose and obey the truth connects the person with a truth that transcends the person and every earthly power. Therefore, it grounds the immunity of human conscience from any encroachment by any human authority from which that coercion may come. The proximity of the truth to one's conscience creates the duty to search for it, first, and, then, sustains the right to the freedom necessary to pursue that search. "Freedom of conscience, rightly understood, is by its very nature always ordered to the truth."[113] "It is in this relation to objective truth that freedom of conscience finds its justification inasmuch as it is a necessary condition for seeking the truth worthy of man and for adhering to that truth once it is sufficiently known."[114]

This subservience of freedom of conscience to the moral duty toward the truth, in the case of the right to religious freedom, explains a strong accentuation of religious obligation which, more than accompanying the right, justifies it and gives it finality—so much so that John Paul II can even say at one point that the right to religious freedom is "a right as a function of a duty . . . the most fundamental of the rights in function of the first of the duties; which is the duty to move towards God in the light of the truth. . . ."[115]

The stressed "requirement of an honest relationship in regard to truth" responds to the pope's preoccupation with the risk that the doctrine on the universal right to religious freedom may mistakenly strengthen any of the erroneous modern conceptions of freedom, based on the illusion of absolute human autonomy. A right relation to objective truth is both a universal obligation and a universal human possibility: "Conscience . . . is not an absolute placed above truth and error. Rather, by its very nature it implies a relation to objective truth, a truth which is universal, the same for all, which all can and must seek."[116]

The "requirement" of a correct relation to truth implies already a warning against current forms of "illusory freedom." But the "warning" deducted by John Paul II from the line of the Gospel of John has still another dimension: It is also an admonition against a presumption of self-sufficiency of the individual conscience in the formation of moral judgments. Freedom is to be reaped in the future, a gift of the truth. Therefore, before the encounter with the truth the conscience is less than free. The stress on a dutiful conscience, strongly bounded to follow the truth, goes hand in hand with a critical distrust of the human capacity to fulfill successfully such obligation without external help. There is a gap between finding oneself obliged and having in oneself the full capacity to discharge the duty rightfully. The claims of the law imprinted on everyone's heart are powerful enough to oblige each one to respond to the longing for the truth and to bring judgment upon those who do not resolutely enter the quest. However, a merely personal grasping of what that law demands in concrete cannot be trusted to guide the search all the way; owing to human limitations and cultural conditioning, the individual conscience most probably will misconstrue and distort those demands.

Even Christians cannot completely trust their own individual capacities; their personal perceptions of impending moral obligations can be equally misleading. Because their obligation to the truth is also particularly exacting, their susceptibility to error is of even more serious consequence. But they also have the support of revelation for moral guidance:

> Faced with the obligation of following their own conscience in the search for the truth, the disciples of Jesus Christ know that they may not trust only in their personal capacity for moral discernment. Revelation enlightens their consciences and enables them to know that freedom which is God's great gift to mankind. Not only has he inscribed the natural law within the heart

> of each individual, in that "most secret core and sanctuary of a man (where) he is alone with God," but he has also revealed his own law in the Scriptures. Here we find the call, or rather the command, to love God and to observe his law.[117]

The full awareness of the weight of the duty and the self-knowledge of the limitations of one's conscience must create in the Christian faithful an attitude of modesty and humility, critically doubting one's individual—possibly individualistic—presumptions and submitting readily to the objective commandments revealed in the Scriptures—unambiguous absolute moral norms, needing or admitting no discussion or adaptation—which God wants us to have as guides more than our limited moral perceptiveness.

Furthermore, this stance above the personal searches of the individual conscience is mediated to the individual Christian through the church's magisterium, as John Paul II describes in a deductive sequence:

> In searching for the truth the Christian has recourse to divine revelation, which in Christ is present in all its fullness. Christ has entrusted the church with the mission of proclaiming this truth, and the whole church has the duty of remaining faithful to that truth. My most serious responsibility as the successor of Peter is precisely this: to ensure this constant fidelity by confirming my brothers and sisters in their faith.[118]

Once again we see how a basically pessimistic theological anthropology ties in with an ecclesiology that strongly stresses the role of moral authority. Both are in a tight interrelation with a specific bias in the interpretation of the demands and prerogatives of the right to freedom of conscience and of religion.

In his endorsement of the right of religious freedom, John Paul II tries to balance the dangers of a unilateral drive for individual self-determination, with the reassertion of a universal duty, and the denunciation of any obstacles to a resurgence of religion and religious values in the lives of individuals and societies. The axioms of his anthropology give support to this partiality in the measure they determine the supremacy of truth over freedom, and, among the constitutive elements of the person through which human dignity is expressed and honored, the prevalence of the duty toward the truth first and foremost, over openness to freedom. This deliberate ideological effort to bring the notion of truth again to the foreground of the cultural understanding of the human person intends to question and correct the primordial role given to freedom as the originating notion of the modern understanding of the person. Through the exploration of the dialectic between freedom and truth, mostly in the context of developments on the doctrine of religious freedom, John Paul II states a very critical position before the individualistic tendencies of the liberal social philosophies of the Enlightenment. The negative judgment on contemporary culture focuses on the deplorable consequences of those tendencies, patent today in liberal societies.

The teaching of John Paul II in the context of the second moment has effected, thus, an adjustment on the relationship of the person in society to freedom prevailing in *Dignitatis Humanae.* The optimistic view of the declaration had confidence in the power of the truth to affirm itself before free people who would not fail to recognize and embrace it. John Paul II's pessimistic evaluation sees notions and practices of individual freedom so distorted that, if it is not helped (redirected to *true* freedom by the force of duty and the guidance of authority), it will stray further away from the truth. Truth is thus a condition for freedom. Instead of underlining that only through freedom freely exercised can the human person be expected to arrive at the truth, John Paul II states emphatically that the human person in the present condition only attains freedom through the recognition and obedience to the truth.

CONCLUSION: ACCENTS AND UNCLARITIES

The advocacy of the civil right to religious freedom by John Paul II was relentless during the first part of his pontificate, in which the church had to face the pressing threats of the second moment. He consolidated the leadership role of the church in the promotion of human rights throughout the world and gave concrete visibility to the radically changed official attitude of the church toward personal rights in matters religious effected by *Dignitatis Humanae.* The holder of papal office, which for so long and until recently had opposed the juridical recognition of the civil right to religious freedom, he turned the demand for a scrupulous respect of that constitutional right into one of the most insistently repeated topics of his public addresses to political authorities all over the world and of the church's official social teaching in general.

Addressing the challenges of the second moment, the pope applied efficiently doctrine established by *Dignitatis Humanae,* but, at the same time, he has also introduced a personal mark on the interpretation and development of that teaching. Easily apparent, distinctive characteristics of his approach are a supreme preoccupation with the defense of the free activity of the church, the stressing of religious freedom as the first of human rights, a reemphasizing of the role of truth as the basis of the whole argument, and, finally, a pattern of preferred or even selective quoting of the text of *Dignitatis Humanae.*

In the context of the second moment, it is by necessity that he bolsters the claim for the freedom of the church. His pastoral solicitude as universal pastor of the church, which heightened the sense of urgency to do something about the situation of persecution and discrimination suffered by Christian believers and the institutional church, and his first-hand experience of the formidable threat for the church constituted by communism, explain the concentration on the promotion of the free exercise of religion. He wants to demand respect for these universally accepted human rights in the most unmistakable way possible, so it is understandable that he focuses the claims on the most urgent and leaves some nuances or qualifications out, even at the price of incurring some imbalance. The priority and emphasis given to the protection of the prerogatives of believers do not imply oblivion or less regard for those rights and protections that, going beyond the restricted guardianship of the particular religious prerogatives of the Catholic church, apply to non-Catholics, believers and nonbelievers alike, and are equally part of the full scope of the doctrine of the right to religious freedom. There is no doubt about the pope's commitment to the universal right of religious freedom as the council defined it—immunity of all persons from state interference in matters of religious belief (or unbelief) and practice (or nonpractice), in private or in public. However, these emphases and omissions continued to shift the focus back to the interests of the church, debilitating somewhat the statement of self-restraint and non–self-centeredness that had been, from the perspective of church-society relationships, the great progress and promise of the first moment of *Dignitatis Humanae*. And any formulations that too easily equate the right to religious freedom with just the rights of the church bring ambiguity, ambiguity that opens the way for the return of suspicion, especially in environments still marked by the battles and the prejudices of the first moment. These doubts can be sufficient to cool, in those circles, the good will toward a greater social role for the church, as well as dispositions for dialogue and cooperation. John Paul II's forceful confrontation of the challenges of the second moment has significantly advanced the cause of religious freedom, but, indirectly, as a byproduct of the second moment, it may also have conveyed in other historical contexts a certain regression of the attitude of the Catholic Church regarding the modern world.

The innovation of ranking religious freedom as the first human right falls under the same kind of ambivalence. On one hand it may (or may not) enhance the public impact of the advocacy for religious freedom,[119] but, on the other, it also can insinuate privilege. This ordering of human rights, justified by the especial excellence of the transcendent dimension of the human spirit, can only be advantageous for believers, and it opens the way for the risky possibility of setting religious freedom apart from other freedoms and turning it into not just the prime but the sole concern of the church.[120] John Paul II does not intend to do that; he stresses precisely the intimate connection of all human rights. The elevation of this one to a special status in his argument is not done to separate it above the others. Instead, it is done for the benefit of the other rights because of its claimed special role as basis and support of the other political-civil rights. Nonetheless, it is hard to prove that, in all circumstances, actual respect for religious freedom is the litmus test for the general respect for human rights. Political persecution and curtailment of civil freedoms can go hand in hand with unrestricted freedom for the church, for instance in cases in which the church is socially hegemonic and sides with the status quo, allying itself with the state against an opposition animated by anticlerical or atheistic ideals, as it has happened sometimes this century with dictatorships in Latin America and Europe.[121] The argument seems to have focused too exclusively on the concrete situations of the second moment.[122] It may not work so well with some kinds of rightist totalitarianism as it does with communism.

In the usual theological explanation of John Paul II, the duty to pursue one's religious obligations is put forward more resolutely than the individual right to freedom of religion. At the level of the grounding of the right, he applies his repeatedly explored view of the dialectic between freedom and truth. That invariably results in propositions that tend to make the right functional to the duty and to define freedom as instrumental to the truth. And this again creates some vagueness, especially if there is no clear distinction of levels between the ontological and the moral and the moral and the civil. If that ordering of freedom to truth were pushed to its extreme, freedom would lose its justification when it rejects or ignores objective truth, and the right to religious freedom would become dependent in some way on the active realization of this connection to the truth. The basic issue at this level of the foundation of the right to religious freedom has to do with the kind of definitive answer to the following question: Where does human dignity ultimately rest in the person? Is that last layer human freedom, a freedom inherent to every person, which can be used well and fulfilled according to its intrinsic orientation, or not, but which, in either case, cannot be tampered with by any external power? Or is it the person's relationship with transcendent truth—truth to be accessed and embraced through freedom only, but to which freedom is only instrumental? John Paul II is clearly more on the side of the latter. This position raises difficulties inasmuch as it does not make it so immediately obvious that such freedom continues to be protected even if used against its own intrinsic orientation: Only freedom can actuate that relationship with the truth; there is no other way through which it can be reached. Freedom is integral to the attainment of the truth; however, freedom, only instrumental, loses its own justification when in a state of refusal of the truth. This vagueness at the level of the grounding of the right adds to the residual ambiguity raised by the other emphases of his formulations. The issue becomes whether John Paul II's theology of religious freedom, with all its accent on the direct protection of the freedom of the church and the rights of religious practice, also appreciates and promotes to a degree sufficiently unequivocal the right to freedom of those who do not believe or are indifferent toward religion.

The use John Paul II makes of the text of *Dignitatis Humanae,* in other words which passages are highlighted and quoted more often, is determined both by his own methodological and theological preferences and by the practical goals he is pursuing in the current historical context. The much lesser weight of the references to the dimension of religious freedom explicitly protective of the immunity of the nonbeliever and of the religiously indifferent is, thus, a natural counterpart of the tactical pastoral choices of the second moment. However, it is not just a matter of political persecution that he tries to counter with a tendentiously exclusive emphasis on the rights of religious faithful to discharge freely their moral duty toward the truth. The bias equally has to do with his great distrust of secularity (and, of course, a total rejection of secularism) of any social assertion autonomous from religion and with the fear that tendencies of indifferentism may further infect the faithful. So, in his promotion of religious freedom, he is extremely careful to dispel any possible doubt about the fact that the right correctly understood does not, in any way, give permission or even a slight excuse for anyone not to consider responsibly the truth concerning religion.[123]

This precaution is probably one important reason why he systematically skips, in his quoting, the final part of *Dignitatis Humanae* number 2 on the rights of those in error. In the short address of his general audience of April 17, 1985 we find his typical way of using this number of the conciliar declaration. What he considers to be "the essential argument in favor of the right to religious freedom" is the middle part of number 2, the sentences stating the moral obligation to search for the truth and embrace it. These sentences follow, in *Dignitatis Humanae,* the statement of the freedom as an immunity (not quoted) and are followed by the explicit qualifications that this is a freedom independent of any subjective attitude of mind, and, therefore, includes also those who do not carry out their obligation, qualifications over which John Paul II jumps to quote, immediately after, the part of number 3 on "the duty and consequently the right to seek the truth."[124] The ignored clause is one of the most significant statements of the development of doctrine effected by the declaration. It addresses primarily the church itself, makes explicit a correction of past actions, and brings the traditional stance of reverence for freedom of conscience to a further level of greater respect for the autonomy of each person's responsibility for his or her fundamental religious choices. So, it is an indispensable part of the elements that signal the radical change in the demeanor of the church in its relationship with the secular world, which I have summarized as the consequences and implications of the first moment of *Dignitatis Humanae*.

The circumvention does not mean that he questions the rights of those who do not believe. John Paul II continues to call for respect for people who think differently,[125] to set rules against intolerance on the part of religious people,[126] and to hold the state to a standard of scrupulous respect for the freedom of conscience of all, even in the case in which one particular religion enjoys a special status, although, in this last case he has primarily in view the protection of Christians in Muslim countries.[127]

What the pope does not want to promote tolerance for is resignation with indifferentism: "It is quite clear that freedom of conscience and of religion does not mean a relativization of the objective truth which every human being is morally obliged to seek."[128] In addition to the specific demands of the second moment, the priority for him now is not so much to dispel fears of church-induced intolerance (as it was the case of the first moment) but rather to contradict what he thinks is a culture of freedom totally gone astray, to protect the faithful from the contagion of erroneous conceptions, and to reverse the cultural tide of relativism and indifference. The acute preoccupation with secularism and indifferentism leads him, even through this kind of selective quoting, to intensify the role of the truth in such a way that the right to freedom is made subservient to the duty toward the truth. In doing this, he also recovers the centrality of the concept of truth in the arguments for religious freedom, something that was an absolute in the approaches previous to *Dignitatis Humanae*. Perhaps some of his less-nuanced propositions have gone too far to one side in his effort to prevent excesses on the other.

These tactical options do not take sufficiently into consideration the kind of unmerciful scrutiny to which the Catholic Church is still subject, on this area, by many in an increasingly secularized society, especially those groups which the church more strenuously opposed in the political controversies finally settled by the first moment.[129] Inside the church, such expressions reinforce the self-assurance of an attitude that does not favor the change of mentality and mood in the church itself still necessary for a more fruitful dialogue and collaboration in society. The aggregated risk is that, with the good intention of warning about dangerous tendencies, John Paul II may be allowing further alienation of secular society from the church, and contributing to the revival of old prejudices and suspicions, precisely those that *Dignitatis Humanae,* after so many pains, was able to begin to diffuse.

Pope John Paul II is firmly convinced of the indispensability of the social contribution of religion. Only people who practice religion, orient their moral lives by religious values, and try to implement them publicly in the whole community can offer the solution for the problems of humanity. The crucial goal is to bring more religious influx into the life of society by empowering believers and churches to make their contributions more effective. As he is dealing with the challenges of the second moment, the authentic problem he perceives goes beyond the disquieting reality that some people are not allowed to practice religion. The gravity of the situation resides not just in the fact that many people are suffering infringement of a basic human right but also in that fewer and fewer people are practicing religion so many societies are being deprived of the beneficial influx of religiously grounded values. The ultimate enemy is not the totalitarian government that disrespects human dignity by refusing freedom of religious practice but the whole antireligious mentality that wants to drive religion away from the public realm; the former is just a more violent form of the latter. In fact, from this perspective, the greatest danger is not posed by those who starkly oppose religious faith—in those situations, religious fervor usually increases—but by the mollification of religious belief and practice among the faithful, influenced by the indifferentism pervasive in the general culture. Promotion of religious freedom is not just a matter of safeguarding civil rights of people; it is the way of addressing the present problems of humanity. In the end, the great benefit for the common good of a scrupulous respect for religious freedom is the opening up of the way for an unimpeded contribution of religious faith to the rebuilding of the moral fabric of society.

Broadening the ambit of signification of religious freedom, taking it out of the somewhat narrow frame of immunity into a context that includes the more fertile concept of religious freedom as empowerment, is an enrichment of the doctrine. However, great care has to be taken that this in no way weakens the unalterable commitment to the defense of the freedom of the person as something absolutely untouchable, not even in the name of the truth—the great progress of *Dignitatis Humanae.* The highlighting of the aspects of empowerment cannot dispense with the unambiguous restatement of all the universal guarantees of the freedom as immunity. The focus on immunity only was narrow because it had to go very deep. As the focus can be widened, the depth cannot be compromised, or it might start looking like a step back. It is very important to continue to ground the right on a dignity unequivocally intrinsic to each person on something that opens no possibility of being conditioned on anything other than the mere being a human person. When the dimension of empowerment is stressed, reasserting the commitment to the dimensions of immunity also helps to avoid suspicion that the claim for religious freedom may be just a pragmatic way of opening the way for religion, now that the tables were turned against the church. It further reminds the church of the restraint that, in view of history and of the ultimate character of its assertions, it should always exercise in the social ministry for which it looks to be empowered.

Although John Paul II engaged fully the challenges of the second moment, he did not limit his defense of human rights, particularly the right to religious freedom, to the legal dimension and the scrupulous respect for the laws already in place or to be enacted. He set the juridical question in a context of values, intimately connected to the culture of society.[130] This progressive enlargement of the reach of the issue has allowed him to move, still within the context of promotion of religious freedom, from the critique of totalitarian governments that do not respect the principles and the laws protecting religious freedom, to the societies and cultures in which, although the constitutional guarantees are all in place and function in their strict limits, the deepest values of religious freedom are equally at risk. From a question in the political-juridical area of the relations between church and state, the issue at stake is expanded to the larger framework of an ideological-cultural dispute at the level of the place and role of religion in society. The defense of the civil right to religious freedom became an opportunity for John Paul II to expose his criticisms of the political and social philosophies of modernity predominant in contemporary societies, especially those aspects of them that are at the root of political practices hostile to, or just indifferently dismissive of, religion. Even though he keeps the focus on the immediate political battle of the second moment, his recognition of where the ultimate enemies and most dangerous threats to religious freedom are is actually already more complex and deeply penetrating than a simple indictment of communist regimes. This way, while still thoroughly committed to the problems of the second moment, he was already preparing the way for the shift of focus to the issues that will become the center of his attention in the years after, when the third moment starts to unfold.

His theological formulation and development of the doctrine of *Dignitatis Humanae*, in its accents but also in its limitations and disadvantages, uncovered with a new sharpness the intimate connections between the kinds of doctrinal approaches to the right to religious freedom and basic options in the larger area of the relationship between church and society.

Through the first part of his pontificate, John Paul II's attitudes and views were certainly conditioned by biases and interests typical of the second moment. But as he was successfully pushing for the resolution of this impasse, he was also gradually casting those specific issues in a larger cultural and ideological context, as well as affirmatively positioning the church before other modern challenges mounted by pluralistic secularized societies. The demise of communism has given him, afterwards, the opportunity to confront with greater focus the latter problems, characteristic of the third moment of *Dignitatis Humanae*. In doing that, he has not been less outspoken and much of his teaching on these issues has been in close continuity in terms of themes and style with the doctrinal guidelines framing his persistent advocacy of religious freedom.

John Paul II and the Third Moment: Mistrust of Secular Pluralism

The fall of communism radically altered the sociopolitical context that had been the point of convergence for the teaching of the Catholic Church on religious freedom since Vatican II. It marked, in my heuristic arrangement, the end of the second moment of *Dignitatis Humanae* but not the end of religious freedom as an issue deserving continued attention on the part of the highest office of the church. In the encyclical *Centesimus Annus,* published in 1991, John Paul II writes that it is still necessary to plead for the rights of the human conscience that totalitarian regimes had so bluntly disrespected for "the recognition of these rights represents the primary foundation of every authentically free political order." He gives three reasons why it is important to reaffirm this principle:

> a) because the old forms of totalitarianism and authoritarianism are not yet completely vanquished; . . . b) because in the developed countries there is sometimes an excessive promotion of purely utilitarian values; . . . c) because in some countries new forms of religious fundamentalism are emerging which covertly, or even openly, deny to citizens of faiths other than that of the majority the full exercise of their civil and religious rights.[131]

The tearing down of the Berlin Wall was not the end of persecution of the church and discriminations against Christians by hostile governments everywhere in the world, so the pope will continue to call for religious freedom in places where the remaining governments of communist inspiration still insist on discriminating against the church.[132] He persists with general appeals to political authorities on behalf of the rights of conscience of minorities, but the victims of religious discrimination that are now most in his mind are the Christians who live in countries of Muslim majority in which the faithful of other religions have no religious rights[133]—the third reason above.

It is the second reason, however, that points to what will become now the central issues of his consideration of religious freedom, constituting thus the distinguishing characteristic of the third moment. The exhilarating events in Eastern Europe in 1989 shifted the primary critical attention of the pope from the governments of the East to the societies of the West, as he explicitly recognizes in a sentence of his address to the Cardinals and the Curia on the Christmas of 1993. Referring to the recent publication of *Veritatis Splendor,* he describes the priorities of the two phases: "In the past it was necessary to say the truth about man to Eastern Europe, beyond the Berlin Wall; now it is necessary to corroborate such truth also to the man who lives in the west and looks with interest towards east."[134] Through the shift of historical-geographical foci from the second to the third moments, solicitude for the truth provides the element of continuity. The dialectic between freedom and truth will continue to be his favorite way of systematizing his approach.

Freedom, therefore, did not lose centrality, but now, instead of the lack of freedom in totalitarian states, John Paul II is concerned primarily with the bad uses of freedom in "free societies." Already at the beginning of 1989 he confessed his "anxiety about the way that certain societies abuse this freedom which is so longed for in others."[135] A few years before, he had already warned that religious freedom is threatened not just by legal constraints or other external restrictions, but also by cultural trends typical of liberal societies, such as habits and ways of thinking contrary to the gospel, a climate of materialism or religious indifferentism, and fallacious and individualistic conceptions of freedom.[136] It is vital for these societies that believers put forward a view of the world inspired by their faith.[137]

The processes of the changes in the East testified to the great power of religion for social transformation. The recognition of the pivotal role the churches had played in some of those countries and the perspective of an unobstructed expression of those religious energies made John Paul II think of a rebirth of the influence of religious faith in the West too: "It seems that beneath our very eyes a 'Europe of the spirit' is being reborn, in line with the values and symbols which have wrought it, from 'this Christian tradition which unites all peoples.' "[138]

In this initial optimistic look, he offered praise for cultural pluralism and pluralistic democracy, but he also pointed out that it is indispensable for society to maintain the relation to transcendent values and that the human person cannot forget his or her reference to God without grave consequences.[139] The new situation is both a time of opportunity and also of great risks, "an hour of truth for Europe." The old continent, caught between the void left by the crumbling of ideologies and the reawakening of the memory of its historic Christian roots, is challenged to redefine for itself the value and meaning of freedom, and that implies redefining itself before the question of God.[140]

Critical warnings about the dangers of liberal democracy will permeate his approach to the third moment. On one hand, he recognizes the possibilities allowed by democracy for a greater civic influence of religion, sees the positive role of a free confrontation of diverse conceptions of the world, and encourages participation of the church in the public dialogue. On the other, he decries the "moral crisis of democracies" created by the "temptation that exists today to found democracy on *moral relativism*."[141] The move from the second to the third moment, it quickly becomes obvious, consists of a shift of the focus from the area of church-state relations (in which the matter of religious freedom was primarily an issue of juridically and effectively guaranteeing personal immunity from political power) to the realm of the relationship of the church with democratic pluralistic societies.

The chief challenge now is to keep religion a fully equal partner in the public debates of civil society. One of the aspects of a "spreading 'practical atheism' " in society is the "bias towards indifferentism and the elimination of any real reference to binding truths and moral values," which, in the name of harmony and a desire to find common ground, "tends to restrict the contribution of those whose moral conscience is formed by their religious beliefs."[142] Therefore, fostering religious freedom in this new context means primarily counteracting the tendencies for total privatization of religion.[143] John Paul II reaffirms, for that goal, the social function of the empowerment dimension of religious freedom, which he had consistently stressed in his advocacy for the right to religious freedom in the context of the second moment.

More concretely, the crucial goal of John Paul II for the third moment will be to reassert the role of religion in the formation of consciences and to preserve its capacity to influence fundamental choices of public morality. These concerns are still directly linked to the ambit of religious freedom but its range has been broadened beyond the issues of a strictly juridical-political concept of a constitutionally guaranteed immunity. Although John Paul II has, in the past, frequently combined in one single proposition the two concepts of freedom of conscience and freedom of religion,[144] now he gives more weight to issues more strictly connected to freedom of conscience, as he stresses that the domain protected by the right to freedom of religion and freedom of conscience includes also the public expression of all intimate personal convictions. Freedom of conscience and religion actually has to grant the daily ability of every person to regulate his or her whole life according to the demands of that freedom. Such freedom "is not limited . . . to the ability to perform rites; it is the right of every man to express at the social level what he has in him of the most profound and not to suffer any harm or inconvenience for that."[145]

Attention to this expanded notion of freedom of conscience and religion serves the promotion of a continual enrichment of pluralistic societies through the respectfully welcomed diverse contribution of individuals. It calls all people to their responsibility to foster a climate of freedom in pluralism without closing out the equal participation of deeply ingrained personal beliefs.

At this time, John Paul II speaks in a very confident and constructive tone on the possibilities of democratic polity. He values the confluence of a pluralism of conceptions of the world, which include religious, atheistic, and agnostic views, and looks for increased participation and dialogue.[146] But he is already also making strong denunciations of the culture of liberal democracies, because it is supportive of profoundly distorted rules of participation, corrupted by views of the human person contradictory to the principles of freedom of conscience and religion, and, in fact, engaged in spreading erroneous conceptions of morality and moral practice. This is the perspective that will prevail in his development of topics typical of the third moment, namely the challenges to the public role of religion, concrete questions of public morality, and the relationship of civil law with moral law.

While the celebrations in and about Eastern Europe were still echoing, John Paul II was aware that the great risk for the newly politically liberated societies would be to absorb uncritically the worst of the culture of liberal democracies. So, he does not pass up the opportunity to sound an early warning about unwise emulation of wrong uses of freedom:

> Unfortunately, Western democracies have too often not known how to use the freedom achieved not so long ago at the cost of hard sacrifices. One can only regret the deliberate absence of any transcendent moral reference in the government of the so called "developed" societies. Despite generous impulses of solidarity, a real concern for the promotion of justice and a continuing concern to implement respect for human rights, one cannot but notice the

> presence and the diffusion of counter values, such as egoism, hedonism, racism and practical materialism.[147]

The solution is clear and it is the same for both East and West: "All Europeans are providentially called to rediscover the spiritual roots which have created Europe."[148] Only in religion can contemporary societies find guidance to overcome the deficiencies ultimately induced by secularism. If the Christian substrate were to be marginalized in its role of ethical inspiration and social intervention, not only the heritage of the European past would be denied, but the future of the European person would be gravely compromised.[149]

Reproach of Western social culture is nothing new in the teaching of John Paul II.[150] His reproach appeared long before 1989, which suggests that this critical stance is not just a matter of responding to a particular conjuncture but, rather, corresponds to deep philosophical and theological convictions of his, the same convictions that oriented his development of the teaching on the right to religious freedom during the second moment. For instance, already in 1980 he had pointed out that "some kinds of 'freedom' do not really deserve the name," specifically when freedom is confused with materialistic consumerism or moral permissiveness as it is typically in liberal capitalist democracies. He encourages then a more proactive role of organized society in the protection and promotion of morality.[151] The concrete illustration with which he concludes the denunciation "of this mistaken idea of freedom" is the generalized acceptance of abortion.

There is, thus, a clearly and consistently mapped out chain of consequences: societies that steer away from their spiritual roots and deny religion its due public influence end up captive of illusionary and pernicious conceptions of human capacity and freedom, which, in turn, create and support a culture of general amorality, most visible and with the most harmful consequences in the areas of the ethics of life. These topics will be the subject of the most important documents of John Paul II in the decade after the fall of communism. They are the issues that took the forefront of his teaching on church-society relationships in recent years, the core of his approach to the third moment.

The main directions of the engagement of John Paul II with the challenges of the third moment are in consistent continuity with what had been the fundamental principles guiding his development of the doctrine on religious freedom during the height of the second moment. Now, the application to a new context will make the consequences and implications of those basic assumptions for the relationship of the church with society appear more distinctly. The combat against the social impoverishment caused by secularism, one of the main driving forces of his ideological battle against communist regimes, is still setting the general orientation for his programmed critique of liberal pluralistic democracies.

The elected points of principal contention with contemporary societies continue to be issues directly and indirectly connected to the doctrine of *Dignitatis Humanae*. Consequently, the way John Paul II confronts these challenges provides for a deeper understanding of his interpretation and development of the teaching of the conciliar declaration. At the same time, the lines of force of his previous appropriations of the recent Catholic tradition on religious freedom during the second moment are helpful guides now for a better comprehension of his actual choices and of the prevailing directions of the current attitude of the papacy toward the world. The uses of *Dignitatis Humanae* by John Paul II in the second and third moments illuminate each other.

Centesimus Annus: An Assessment of the Condition of Freedom

The first systematic attempt by John Paul II to formulate the new challenges of the third moment and, simultaneously, to position the Catholic Church before them, was the encyclical *Centesimus Annus*. There, he takes the opportunity of the celebration of the first centenary of *Rerum Novarum* "to propose *an analysis of some events of recent history* . . . in order to discern the new requirements of evangelization" (*CA*, no. 3). It is, thus, an exercise of interpretation of the past for the benefit of the ensuing future. The analysis unfolds in three steps. First, he uncovers the fundamental reasons why communism collapsed. In this part of the analysis, he reveals in a systematic and more explicit way the bases of the opposition to communism that, sometimes only implicitly, guided his defense of the right to religious freedom during the second moment. History has vindicated his analysis. Then, he applies those insights to diagnose the virtues and vices of contemporary societies, setting, finally, the task of the church for the third moment as both a function of judgment and denunciation of the shortcomings of liberal democracies and a role of proposing alternative solutions.

What Made Communism Collapse? For John Paul II, the fundamental error of socialism is anthropological, and it has to do with a mistaken concept of the nature of the person caused by atheism. Atheism causes great impoverishment in each person's perception of him or herself, because God is the foundation of the person. That, in turn, translates into a deficient social organization, without reference to the person's dignity and responsibility (*CA*, no. 13). When this deficient social order, based on a defective conception of the human person, is imposed by a militant atheism with an aggressive political agenda, it further impoverishes the moral and spiritual life of peoples and nations, by cutting off their experience from a cultural tradition deeply shaped by religious faith (*CA*, no. 24). The result is a totalitarian culture lacking, or purposely ignoring, adequate answers to the most fundamental human questions, and so condemned to succumb to its own spiritual emptiness.

If the big error of communism was its denial of religion and of the spiritual dimension of the human person, it is no surprise that it was the reawakened forces of religion that brought it down. The role of the church was, consequently, crucial in the political transformations of the late eighties in Europe, and also, all through that decade, in other parts of the world (*CA*, no. 22).

Atheism, the first cause and source of all errors and evils of the social model that collapsed in 1989, "is also closely connected with the rationalism of the Enlightenment, which views human and social reality in a mechanistic way. Thus there is a denial of the supreme insight concerning man's true greatness, his transcendence in respect to earthly realities" (*CA*, no. 13), which, then, gives rise to "an understanding of human freedom which detaches it from obedience to the truth, and consequently from the duty to respect the rights of others" (*CA*, no. 17). Leo XIII, at the end of the nineteenth century, in *Rerum Novarum* and other documents, had already attributed the origin of the evils he was denouncing to this conception of freedom, John Paul II notes (*CA*, no. 4).

John Paul II uncovers in this way the origins of modern totalitarianism. Although it appears as a denial of freedom, actually it

> arises out of a denial of truth in the objective sense. If there is no transcendent truth, in obedience to which a person achieves his full identity, then there is no sure principle for guaranteeing just relations between people. . . . Thus, the root of modern totalitarianism is to be found in the denial of the transcendent dignity of the human person who, as the visible image of the invisible God, is therefore by his very nature the subject of rights which no one may violate—no individual, group, class, nation or State. (*CA*, no. 44)

Moreover, any voluntaristic political program that intends to establish a durable regime on these philosophical bases, as was the case of the communist regimes, has necessarily to make use of practices of religious discrimination and persecution. It is something intrinsic to its own ideological makeup and logic of affirmation and survival.[152]

In this perspective, religious freedom was a crucial point of conflict between the church and totalitarianism; neither side could afford to take it lightly or to compromise. For the church, more was at stake than just the freedom for its mission. When it defended religious freedom it wanted to preserve the most basic conceptions of the person and society. Only upon them can a right ordering of the whole human living in the world be structured. For totalitarian regimes, stifling religious freedom was crucial to preserving their own particular conception of the world and to being able to sustain the political implementation of their social model. This fundamental incompatibility allows John Paul II to advance, at the conclusion of his analysis of the principles and practices of communism, a justification of the strategy he followed in the second moment, which emphasized the freedom of the church and highlighted the right to religious freedom as prominent among human rights:

> [T]he totalitarian State tends to absorb within itself the nation, society, the family, religious groups and individuals themselves. In defending her own freedom, the Church is also defending the human person, who must obey God rather than men (cf. Acts 5:29), as well as defending the family, the various social organizations and nations—all of which enjoy their own spheres of autonomy and sovereignty. (*CA*, no. 45)

In all this, John Paul II seems to be settling the scores in the decades-long conflict of the church with communism, centered in great part on issues of religious freedom. His analysis makes explicit the reasons why, in the years before, he had tried to set the upholding of the civil right to religious freedom in a larger doctrinal framework, capable of addressing the roots of the problem too, not just the juridical issue. But this is not an exercise of vindication of personal views, relishing the fact that history proved him right decisively and in a short time. Bringing more clarity to the recent past is also a way to search for a ground in tradition from which to face the challenges of the new social context in which the Catholic Church now lives and ministers. That is why he went as far back as the nineteenth-century papal condemnations of absolutist liberalism. If the political situations and the challenges faced by the church in each of these two moments are quite different, the erroneous conceptions at the root of the philosophies and practices contrary to the Christian view of the human person and of human society are very similar, if not entirely the same. If the same root-causes that inspired and, eventually, doomed communism are also active in many traces of the dominant culture of Western democracies, they threaten, therefore, no lesser future troubles. A last explanation of the ideological bases of the conflict of the second moment actually functions, in this encyclical, as a laying down of the fundamental bases for a critical confrontation of the main vices of contemporary pluralistic societies, the great concern of the new third moment.

The Threat of a Secularist Culture of Freedom. A mistaken conception of the relationship between freedom and truth is the immediate common basis of the errors denounced by John Paul II in both moments. Denial of objective truth gave rise to totalitarianism and is also generating the agnostic moral relativism, a typical flaw of modern democracies, which expresses itself in the idea that the truth is determined by majority (*CA,* no. 46).

Because this principle excludes some people from social participation, namely those who have their positions inspired by religious values and justify them on divinely revealed truths, John Paul II considers that the principles of religious freedom are also threatened in these societies, to the point where he says bluntly that "a democracy without values easily turns into open or thinly disguised totalitarianism" (*CA,* no. 46).

It is not only disregard for objective truth that likens capitalist democratic societies with totalitarianism; their consumerism does that too, in the measure in which, no less than Marxism, it expects to satisfy all human needs by means of material things, forgetting spiritual values (*CA,* nos. 19 and 36), and, thus, weakening "the entire socio-cultural system, by ignoring the ethical and religious dimension" (*CA,* no. 39).

The real center of the problem of the dominant culture of liberal pluralistic democracies—a culture that, at this same time, he called narcissistic[153]—is secularism, the disregard for the transcendent dimension of the human person, and the consequent moral relativism; that is also the target, in this instance, of the pope's teaching.

The Church's Alternative Solution. In the present context, it keeps being necessary to maintain that the recognition of the rights of religious freedom and freedom of conscience "represents the primary foundation of every authentically free political order."[154] The goal of the church continues to be the promotion of authentic human freedom, for freedom is what humankind was created for (see *CA,* no. 25).

However, John Paul II's sensitivity to the concrete dangers of mistaken ideas of freedom current in our world never lets him make a statement defending human freedom without immediately adding the same kinds of qualifications we have seen before, now in an even starker form. Freedom is the end of created humankind, but "*obedience to the truth* about God and humankind is the first condition of freedom" (*CA,* no. 41). The emphasis on truth makes it even the primary human referent: "Man remains above all a being who seeks the truth and strives to live in that truth" (*CA,* no. 49). Failure to respect this relation of dependency creates situations of oppression and alienation.[155]

Faithful to its role of respecting and promoting freedom, the church has, first of all, to propose and uphold the truth[156] in openness and dialogue with others certainly but without shying away from the duty of affirming its owned truth in service of freedom. John Paul II underlines that this repeated proposition of the truth about the human person and society, like the whole teaching in social questions since *Rerum Novarum,* has not been done by the church "in order to recover former privileges or to impose her own vision. Her sole purpose has been care and responsibility for the human person, who has been entrusted to her by Christ himself" (*CA,* no. 53). In the conjuncture of the third moment, the church continues to express a solicitude for society that is part of its own mission. A firm stand against relativism is nowadays the way to defend society from its worst self-destructing tendencies, for when a culture rejects "any exchange or debate with regard to the truth about man, then it becomes sterile and is heading for decadence" (*CA,* no. 50).

What the church offers out of its own particular sense of responsibility is also a contribution that responds to a dire need increasingly being felt by all:

> The world today is ever more aware that solving serious national and international problems is not just a matter of economic production or of juridical or social organization, but also calls for specific ethical and religious values, as well as changes of mentality, behavior and structures. The Church feels a particular responsibility to offer this contribution. (*CA,* no. 60)

The pope expects collaboration in this task from people who profess no religion, and, especially, from other religions (*CA,* no. 60), but the contribution of the church is seen as unique and irreplaceable. We encounter again at this point the basic principles of John Paul II's theological anthropology, namely, the firm conviction that "a person's true identity is only fully revealed to him through faith" (*CA,* no. 54), a conviction that immediately establishes the church in a privileged position since it "receives 'the meaning of the person' from Divine Revelation" (*CA,* no. 55). The church's teaching on the dignity of every human being and on a conception of society respectful of the transcendent dimension of the person is, thus, fully theological in its sources and will tend to keep that character in the arguments and the language used.[157]

Identifying the refusal of the transcendent at the root of important traits of the social models characteristic of both the second and the third moment distances the church equally from both of them. The contents of a revealed vision of the person, in turn, provide the church with an alternative solution, which, faithful to its sources, the church elaborates and proposes in theological terms, as John Paul II had already tried to establish for the foundation of the right to religious freedom. *Centesimus Annus* sets the contribution of the church in contrast with the two options, one already tried and conclusively dismissed, the other still active but equally inadequate:

> The theological dimension is needed both for interpreting and solving present-day problems in human society. It is worth noting that this is true in contrast both to the "atheistic" solution, which deprives humankind of one of its basic dimensions, namely the spiritual one, and to permissive and consumerist solutions, which under various pretexts seek to convince man that he is free from every law and from God himself, thus imprisoning him within a selfishness which ultimately harms both him and others. (*CA*, no. 55)

Equidistant between two alternative social systems has been a continual positioning of Catholic social teaching in the twentieth century, in spite of periods of greater approximation to some aspects of one or the other. But here John Paul II does not focus on capitalism and socialism as economic or political systems. He is looking at cultures and orderings of values. It is not a matter of proposing a middle way, but, rather, the stating of an equal rejection of atheism and moral relativism, both of which are forgetful of the transcendent truth about the human person.

The basic contention of the encyclical is that all present social problems have their root in the modern turn to secularism and that solutions can only come from a return to religiously inspired values. A certain correction to erroneous tendencies of modernity is necessary to steer democratic societies away from impending distresses. The analysis of the reasons for the collapse of communism and the diagnoses of the social ailments of the "free societies," together with the theological conception, which John Paul II developed during the second moment (which he again synthesized in *Centesimus Annus*), positioned him to engage the concerns of the third moment.

The next two major encyclicals of his pontificate would very much define the kind, the intensity, and the points of greater anxiety of his approach to the challenges mounted by the shortcomings of liberal democracy. This response by John Paul II has also decisively determined the way the church is being perceived in the third moment, with some significant contrasts relative to the great expectations the end of the first moment had created within and without the church. Fuller consequences of the experience, personal and institutional, of the second moment can then be evaluated.

VERITATIS SPLENDOR AND *EVANGELIUM VITAE*: REJECTION OF THE CULTURE OF DEATH

What in *Centesimus Annus* were concerns and warnings about fundamental flaws of the dominant culture and supporting ideologies of Western democracies became in *Veritatis Splendor* and *Evangelium Vitae* clear indictments and stronger condemnations. Focusing on issues of morality (the first on current tendencies in moral theology and the second, more concretely, on questions of bioethics), these documents present a very negative picture of the contemporary world, of, more precisely, the ethical environment of liberal pluralistic culture. The general tone is more of countercultural denunciation and rejection than of openness to dialogue. The strategic option seems to be the closing of the ranks of the church to preserve it as much as possible from contagion and to stiffen its force as a bulwark of resistance and agent of regeneration.

More than any radically new positions, these encyclicals stress and make more concrete points already announced in *Centesimus Annus* and earlier through the teaching of the present pope. The theological guidelines, methodological preferences, and favorite emphatic formulations of his system of theological grounding of the right to religious freedom reappear with greater sharpness and intensity. Principles related to *Dignitatis Humanae* are here directed very pointedly to a critique of the culture of secularized pluralist democracies, with emphasis on morality, especially the ethics of life. The inescapable incisiveness of many propositions in these encyclicals, their general tone, and the public impact they had gave them the role of decisive hermeneutical key for the positioning of John Paul II on church-society relationships.

Breach Between Freedom and Truth. A wrongful and pernicious conception of human freedom is once again exposed as the source of all evil. A cultural and moral mindset carries the concept of subjectivity to the extreme of equating personal dignity with overvalued autonomy. From this distorted estimation of autonomy issues an individualistic notion of freedom, which isolates and absolutizes the individual. Finally, this freedom "no longer recognizes and respects its *essential link with the truth*."[158] It upholds, rather, a primacy over truth "to the point that truth itself would be considered a creation of freedom."[159]

John Paul II suggests an ultimate explanation of this breach between freedom and truth in the terms of a tendentiously pessimistic theological anthropology:

The effects of original sin cloud human recognition of the truth and misdirect the human person to illusory forms of freedom.[160] Supported in, and supportive of, subjectivism, utilitarianism, and relativism (*VS*, no. 106), this notion of freedom distorts gravely the criteria for individual moral decision making. Instead of the truth about good and evil, the point of reference becomes only one's "subjective and changeable opinion or, indeed, . . . selfish interest and whim."[161] The result is "a relativistic conception of morality."[162]

Aftereffects are visible not only at the level of individual morality. Its consequences end up shaping the whole culture and influencing human living at all levels: "This view of freedom leads to a serious distortion of life in society."[163]

Disrespect for the Right to Life is a Threat to Democracy. The associated tendencies to subjectivism, utilitarianism, and relativism have even begun to overthrow the most basic values that shaped and distinguished modern Western societies. A conception of freedom in total refusal of the demands of the objective moral order is creating a dramatic contradiction between reiterated declarations defending "the value and dignity of every individual as a human being" and the "tragic repudiation of them in practice," especially of the right to life. All this occurs precisely "in a society which makes the affirmation and protection of human rights its primary objective and its boast" (*EV*, no. 18).

It is not just because *Evangelium Vitae* particularly targets issues of bioethics that John Paul II elects the right to life as the crucial point of contention with the modern culture of freedom. Since the ideological bases of this culture support, and even actively promote practices such as abortion and euthanasia, the current notion of freedom is directly responsible for the rise of what he calls the "culture of death." In it, "any reference to common values and to a truth absolutely binding on everyone is lost, and social life ventures on to the shifting sands of complete relativism. At that point, *everything is negotiable, everything is open to bargaining:* even the first of the fundamental rights, the right to life" (*EV*, no. 29).

The offenses against life are, thus, a proof and a symbol of all the dangers to which this conception of freedom exposes the tradition of democratic social living.[164] Such attacks "represent a *direct threat to the entire culture of human rights.* It is a threat capable, in the end, of jeopardizing the very meaning of democratic coexistence."[165] Under the reign of relativism, "democracy, contradicting its own principles, effectively moves towards a form of totalitarianism."[166]

Although, at the beginning of the third moment, liberal democracies stand victorious after the crumbling of the most obvious threats to human rights posed by communism (especially religious freedom), the menace hanging over them, in the view of John Paul II, is not less serious now; it can even be more ominous because it does not derive from an external enemy but resides right within the ethical tendencies commanding developed societies. The impending danger comes from "*the risk of an alliance between democracy and ethical relativism,* which would remove any sure moral reference point from political and social life, and on a deeper level make the acknowledgment of truth impossible."[167]

The pope speaks again of impending totalitarianism, hindrances to human rights, denial of religious yearning—language and concepts that still strikingly evoke the context of the second moment. Promotion of religious freedom is not over and done with, because, albeit under quite different appearances, it continues to be at risk. The new political circumstance constitutes thus another round of the friction between post-Enlightenment political ideologies and the Catholic Church, between the different forms and upshots of modern secularization and the claims to free expression of religion in society.

Strategies to Counteract Ethical Relativism. We have seen the essential thrust of John Paul II's diagnoses and denunciation of the evils of the present age. He signals the problems already being felt, identifies their sources, announces even worse predictable consequences if the present cultural route continues, and selects the most urgent points of action. Through emphatic stress on the evil of assaults against life, he hopes to mobilize the outrage of the church and, hopefully, of the whole society, so they will question down to its roots the culture that consents to such practices. His goal is an immediate change of the situation. As promptly and effectively as possible, he wants to stop the concrete offenses against the dignity of persons and reverse the trend of moral degradation. To understand how John Paul II intends to develop the counteroffensive, it is necessary to look now at the resources, the strategies, the means of implementation, and the concrete proposals he trusts to turn around the current course of events.

If at the source of all these problems he recognizes the divorce of freedom from the truth, it is necessary to counteract this breach immediately by reaffirming, against the grain of contemporary culture, the "fundamental dependence of freedom upon truth."[168] That brings nothing substantially new; he just keeps reasserting a principle that has been almost a refrain in his teaching. He tries to make it ever more peremptory by using as strong an absolutist language as he can find: "[T]here can be no freedom apart from or in opposition to the truth, the categorical—unyielding and uncompromising—defense of the absolutely essential demands of man's personal dignity must be considered the way and the condition for the very existence of freedom."[169] His acute preoccupation with morality leads him to a greater emphasis on the actual living out of the truth. Renewed obedience to the truth is absolutely necessary, not just as an allegiance of the mind but as concrete practical conformity: To enjoy authentic freedom, it is indispensable not just to be in the truth but also to do the truth.[170] And this is not limited to ethical living but extends also to the life of faith: "Worship of God and a relationship with truth are revealed in Jesus Christ as the deepest foundation of freedom."[171] As we have seen, John Paul II prefers and has developed a theologically rich doctrine of freedom. Here he does not just ground freedom on truth but, appealing to revelation, he connects it also to the worship of God.

The urgency and the reach of the threats justify the drive to more emphatic statements. Together with it, however, continues—or even augments—the potential for ambiguities already raised by his pronouncements in the context of the defense of religious freedom, which conditioned freedom by some kind of fidelity to the truth.[172] A case in point is a sentence about the erroneous conscience. After stating the general principle that "it is always from the truth that the dignity of conscience derives," John Paul II reiterates, in an even more explicit way, a sentence of *Gaudium et Spes* number 16, which in itself may stand already in some tension with the last proposition of *Dignitatis Humanae* number 2: "Conscience, as the ultimate concrete judgment, compromises its dignity when it is *culpably erroneous,* that is to say, 'when man shows little concern for seeking what is true and good, and conscience gradually becomes almost blind from being accustomed to sin.' "[173] The focus here is the moral conscience not the basis for a civil right to religious freedom, but still this qualification brings back a certain unclarity about the foundation of the right to freedom of the individual conscience. The critique of cultural tendencies favorable to subjectivism is utterly pertinent, but statements of this kind do not sufficiently guard against accusations that the church continues to be animated by a profound suspicion of freedom and not just committed to correct its distorted abuses. The lack of nuance serves extremist positions on both sides more than it encourages an exercise of careful discernment to separate what is worthy of promotion of right human liberty from the excesses of libertarianism.

As a general methodology, the same systematic construct—based on a theological anthropology anchored in Christology—in which John Paul II has founded the right to religious freedom during the second moment, provides, in the third moment, the resources for an alternative to the relativism of contemporary liberal pluralistic culture. This right conception of freedom revealed in Jesus Christ is now entrusted to the church and, in an especial way, to the care of the magisterium. The nature of the mission of the church provides both the means and the duty to denounce but also to correct today's culture. The pope assumes the task of clearing the way for the truth proposed in revelation, so that it may be heard in society and actualize its effective power there, in belief and action. The way he carries it out passes through the strategies of a rebuttal of secularism, a theological grounding of moral freedom, and concrete options about the ways the church should look to influence society.

Secularism, the Deepest Root. Although John Paul II centers the issues of the third moment on a basic cultural and ideological erroneous conception of the relationship between freedom and truth, he sees the real ultimate source of the problems (as he already had for the second moment threats to religious freedom) in the modern decline and growing rejection of religion, as he says in *Evangelium Vitae:*

> In seeking the deepest roots of the struggle between the "culture of life" and the "culture of death," we cannot restrict ourselves to the perverse idea of freedom mentioned above. We have to go to the heart of the tragedy being experienced by modern man: the eclipse of the sense of God and of man, typical of a social and cultural climate dominated by secularism.[174]

The way the evils of moral relativism are also finally attributable to secularism shows how the axioms of his theological anthropology continue to guide his perspective on the contemporary world and to determine his moral theology. Secularism not only damages the strictly religious relationship, denying the reverence due to God, it also greatly impairs the rightful honoring of the human person. The religious relationship is the source of all meaning and veracity about the human person (*EV,* no. 22), and thus its withering opens the space for an idolatry of the individual (*EV,* no. 64), and leaves persons and society captive of what is less than divine and also less than human.

In the end, as we see in the present predicament, the most consequential effect of modern secularism has been the progressive degeneration of morality and widespread ethical confusion, of which the disrespect for human life is the most distressing representation.

John Paul II stresses a direct connection between the permissiveness of contemporary moral conscience regarding attacks on human life and secularism in a radicalized way, presenting the former as the final uncovering of the whole truth about the latter. It is not a matter of excesses of tendencies but a question of direct intrinsically necessary consequence. This way, no resolution can be achieved by trying to correct tendencies or compensate for deviations; this method would never get to the permanent source of the problem. Only the reversal of secularism can change what it has induced and keeps controlling—a "moral conscience of society," which strongly conditions the moral judgment of individual consciences vulnerable and dependent in the face of whatever social pressure from the culture that surrounds them (*EV,* no. 24). Secularism, for as long as it prevails, creates by itself a dynamic of human impoverishment and moral degeneration. It entraps a culture in a

> sad vicious circle: when the sense of God is lost, there is also a tendency to lose the sense of man, of his dignity and his life; in turn, the systematic violation of the moral law, especially in the serious matter of respect for human life and its dignity, produces a kind of progressive darkening of the capacity to discern God's living and saving presence. (*EV,* no. 21)

Such an uncompromising view has the virtue of courageously addressing the roots of the issues. Its disadvantage resides with the rhetorical exaggerations and lack of nuance to which it may easily lead. Governed by a heightened sensibility to questions of bioethics and their impact on public morality, John Paul II's analysis overlooks any sustainable humanistic values associated with the modern trend behind secularism. His application of the term secularism is expansive; it is not limited to an aggressive denial of God, a militant atheism, but also includes just as well any loss of the sense of God. This broad use of the negative concept unwillingly risks heartening integralist views based on a fundamental questioning of any secular world view, or even of any radically secular politics. It is an approach that automatically encourages ecclesial responses to side more with an overall intransigent resistance and opposition, setting up and strengthening an external counterinfluence, than to side with the efforts to search common ground. It presents a church predisposed more to rejection and separation than to dialogue and mutual interchange. The adopted premise seems to be that only a counterculture actively rejecting the secularist premises can, from the outside, break this negative cultural circularity, which continues to distort moral formation, and hopefully open again the ways to God and full respect for human dignity in modern society.

The judgments of John Paul II in these two encyclicals are very blunt and severe, without much nuance or effort to accommodate. They set his view of the relationship between the church and modern advanced societies into a dualistic framework. He makes it seem that, in the spectrum of worldviews in society, there are no intermediate mixed positions integrating mutual concessions and acceptable compromise, that there is nothing common in the space between the edges of atheism and an explicitly religious outlook on life. Only the incompatible and reciprocally antagonistic extremes count. Whatever is outside a religious view of reality and a religiously inspired morality will inevitably, in this perspective, set humanity on the way to moral depravity and ethical blindness.

Consequently, in the present circumstances, John Paul II does not believe that much help can come from outside religion. For, if it is the rejection of religion, and the promotion of secularized views of the world that are primarily responsible for the current problems, any conception informed by secularism can hardly be expected to offer any positive contribution to the solution. This helps to explain his almost exclusive reliance on theological arguments, and also his openness and encouragement to dialogue and collaboration with other religions,[175] but no similar expression of interest in dialogue with secular movements. In this radically sharpened picture there is no space for a secular culture that still may be deeply influenced by religiously inspired values and, therefore, worth listening to and cooperating with.

This tendentiously dualistic scheme makes too much of a negative judgment on secular culture. It is also unwarranted: It makes claims for the church that the history of the development of human rights and the whole unfolding of the first moment, from its most early beginnings to its conclusion, cannot support. Finally, it is impoverishing: Dismissing at the start any contribution by the other makes dialogue impossible not just because there is no openness to learn but also because the other has no incentive to listen after being so depreciated. Even if the church has little to learn from secular views, at least it may profit from critical confrontation. To submit itself to a reasonable amount of questioning and suspicion will help the church to purify its service to the tradition, as the secular developments that forced and inspired *Dignitatis Humanae* prove. Commitment to religious freedom, as the council defined it, demands also a commitment to develop a space of plural contributions to help all to better search for the truth.

The sense of urgency about imperative moral issues and the radicalized dualistic view of an irreconcilable cultural divide behind them justify, thus, the extremely harsh terms used in the condemnation of contemporary society in *Evangelium Vitae*. A conscience that submits to this culture is "on the path to the most alarming corruption and the darkest moral blindness."[176] The contemporary situation of crisis is regularly described in terms of a battle, "a dramatic struggle between the 'culture of life' and the 'culture of death.' "[177] Such language, in its marked separation of camps and little nuance in judgments, however, cannot avoid evoking some of the siege mentality of a countercultural church resisting the tide of the times that was so typical of the nineteenth-century papal condemnations of doctrinaire liberalism. The small positive signs and reasons for optimism in these societies and cultures recognized by the pope are first of all groups that act counter to the culture of death, enclaves resisting the dominant tendencies (*EV*, no. 26). John Paul II makes reference also to a few good recent developments—namely, opposition to war and to the death penalty and ecological awareness—but the conclusion continues to be pointedly dualistic:

> This situation, with its lights and shadows, ought to make us all fully aware that we are facing an enormous and dramatic clash between good and evil, death and life, the "culture of death" and the "culture of life." We find ourselves not only "faced with" but necessarily "in the midst of" this conflict: we are all involved and we all share in it, with the inescapable responsibility of *choosing to be unconditionally pro-life*. (*EV*, no. 28)

Truth in Christ is the Only Solution: The New Evangelization. The preference of John Paul II for a theological grounding of his social doctrine and his tendency to emphasize the unique and indispensable contribution of revealed religion for a right ordering of life in society has already been seen in his approach to religious freedom in the second moment. In the third moment, those propensities are further stressed with the radicalized negativity assigned to secularism. John Paul II, thus, uses even stronger language in his claims of uniqueness and exclusivity for the solutions grounded on revelation.

In the third moment, when the problems center on ethical issues, only ("only" is the operative word in these affirmations) religion and religiously inspired morality can save the world out of its present condition:

> Only God, the Supreme Good, constitutes the unshakable foundation and essential condition of morality. . . . The Supreme Good and the moral good meet in *truth:* the truth of God, the Creator and Redeemer, and the truth of man, created and redeemed by him. Only upon this truth is it possible to construct a renewed society and to solve the complex and weighty problems affecting it, above all the problem of overcoming the various forms of totalitarianism, so as to make way for the authentic *freedom* of the person.[178]

No secular humanism can provide a sufficient response, for they all lack the necessary answers. "The decisive answer for every man's questions, his religious and moral questions in particular, is given by Jesus Christ, or rather is Jesus Christ himself."[179]

In spite of this emphasis on the indispensability of revelation, even in these encyclicals there are some concessions to the role of human reason and natural law as source and foundation for moral norms, of guidance in moral discernment, and, especially, as a basis for dialogue with modern culture. In *Evangelium Vitae* he makes a qualified opening to the possibility of every person being able to accomplish, through sincerity of heart and use of reason, the same kind of moral wisdom offered in Christian revelation.[180] In *Veritatis Splendor,* John Paul II recognizes that, "in response to the encouragement of the Second Vatican Council, there has been a desire to foster dialog with modern culture, emphasizing the rational—and thus universally understandable and communicable—character of moral norms belonging to the sphere of the natural moral law."[181] As a service to this end, he praises the efforts of some moralists who "rightly recognize the need to find ever more consistent rational arguments in order to justify the requirements and to provide a foundation for the norms of the moral life" (*VS,* no. 74).

The lesser weight of this line of reasoning within the thought of John Paul II, even if a significant degree of ambivalence prevails, is, however, clear:

> Some people, however, disregarding the dependence of human reason on Divine Wisdom and the need, given the present state of fallen nature, for Divine Revelation as an effective means for knowing moral truths, even those of the natural order, have actually posited a complete sovereignty of reason in the domain of moral norms regarding the right ordering of life in this world. (*VS,* no. 36)

We are quickly brought back to the dominant perspective of his theological anthropology.

In any case, the church is in a privileged position and may claim a leading role in the moral renewal of society, for it "offers to everyone the answer which comes from the truth about Jesus Christ and his Gospel" (*VS,* no. 2), the only capable solution for our contemporary problems.

From Jesus Christ, the church has received the mandate to evangelize, to spread the message through all the earth, to push the frontier of the proclamation of the gospel ever deeper into every culture and nation. In the immediate, however, the great concern of John Paul II is to renew the acceptance of its message in the societies of "Christian" nations, to promote there a "new evangelization."[182] Using the approaching of the millennium as an extra mobilizing incentive,[183] he has tried to motivate the church, especially in Europe, to renew its presence in these societies and cultures that have been shaped and developed under Christian influence but have been drifting away from that inspiration.[184] In the apostolic letter in which he presented the objectives and the program of the preparation of the great jubilee of the year 2000, he points out the troubling signs of growing "religious indifference" and "widespread loss of the transcendent sense of human life" in cultures in which the Christian faith has been present for almost two millennia. So, he questions the quality of the testimony being given by Christians and wonders "to what extent the sons and daughters of the church, too, . . . have . . . been shaped by the climate of secularism and ethical relativism."[185] These are the two adversaries he always pairs together when he speaks of the new evangelization, a program that is, therefore, as much directed to the inside as to the outside of the church.

John Paul II wants to encourage the construction of a new culture, protective of the patrimony of convictions and values of the European Christian heritage, nowadays threatened by the pressures of secularization and forms of practical atheism.[186] To the "strong currents of 'counter-evangelization,' which try to undermine the Christian roots of our civilization" he wants to respond with a "new élan of evangelization,"[187] an effort "to promote the presence of the evangelical leaven in the present and the future of Europe, especially before attempts, not so disguised, to marginalize faith and the saving truth from any manifestation of public life."[188]

This crisis of civilization is not limited to excluding God from social life, however. The need for change includes also the moral aspect. The "formidable challenge to undertake a 'new evangelization' " includes, thus, a program of strong promotion of the moral requirements of the Christian faith, for

> dechristianization, which weighs heavily upon entire peoples and communities once rich in faith and Christian life, involves not only the loss of faith or in any event its becoming irrelevant for everyday life, but also, and of necessity, *a decline or obscuring of the moral sense.* This comes about both as a result of a loss of awareness of the originality of the Gospel morality and as a result of an eclipse of fundamental principles and ethical values themselves.[189]

A situation like this leaves the church, and particularly the hierarchy, with a particular responsibility: "As Pastors, we have a duty—a task integral to the new evangelization—to *rekindle awareness of fundamental moral truths* as the necessary ethical foundation for a society worthy of man."[190] If ordinarily "*evangelization*—and therefore the 'new evangelization'—*also involves the proclamation and presentation of morality,*"[191] the present moral decay of traditionally

Christian societies reinforces even more the importance of this dimension of the church's announcement of the truth in the teaching of John Paul II. A preoccupation with morality, especially the respect for the absolute moral norms of divinely revealed commandments, has become the center of his social teaching in the third moment. Adherence to the truths of faith and actual respect for moral obligations are considered to be equal requisites to keep the unity of the church.[192] One more piece of evidence can be seen in his current attribution to moral norms of the same foundational role for the solidity of society that he had before attributed to religious freedom: "In the end, only a morality which acknowledges certain norms as valid always and for everyone, with no exception, can guarantee the ethical foundation of social coexistence, both on the national and international levels" (*VS,* no. 97).

The Necessary Guidance of the Magisterium. It is in the deposit of revealed truth, particularly in its moral norms, that contemporary culture can find solid ground and firm direction to recover the right path of freedom. By contrast to the general disorientation and the ever more visible consequences of relativism, "the Church, in her life and teaching, is thus revealed as 'the pillar and bulwark of the truth' (1 Tm 3:15), including the truth regarding moral action" (*VS,* no. 27). John Paul II restates the traditional theological justifications for the continuing authoritative guiding function of the church hierarchy in moral matters,[193] both within and without the church,[194] and further justifies it with the example of the important moral teaching of the popes of the last two centuries (see *VS,* no. 4).

Together with the affirmation of a concretely binding objective truth as the way to respond to moral relativism, we find in these encyclicals a renewed accent on the role of the authority of the church's magisterium as another way to counterbalance the reigning conception of freedom, believed to imply absolute moral self-determination, the proximate source of all social evils. John Paul II, both in his pastoral ministry and in his government of the church, has emphasized the authoritative function of the restricted group of the highest hierarchical officials. Such stress on authority, even within the church, is intense because he believes that the cultural vices of relativism and undue claims of autonomy have tainted virtually all people. Not even the church's faithful have stayed immune: "[T]oday's growing secularism" constitutes

> a mentality which affects, often in a profound, extensive and all-embracing way, even the attitudes and behavior of Christians, whose faith is weakened and loses its character as a new and original criterion for thinking and acting

in personal, family and social life. In a widely dechristianized culture, the criteria employed by believers themselves in making judgments and decisions often appear extraneous or even contrary to those of the Gospel. (*VS*, no. 88)

Fortunately, "Christians have a great help for the formation of conscience *in the Church and her Magisterium*" (*VS*, no. 64). It is not so much the church at large but its magisterium that constitutes today the bulwark of truth against moral relativism. There is not much trust in the capacities of the individual conscience, in society and in the church, to resist the baneful influence of the pervasive relativistic culture, to stand up against the distorted social moral conscience. The only safe path for people in search of true freedom is to obey the truth and subject themselves to objective norms of revealed morality as they are proposed and applied by those who have a particular divine guarantee of assistance in moral discernment. "Experience teaches in any case," he said a few years before, "that liberty is deployed best when it holds to the rules of the moral law and follows guidelines laid down by the shepherds of the people of God."[195]

This is the ecclesiological facet of the theological approach of John Paul II to the challenges of the third moment, another application of his theology of freedom, first developed to justify and ground the right to religious freedom in the second moment. The elements of the system are already familiar: A pessimistic theological anthropology paired with a negative judgment of modern cultural tendencies as a whole leads to a gloomy perspective on the present condition of human freedom and the culture of contemporary society that necessitates a forceful involvement of the church. The character of its intervention is determined by the conviction that the only way out of the present social (and also ecclesial) predicament is the reinforcement of a top-down, obedience-to-authority approach to moral formation within and by the church.

The Role of Civil Law in Service of Morality. At the social and political level, in issues of public morality, John Paul II favors also the role of authority and civil law in the promotion of a greater observance of moral norms. His denunciation of contemporary societies targets cultural tendencies disrespectful of human life and legislation that sanctions and makes socially acceptable—and thus encourages—those practices.[196] Having particularly in mind the case of abortion, the pope denounces the 'conspiracy against life,' which gathers support at the cultural, social, political, and also juridical levels (*EV*, no. 68) and ends up giving juridical recognition to the absurd cultural constructing of "crimes against life as legitimate expressions of individual freedom, to be acknowledged and protected as actual rights" (*EV,* no. 18). Such preposterous conclusions indicate key flaws in the process of political and legislative decisions.

On this basis, John Paul II makes a very critical judgment on currently prevailing understandings of democracy, namely the ideas that tolerance and respect for everybody necessarily imply that democracy has to succumb to ethical relativism, or that any reference to objective moral norms denies democracy in favor of authoritarianism. The acknowledgment of admissible historical reasons that may explain why some people see ethical relativism as the only effective protection against intolerance and totalitarianism does not stop him from pointing out that such a position ends up creating as much evil as the one it wants to prevent.[197] Democracy is a process but it cannot become purely procedural—as if it could provide, merely through its morally neutral workings, a moral orientation for society. Only a democracy firmly grounded in values can fulfill its objectives and accomplish its professed advantages. For that to happen, "the basis of these values cannot be provisional and changeable 'majority' opinions, but only the acknowledgment of an objective moral law which, as the 'natural law' written in the human heart, is the obligatory point of reference for civil law itself."[198] This point of reference is also constituted by the revealed content of objective moral law, which obliges both individuals and political officials in their public functions, as John Paul II notes in *Veritatis Splendor*. "The commandments of the second table of the Decalogue in particular . . . constitute the indispensable rules of social life," and although they are very general, they are supposed "to be specified and made more explicit in a detailed code of behavior." Thus, these commandments "entail specific demands to which both public authorities and citizens are required to pay heed."[199]

In a context of pluralism that is not only political but also a pluralistic concept of morality, how can the principle that the civil law has to have a point of reference in the moral law be applied? What can it mean in terms of the concrete degree of conformity of the two laws? This is one of the central issues of the third moment. And it is also a problem to which the framework of parameters set by the doctrine of *Dignitatis Humanae* can offer guidance more directly. It is thus a privileged point of evaluation of where the work of development and interpretation of *Dignitatis Humanae* by John Paul II all through his pontificate has led the general attitude of the church in pluralistic societies, compared with the possibilities *Dignitatis Humanae* seemed to have opened at the end of the first moment. A more detailed analysis of the pronouncements of John Paul II is, then, justified.

To respond to this cultural and political situation, John Paul II sees the "need to recover the basic elements of a vision of the relationship between civil law and moral law,"[200] proposing a "doctrine on the necessary *conformity of civil law with the moral law,*" which, he asserts, "is in continuity with the whole tradition of the Church" (*EV,* no. 72). One of the basic principles of this tradition states that "the purpose of civil law is different and more limited in scope than that of the moral law" (*EV,* no. 71) as he starts by reaffirming. He proceeds, then, to elaborate on what cannot be left out of that limited scope. Drawing the line at the protection of fundamental human rights, he makes a special mention of the right to life. He continues by stating the classic reasoning for allowing for a discrepancy between the two laws, but he immediately qualifies it, in line with his criticism of misconceptions of democracy, in a way that denies any weight to arguments based on majority opinion:

> While public authority can sometimes choose not to put a stop to something which—were it prohibited—would cause more serious harm, it can never presume to legitimize as a right of individuals—even if they are the majority of the members of society—an offense against other persons caused by the disregard of so fundamental a right as the right to life. (*EV,* no. 71)

Finally, he names the concrete cases he has in mind, highly contested in the current public controversies about standards of publicly enforced morality: "The legal toleration of abortion or of euthanasia can in no way claim to be based on respect for the conscience of others, precisely because society has the right and the duty to protect itself against the abuses which can occur in the name of conscience and under the pretext of freedom" (*EV,* no. 71).

John Paul II leaves no doubt that his campaign against the cultural tendencies disrespectful of human life looks not just at the moral education of individual consciences and to advance in society favorable dispositions regarding the defense and promotion of life, but he also has as its goal changes in civil law and the enlistment of the juridical function of the state to patronize and enforce, even if against popular sympathy, stricter protections to the fundamental human right to life.

The question of the relationship between moral law and civil law has to do with the difficulty of harmonizing, in pluralistic societies like the ones in which we are living in the West, the requirements of two of the church's fundamental ethical principles: respect for the freedom of individual consciences and obligation toward an objective moral law, natural and revealed, that is not relativistic. Different attempts to deal with the tension between the two principles result in opposed tendencies, each determined by which of the two principles is actually given operative supremacy. The accentuation of conformity between the two laws means that primacy is given to the moral obligation. In matters of insoluble pluralism, if greater disharmony between the two laws is allowed, it signifies that freedom of individual conscience gains actual prominence. The relative valuing of the two principles, freedom or obligation, determines also different kinds of pedagogical and political strategies of promotion of moral values in the social order.

Regarding the first alternative (conformity vs. disharmony), it is clear that the preference of John Paul II is for as much conformity as possible, in correspondence with his general position of favoring the priority of truth over freedom. As to the ways of addressing the political challenge of reversing the tide of moral relativism, he moves, not without some inconsistency, in *Evangelium Vitae* between two different basic approaches. In a few instances he calls for a grassroots persuasive campaign to awaken people to the necessary moral correction and, thus, transform the prevailing values of the dominant culture of society from within. More frequently, however, he appeals to a top-down, legislation-enforced change, using the power of the state to compel upon society higher standards of morality than the ones the majority may be inclined to adopt.

The top-down approach consists, in the papal magisterium, of direct appeals to the conscience of public officials. (In concrete cases, this includes resorting to direct and public political pressure upon elected officials or active intervention in electoral campaigns.) When denouncing the claim that the legally established norms of social order should be determined simply by the will of the majority, John Paul II refuses also the consequent idea that legislators and public officials should remain in a position of total moral neutrality, setting aside their own personal convictions. John Paul II does not accept the pretension of the prevalent democratic culture to separate sharply the private and the public realms, forcing politicians, in particular, to turn their personal responsibility over to a civil law decided by a simple procedural rule of majority, and, thus, to forsake the dictates of their own personal consciences when acting in the public sphere (*EV*, no. 69).

On the contrary, he encourages individuals and groups to engage in social activism and enter political life guided by their own moral principles and motivated by the defense and promotion of a culture of life (*EV*, no. 90). Although aware of the limitations imposed by pluralistic democracies, the pope addresses political leaders directly, even invoking the allegiance of those who are Christians, calling them to listen to the truth in their consciences and to use their offices in the service of the respect for life, the crux of the contemporary moral crisis:

> The Church well knows that it is difficult to mount an effective legal defense of life in pluralistic democracies, because of the presence of strong cultural

> currents with differing outlooks. At the same time, certain that moral truth cannot fail to make its presence deeply felt in every conscience, the Church encourages political leaders, starting with those who are Christians, not to give in, but to make those choices which, taking into account what is realistically attainable, will lead to the establishment of a just order in the defense and promotion of the value of life.[201]

These "courageous choices in support of life" to which the pope summons civil leaders include, even especially demand, public testimony, "especially through *legislative measures*."[202] John Paul II calls legislators in a particular way to their sense of personal responsibility. Those who decide at this highest level, constraints of democracy notwithstanding, are reminded of a hierarchy of obligations they have to follow in their resolutions.

> In a democratic system, where laws and decisions are made on the basis of the consensus of many, the sense of personal responsibility in the consciences of individuals invested with authority may be weakened. But no one can ever renounce this responsibility, especially when he or she has a legislative or decision-making mandate, which calls that person to answer to God, to his or her own conscience and to the whole of society for choices which may be contrary to the common good.[203]

He then explains the reason for his insistence on the role of the civil law: "Although laws are not the only means of protecting human life, nevertheless they do play a very important and sometimes decisive role in influencing patterns of thought and behavior." Concluding, he returns to his earnest directly personal appeal: "I repeat once more that a law which violates an innocent person's natural right to life is unjust and, as such, is not valid as a law. For this reason I urgently appeal once more to all political leaders not to pass laws which, by disregarding the dignity of the person, undermine the very fabric of society" (*EV,* no. 90). This is the strategy that goes directly to the top, that favors the direct urging of the holders of political power to change legislation that confirms and even further advances the declining of moral values in society.

But in the same encyclical John Paul II also makes suggestions of a different approach to the challenge of moral relativism in democratic pluralistic societies. In those passages, he favors a cultural transformation at the level of society, not so much an intervention in and through power politics. He aims at doing that primarily through changing mentalities and moral sensibilities, not through attempts to change legislation immediately and directly. "The first and fundamental step towards this cultural transformation," John Paul II writes, "consists in forming consciences with regard to the incomparable and inviolable worth of every human life." In order to achieve that, it is the level of cultural misconceptions that has to be addressed, and there the restoration of correct views of freedom is crucial:

> It is of the greatest importance *to re-establish the essential connection between life and freedom*. These are inseparable goods: where one is violated, the other also ends up being violated. . . . No less critical in the formation of conscience is the recovery of the necessary link between freedom and truth. As I have frequently stated, when freedom is detached from objective truth it becomes impossible to establish personal rights on a firm and rational basis; and the ground is laid for society to be at the mercy of the unrestrained will of individuals or of the oppressive totalitarianism of public authority." (*EV*, no. 96)

For the church, in this perspective, the pressing momentous need is "to bring the Gospel of life to the heart of every man and woman and to make it penetrate every part of society" (*EV*, no. 80), beginning within the Christian communities themselves.[204] And so "what is urgently called for is a *general mobilization of consciences* and a *united ethical effort* to activate a *great campaign in support of life. All together, we must build a new culture of life*" (*EV*, no. 95). This is the task of the moment for the whole church, but an especial responsibility falls on every ministry of proclamation of the truth and moral formation. Defense of life has to be promoted

> *in catechesis, in the various forms of preaching, in personal dialogue and in all educational activity*. Teachers, catechists and theologians have the task of emphasizing the anthropological reasons upon which respect for every human life is based. In this way, by making the newness of the Gospel of life shine forth, we can also help everyone discover in the light of reason and of personal experience how the Christian message fully reveals what man is and the meaning of his being and existence. We shall find important points of contact and dialogue also with nonbelievers, in our common commitment to the establishment of a new culture of life. (*EV*, no. 82)

Dialogue, "a serious and courageous cultural dialogue among all parties," is actually a necessary means to face this challenge: "[W]e need to promote a serious and in-depth exchange about basic issues of human life with everyone, including non-believers, in intellectual circles, in the various professional spheres and at the level of people's everyday life" (*EV*, no. 95). John Paul II puts great hopes especially in the cooperation with other churches and other religions in defense of life (see *EV*, no. 91). Although the call is to dialogue and to find points of agreement with others, in the campaign for life there can be no doubts about an unbending commitment to the truth and no concessions to the reigning culture: "In the proclamation of this Gospel, we must not fear hostility or unpopularity, and we must refuse any compromise or ambiguity which might conform us to the world's way of thinking" (*EV*, no. 82).

These two strategies to promote the new culture of life are not necessarily contradictory; they may work concurrently in terms of immediate goals. However, if the ultimate objective is really a cultural transformation, the strategy of dialogue and education for moral conversion of the culture has to be the prevailing one and has to retain all its efficiency. This will happen only if the church protects the credibility of its positions and contributes, through clarity of intentions and openness of processes, to increasing receptivity and trust on the side of its dialogue partners.

Evangelium Vitae, in its general tone and basic tenets, leaves no doubts that John Paul II, in the present circumstance, favors the top-down approach, the seeking of direct political influence. His sense of moral outrage and pastoral and political urgency to do something to stop abortion and similar attacks on human life lead him, first, to a narrow focus on these issues within the whole long-term interests of the relationship of the church with the world, and, then, to opt decisively for the means that seem to promise more immediate results. On another level, this strategy is also more in accordance with his conviction of the barrenness of secularism and of the moral dead end to which it is pushing pluralistic societies. There is less sense in trying to change this culture from within—by walking with it, steering it in the right direction—if you think the path is thoroughly wrong and the only redeeming possibility is to radically reverse the route. It agrees too with his general evaluation of a very deficient capacity for moral discernment on the part of individuals submersed in the relativistic culture, even in many of those who continue to practice the Christian faith but ignore the moral teaching of the magisterium. Thus, for all this, the general stress on authority, undiscriminating obedience to the law, and no encouragement of individual discretion.[205]

The focus of John Paul II's proposal in this encyclical is not the patient formation of consciences, progressively changing the predominant values in culture and, through that change, achieving the transformation of the social consensus. His aim right now is the search for a protection and promotion of traditional Catholic morality by civil law, even if against the grain of the positions of the majority. For that, he appeals directly to the moral and religious conscience of political officials. It is clearly an option privileging, at this particular point, the relationship of church with state, over that of church with society. It evokes, now applied to the right to life, even typical traces of the nineteenth-century approach of the church to the discussion of religious freedom, which was, then, framed between a double stressing of the responsibility of the Christian prince as *defensor fidei,* on one side, and the helpless condition of the *imperita multitudo,* on the other. The first moment of *Dignitatis Humanae* radically reversed the church's strategy on religious freedom, when it abandoned the dependence on power institutions paternalistically governing the masses in favor of respect for freedom of the individual consciences and reliance on persuasion assured of the intrinsic convincing power of the truth. This attitude, however, seems again to be less favored by John Paul II in his promotion of the church's ethic of life. It is certainly necessary to be bold, leave no doubts, and act urgently. But, then, also great care is needed so that trying to win one battle too quickly will not compromise longer-term prospects for the promotion of the church's ethic of life.

The papal option looks to have more chance of immediate success in places where Catholics constitute the overwhelming majority of the population or where the Catholic Church can still amass, alone or with other churches, a significant influence over the powers of the state. However, the societies in which such a strategy may have more impact are also those in which there is more resistance to that kind of use of church influence, because they have been the ones more marked by the stigmas of the first moment. Old fears, prejudices, and mistrusts will, thus, create greater difficulties for an immediate political victory, and, additionally, reawaken and strengthen obstacles to the successful unfolding, in a longer run, of the alternative strategy of dialogue and search for common ground in cultural transformation.

Conclusion: Renewed Defensiveness toward Modernity

John Paul II has continued in the third moment to follow the same lines of development of his teaching on religious freedom and freedom of conscience. After 1989, however, the freedom of conscience that he speaks primarily about is not so much the freedom to practice religion or the freedom of the church, but, rather, the freedom of the moral conscience, the unhindered ability of everyone to form one's own conscience according to the truth and in obedience to the objective moral law. This freedom means concretely the possibility of being preserved from negative overwhelming conditioning by a culture based on wrong conceptions of absolute individualistic autonomy, which, in particular, does not respect the fundamental right to life. Whereas before, the focus of the question was the practice of religion, now it is of moral living.

As the pope expands the application of the same principles he had relied on to sustain the right to religious freedom now to issues of public morality, he makes also more clear a certain shifting of fundamental emphases in the balance of the basic elements of the doctrine of *Dignitatis Humanae.* While John Paul II unequivocally underscores the priority of the duty toward the truth, the declaration, in turn, has affirmed even more forcefully the dignity and autonomy of the individual person and the respect for each one's way and pace of forming his or her own conscience in the personal search for the truth. The recognition of the civil right to religious freedom by *Dignitatis Humanae* signified for the church the renunciation of paternalistic protections by the state and the reliance on persuasion in freedom as the exclusive way to lead people to the truth. John Paul II, however, shows great reservations about the ability of the individual conscience to find its way to the truth. He, therefore, returns heavily to arguments of authority and even to appeals to political authorities to enforce less than consensual options of morality in society.

These tendencies were already present in the second moment, but here their implications become more visible. Before, his defense of the civil right to religious freedom looked for the empowerment of people, stressing the sovereignty of individuals and their consequent immunity from government interference. Now, against individualistic and relativistic ethics, he stresses compliance with norms and submission to external guidance. In the second moment, he still gave priority to the freedom to be able to search and express the truth. In the third moment, greater emphasis goes to the allegiance to the truth. By reasserting the duty of obedience of the person to the higher moral law of revelation taught by the church, he tries to curtail tendencies for exaggerated individual autonomy.

Personal theological views, particular sensibilities to issues, and choices of strategies to engage the world have shaped John Paul II's distinctive approach to the relationship of church with society, the cardinal orientations of which were made patent through the analysis of his teaching on religious freedom and freedom of conscience. In the postcouncil context, the new or restored doctrinal accents, ways of reasoning, and, especially, attitudes toward modernity of such an approach did not bring greater clarity to a somewhat dubious and confusing status of the overall positioning of the Roman Catholic Church before the challenges of contemporary cultural pluralism. Not even John Paul II's teaching is, in itself, unequivocal in this regard. I have pointed to some hesitation in the two encyclicals on approaches to moral questions in society between, for example, relying primarily on authority or on dialogue—although it is very plain, in those particular writings, which one is his favored position. Other pronouncements, however, exhibit the opposite bias, adding to the ambiguity.

For instance, the address to the General Assembly of the United Nations in 1995 has a quite different tone. Here John Paul II seems to step back from his unilateral affirmations that only the recovery of religion and of a revealed conception of the transcendence of the human person as guides for social living can save this world. He professes instead a great deal of trust in the potentialities of dialogue, open discussion, and persuasion, based on common values and experiences. Natural law is both the source of knowledge of universal human rights and the basis for a universal dialogue about those same rights.[206] He reaffirms the ordering of freedom to the truth and the need to acknowledge continually the spiritual human dimension, but in this insistence on the close conjunction of freedom with the truth, he gives prominence to freedom, acknowledges explicitly a legitimate pluralism of cultural, political, and social forms of human freedom, and even says that the truth about humanity is a multidimensional, culturally specified, complex truth.[207] The whole speech presents a commitment of the church to an open, coequal dialogue with others in our pluralistic world. John Paul II even finishes with an optimistic note on the human capacities to build a better future.[208] Compared to the letter and the spirit of *Evangelium Vitae,* this address to the UN is of a quite different tone and substance.

In spite of all the ambivalence in and between many of his pronouncements, the attitude of John Paul II in the third moment, at least what has passed as his basic and habitual disposition regarding contemporary pluralistic culture, is more accurately represented by the traits highlighted with greatest prominence in *Evangelium Vitae.* During his papacy a strong public image of the church has been taking shape, one characterized by less openness to dialogue with secular movements, greater suspicion of liberal freedoms, stronger emphasis on undisputed moral conformity with absolute norms, and low tolerance for dissent or personal experiments in search of the truth. Overall, in the outlook of his teaching on issues of the relationship of the church with society, generally sensed is a certain regression vis-à-vis the overture to the spirit of modernity and the attitude of openness to the contemporary world characteristic of the progressive vitality of Vatican II.

Further, the influence of the pope on the whole demeanor of the relationship of the church with the world and the kind of image it obtains in the eyes of the secular world is not limited to the direct impact of his words and actions. The full consequence of his positions can only be thoroughly evaluated after we take into consideration what kind of concrete practices already present in the church are being stimulated or discouraged, and what are the tendencies, dominant agendas, and images of the church communicated by the movements (organized or not) with which those practices are primarily associated. In this regard, there is a widespread perception that, lately, there has been a greater ascendancy of ecclesial sectors and movements that, greatly suspicious of the "spirit of Vatican II," have been laboring to restore the church to its traditionalist stances and ways of doing things. Many of these groups have made their strategic priority a deliberate and profusely publicized identification with the positions of the papacy, often selectively picked though, in search of an authoritative legitimization for their positions in a claim of faultless allegiance to orthodoxy. Their voices have assumed the role of amplifiers for the teaching of John Paul II. They tend, however, to make a more restricted and radicalized representation of it, since they are more inclined to give one-sided accounts and to overlook the qualifications less favorable to their positions.

John Paul II diagnoses and denounces really serious evils and dangerous tendencies in contemporary liberal democracies. He has done so by deepening the reflection on themes intrinsically connected to the doctrine of *Dignitatis Humanae.* In order to respond to the challenges mounted by the cultural relativism of our times, he has developed, thus, the reflection on freedom of conscience as it applies to the formation of the individual conscience for concrete moral judgments. He is countering refashioned threats to fully human social living by the same external ideological adversaries of the first moment. They configure a new round of the confrontation between the Catholic view of the human person and some incompatible principles of modern liberalism newly expressed in some traits of the political and social culture of contemporary pluralist democracies. There can be no contention with the final goals he pursues and the appropriateness of the ultimate solutions he offers. What may be questioned is whether the tone and the intensity of the condemnations and the strategies for promoting alternatives do not, actually, induce less receptivity for the message of the church in society and, thus, hinder the successful attainment of its social mission in the present circumstances.

Highlighting the negative in modernity is certainly a good corrective to the accusation by some of Vatican II's exaggerated optimism. But John Paul II, especially in pronouncements like *Evangelium Vitae,* approximates himself of views that slide too easily into a black-and-white kind of analysis, overlooking distinctions and nuance, as if there were only two nonoverlapping extremes with all the good on one side and only evil on the other. These approaches, as rhetorically powerful as they may be, tend, however, to encourage rapid but simplistic judgments with no real grappling with the good intentions and honest critical thinking made by many people in the middle, both within and without the church.

As a result of the growing influence of this mindset, once again, the church appears to be gravely tempted, before severe challenges, to retreat into its own fortress, cutting itself off from the progression of secular culture. This retreat would reverse the approach favored by Vatican II of attempting to understand and engage secular culture and to participate, without compromise but through cooperation and dialogue, in the correcting and redirecting of the course of history.

Features of such a conspicuously defensive posture in the reading of the social reality and the consequent public posture evoke from afar some of the nineteenth-century attitudes of the church before modernity, characteristic of the church-society impasse of a century ago. First, there is a renewed sense of siege in a church ever more at odds with the culture of society—especially in the area of the ethics of life—a church in which tendentiously sectarian and integralist groups are the loudest voices. Second, disproportionate importance is being given to a particular issue (in the nineteenth century, religious freedom; now, abortion) that becomes, then, the make or break criterion of all judgments and the focus of totally one-sided extremist positions. Third, insistent block condemnations of whole movements or ideas do not make any differentiation between basic principles and relative applications. All through the nineteenth century and a good part of the twentieth, it was this kind of principled but misguided intransigence that weakened the social influence of the Catholic Church and drove it, in many areas of its teaching, into the isolation of a dead-end of doctrinal immobility, until, finally, the first moment of *Dignitatis Humanae* cleared the remnants of the long standing *équivoques* and opened up new avenues for credibility and dialogue.

John Paul II was never particularly sensitive to the issues of the first moment, as we have seen, and therefore has been less impressed by the lessons learned in the process of opening the Catholic Church to the modern world, which culminated in *Dignitatis Humanae*. Probably for this reason too, he has no misgivings in insisting, in the third moment, on solutions and strategies that could be somewhat reminiscent of past responses of the church to the initial confrontations of the first moment. Typical of the present perceived attitude of the church are the emphasis on the authority of the magisterium in moral issues; the insistence on the primacy of the truth; distrust of the moral discernment of individual people; and the call for a greater role of the civil law in the promotion of public morality. For those still careful to avoid any hint of a return to intransigent antimodern postures, it would be better to keep these traits differentiated as clearly as possible from old nineteenth-century trademark stances: the ultramontane drive to a hypertrophy of papal authority; the axiom "error has no rights;" the concept of "ignorant masses" with which Leo XIII justified the refusal of religious freedom; and expectations based on the union between church and state. It is not just on the side of the external challenges that we can see today that significant similarities with the outlook of the church-society relationship in which Roman Catholicism found itself before Vatican II. The difficulty in adjusting the public role of the church to a context of pluralism and secularization continues too.

We arrive thus at a situation significantly different from the long-term expectations for the encounter of the church with contemporary society raised by *Dignitatis Humanae*. And yet, that which, in the teaching of John Paul II, contributed or just accompanied this development started and unfolded as a continued treatment of fundamental themes of the declaration applied to the evolving challenges to the mission of the church. Was this leaving of the expectations behind a necessary process of growth and change determined by unforeseen challenges to which the direction of *Dignitatis Humanae* could not respond? Or is there an alternative appropriation of the doctrine of the declaration that can address the same specific challenges of the third moment with the same uncompromising defense of nonnegotiable principles, but with a general posture in church-society relations that will more clearly steer the church away from tendencies to return to old public demeanors?

In spite of the parallels between the current predicaments and those before *Dignitatis Humanae*, there is a crucial difference. *Dignitatis Humanae* is now the doctrine approved by an ecumenical council, even if the authoritative interpretation of all its details is not yet fully settled. The current resistance or hesitation does not come from an irreducible official position, but from particular tendencies within the church, albeit with sometimes and in some aspects significant official encouragement and growing influence. There continue to be, however, other powerful voices in the church keeping alive and developing the line of open dialogue in which Vatican II was concluded. The situation, thus, is not a dead end as it was a century ago, but reaching a crossroads. It is a time of decision between alternative emphases, a time of choice between competing historical and theological inspirations for the church's social mission. As much as *Dignitatis Humanae* initially addressed the core of this problematic, competing understandings of its content and implications are again at the center of these renewed tensions in the church. At this point, after having systematized a set of parameters with which *Dignitatis Humanae* may guide the church in the problems of the third moment, and analyzed the process and the consequences of the appropriation of the declaration by John Paul II, it is time to take these two results, compare their form of dealing with the issues at hand, and judge if the new path for the role of the church in pluralistic societies opened by the council can still be sustained as the best option for the encounter with contemporary pluralistic societies.

NOTES

In citing papal encyclicals and conciliar documents in the notes, short titles have been used. Bibliographic information for the documents listed below can be found in the references under the following entries.

Centesimus Annus	John Paul II 1991, May 1
Dignitatis Humanae	Vatican II 1990
Evangelium Vitae	John Paul II 1995, March 25
Redemptor Hominis	John Paul II 1979, March 4
Veritatis Splendor	John Paul II 1993, August 6

1. I will restrict my analysis to the pronouncements made by John Paul II himself or signed by him. Certainly, to the full impact of his papacy contribute also the decisions and statements issued by other institutions of the papal curia, especially, for the topic of this study, documents from the Congregation for the Doctrine of Faith. But these, for reasons of economy of research, even if explicitly stating formal papal approval, will not be considered here.
2. Grootaers 1981, 151, 166–67.
3. For the list of the twenty-four interventions, see Appendix.
4. Wojtyla 1959, 741–42.
5. Wojtyla 1964a, 530–31. In the written observations submitted earlier (see Wojtyla 1964c), he describes this duplicity in terms of two aspects of "religious freedom": the ethical and the juridical (or the ethical and the political, in Wojtyla 1964b).
6. Wojtyla 1964a, 531.
7. Wojtyla 1964c, 766.
8. Ibid.
9. Wojtyla 1964a, 531–32.
10. Ibid. Already in one of the written observations submitted to the commission, when making the same distinction of the two aspects of the issue, he described the second as being a discussion of religious freedom "in sensu politico iurium cuiuslibet *credentis* in civitate." Wojtyla 1964b, 838 (emphasis added).
11. Wojtyla 1964a, 532.
12. Grootaers 1981, 160.
13. Wojtyla 1964d, 301.
14. Wojtyla 1965a, 11.

15. Wojtyla 1965b, 293.
16. Wojtyla 1965a, 11.
17. Ibid., 12.
18. Ibid.
19. The same argument is repeated in the first point of Wojtyla 1965b, 292.
20. Wojtyla 1965a, 12.
21. Ibid., 13.
22. See Grootaers 1981, 159, for the influence of the bishops who lived under communist regimes, and especially Monsignor Wojtyla, in the final formulation of the qualifications to the concept of public order as a limitation to religious freedom.
23. Wojtyla 1965a, 12–13.
24. Wojtyla 1965c, 662.
25. Ibid.
26. Grootaers 1981, 168.
27. The emotional plea of Cardinal Wyszynski, on 20 September 1965, asking the council to pay greater attention to the situation of the church in the East, reveals how complicated was the mutual understanding of the different agendas of the Western and Eastern European bishops on the issue of religious freedom. Wyszynski 1965.
28. See Grootaers 1981, 167: "The secularizing ideology with which Mgr. Wojtyla was confronted in Poland in the years that preceded and accompanied Vatican II is totally different from the process of secularization at work in Western Europe and North America. It is not certain that Mgr. Wojtyla had full awareness of the stretch of that difference." In this regard, it is interesting to see the direction in which an author, very laudatory of John Paul II (and also possessed of an extreme antimodernity bias), pushes this distinctiveness: Buttiglione 1997, 1–17. He describes how the Polish nation resisted secularizing pressures and preserved a sense of spiritual identity based on a Christocentric unifying conception of the person, something that now, providentially through the election to the papacy of Cardinal Wojtyla, the rest of Europe can learn from them. "History has preserved Poland somewhat from the influence of that *ethical immanentism* which has marked the rest of the continent" (8) and so now this part of the history and culture of Europe "reveals itself to be the place where the truth of European civilization, its fundamental Christian character, is most clearly preserved. . . . [T]he history of Poland appears as the only possible salvation for the European cultural heritage" (10).
29. Wojtyla 1964a, 530–31.
30. For the same connection, although with different interests and emphases, see Scola 1984, 289–306, especially 298–302. He delineates first the main lines of the anthropological reflection contained in the conciliar interventions of Monsignor. Wojtyla, which he classifies as an "integral personalism" ("personalismo integrale"), and then looks at the pronouncements on religious freedom as a particular example or a fundamental application of that conception of the person.

31. Wojtyla 1959, 741.
32. Wojtyla 1965c, 660.
33. Ibid., 661.
34. Ibid.
35. Grootaers 1981, 166 mentions the controversies between "incarnationists" and "eschatologists," about more or less "horizontalism" or "verticalism" in the presentation of the mission of the church.
36. Komonchak 1994, 86–88, describes the general distinctive traits of the theological epistemologies of each tendency. The tendencies of Monsignor Wojtyla's personal theological anthropology, as inferred from his conciliar statements on the issue of religious freedom, fit perfectly a typical Augustinian approach. For a quite different point of view on the positioning of Cardinal Wojtyla among the different theologies of the relationship between nature and grace vying for recognition at the council, see Buttiglione 1997, 195–99.
37. See Grootaers 1981, 173–75.
38. Wojtyla 1980.
39. Ibid., 313. Note the reiteration of the connection of freedom to responsibility and truth. After the series of quotations, the concept of "responsible liberty" is again used: "[S]ince love of men demands respect for 'responsible liberty' in the religious sphere. . . ." Ibid., 314.
40. The sentence quoted reads in *Dignitatis Humanae:* "Therefore the right to religious freedom has its foundation not in the subjective attitude of the individual but in his very nature." The passed over following clause continues: "For this reason the right to this immunity continues to exist even in those who do not live up to their obligation of seeking the truth and adhering to it." Vatican II 1987b, 801. The first clause is cited again alone in Wojtyla 1980, 409. The context there shows clearly that what caught his attention in the sentence was the straightforward statement of the foundation of the right on human nature, not the consequence derived from it.
41. Wojtyla 1980, 409.
42. Ibid., 412. Three pages earlier he had called attention to the double approach of *Dignitatis Humanae:* "The Declaration points out in the first place that 'the human person has a right to religious freedom' (number 2), and it bases this statement on primarily rational principles, before proceeding in the second part of the document to expand on it from a theological standpoint analyzing religious freedom in the light of Revelation." Ibid., 409. It seems that, by using now the expression "above all on the nature of faith," he is giving prevailing importance to the theological argumentation.
43. Ibid., 414.
44. Ibid., 414–15.
45. The last non-Italian bishop of Rome had been Hadrian VI, a Dutchman, who was pope from 1522 to 1523.

46. This role was publicly recognized by, of all people, Mikhail Gorbachev himself a few years later. See Gorbachev 1992.
47. John Paul II 1978, October 17, 293.
48. See, for instance, John Paul II 1987, December 8, 496: "My thoughts turn with particular affection to those brothers and sisters who are deprived of the freedom to profess their Christian faith, to all who are suffering persecution for the name of Christ, to those who for his sake must suffer rejection and humiliation. I want these brothers and sisters of ours to feel our spiritual closeness, our solidarity and the comfort of our prayer." Particularly poignant is the comparison between the persecutions and martyrdom of many Christians in the first centuries of the church and the religious persecutions of today, the "kind of *civil* death" ("sorte de mort *civile*") being endured by many, which he develops in John Paul II 1983, August 14, 211.
49. For an analysis of these lines of development in the recent Catholic teaching on human rights, see Hehir 1996, 97–107. Also, Hollenbach 1979, 41–106; Hehir 1986b.
50. Hehir 1995, 174.
51. Hehir 1986b, 256.
52. From *Redemptor Hominis,* no. 17, repeated literally in John Paul II 1984, March 10, 657, without reference to the encyclical. Earlier in number 12 of the encyclical he had already given a sign of the importance he attributes to the differences between the two parts: "[T]he Church in our time attaches great importance to all that is stated by the Second Vatican Council in its *Declaration on Religious Freedom,* both the first and the second part of the document."
53. John Paul II 1978, December 2, 252–57.
54. Ibid., 254. A footnote refers to number 158 of *Pacem in Terris,* which reads: "However, one must never confuse error and the person who errs, not even when there is question of error, or inadequate knowledge of truth, in the moral or religious field. The person who errs is always and above all a human being, and in every case he retains his dignity as a human person. He must always be regarded and treated in accordance with that lofty dignity." John XXIII 1976, 235.
55. John Paul II 1980, September 1, 1254.
56. Ibid.
57. Ibid. The quote is from *Dignitatis Humanae,* no. 2.
58. John Paul II, 1984, March 10, 655.
59. Ibid., 657.
60. Especially when addressing international political bodies, or commenting on juridical declarations on human rights, he continues to develop philosophical arguments and to promote the right in nonconfessional language. See, as an example, the Message for the 1988 World Day of Peace, John Paul II 1987, December 8, 493, which he cares to address explicitly to "the leaders of the nations and the heads of the international organizations, as well as all my brothers and sisters throughout the world. . . ." But, even on those occasions, he always adds some theological

qualifications or some kind of supernatural grounding for the right. His dissatisfaction with the natural-law approach is shown more clearly on the many occasions he felt the need to deepen the theological foundations of the right to religious freedom, and integrate it in a systematic understanding of Christian faith and moral living.

61. Hehir 1995, 174.
62. John Paul II 1978, December 2, 255.
63. Ibid., 256.
64. Ibid., 255.
65. Ibid., 256.
66. *Dignitatis Humanae,* as other civil declarations before, makes no distinction of the plane between religious freedom and the other fundamental human rights. Only after the council proposals were made to define its relation with all the other rights of the person as one of priority (see Pavan 1986, 48–51). John Paul II has particularly stressed this point and developed the reasons for such prominence, but Paul VI had already made remarks alluding to a similar primacy, for instance in *Evangelii Nuntiandi,* n. 39, Paul VI, 1992: "Among these fundamental human rights, religious liberty occupies a place of primary importance." Actually, even John Courtney Murray concludes one of his commentaries on *Dignitatis Humanae* with an observation in the same direction: "Religious freedom itself is the first of all freedoms in a well-organized society, without which no other human and civil freedoms can be safe." Murray 1994b, 199.
67. Although this is a most frequent occurrence, sometimes he does not set it apart. See, for instance, John Paul II 1979, October 2, 262, where he includes the right to religious freedom in the enumeration of "some of the most important human rights" without any special distinction.
68. John Paul II 1990, December 8, 474.
69. Ibid., quoting John Paul II 1984, March 10, 656.
70. *Centesimus Annus,* no. 47.
71. John Paul II 1992, May 9, 1376. For other sentences expressing this preeminence of religious freedom, see, for example: John Paul II 1979, January 12, 49; 1988, March 26, 772; 1990, December 8, 474; 1988, November 15, 1557; 1989, June 5, 1526.
72. John Paul II 1987, December 8, 494.
73. John Paul II 1989, January 9, 543.
74. John Paul II 1979, March 4, no. 17.
75. John Paul II 1981, January 12, 64.
76. John Paul II 1980, December 8, 468. Also John Paul II 1987, December 8, 495: It "sustains and is as it were the raison d'etre of other freedoms."
77. John Paul II 1989, January 9, 543.
78. John Paul II 1995, October 5, 297.
79. John Paul II 1982, September 18, 486.

80. John Paul II 1987, December 8, 493.

81. Ibid., 495. See also John Paul II 1989, October 13, 884.

82. John Paul II 1980, September 1, 1259.

83. Ibid. A similar argument, but from the perspective of the disadvantages of not respecting religious freedom, was reiterated more recently: "Millions of believers cannot be indefinitely oppressed, held in suspicion or divided among themselves without this involving negative consequences not only for the international credibility of those states but also for the internal life of the societies concerned: A persecuted believer will always find it difficult to have confidence in a state which presumes to regulate his conscience. On the other hand, good relations between churches and the state contribute to the harmony of all members of society." John Paul II 1996, January 13, 528.

84. John Paul II 1978, December 2, 256. The inserted quotation is from *Dignitatis Humanae,* which, itself, refers this argument to Leo XIII's encyclical *Immortale Dei.*

85. John Paul II 1989, June 5, 1522.

86. John Paul II 1987, December 8, 495.

87. Religious freedom is a topic touched by John Paul II almost every time he addresses governmental authorities—in an international forum like the United Nations, the European Parliament, or in his visits to particular countries—either to praise the achievements of more accomplished constitutional orders or to censure courageously less than complying governments. The annual address to the diplomats accredited at the Vatican has actually been, through the years, one of the privileged occasions for the development of his thought on this matter. In an annual overview of all areas of the world, he usually names the countries where there are still critical situations regarding this right. Formal speeches of acceptance of credentials of new ambassadors to the Holy See have also been regular occasions to commend, encourage, or demand full respect for the civil right to religious freedom, no matter what their geographic provenance is, and what system of government or national majority religion they represent. See, for example, speeches to the new ambassadors from Iran (John Paul II 1981, November 14, 634), Bangladesh (John Paul II 1985, December 28, 1626), Kenya (John Paul II 1987, January 9, 67–68), Spain (John Paul II 1987, October 17, 877), Turkey (John Paul II 1988, June 13, 2014–15), Finland (John Paul II 1988, October 3, 1022–23), Mauritius (John Paul II 1988, December 12, 1852), Cuba (John Paul II 1989, March 3, 477–78), United States (John Paul II 1989, October 3, 744–46), Czechoslovakia (John Paul II 1990, December 21, 1709–10), Pakistan (John Paul II 1991, January 4, 34–35), Sudan (John Paul II 1991, January 14, 107–08), Singapore (John Paul II 1991, January 24, 182–83), China (John Paul II 1991, June 17, 1693), and Nepal (John Paul II 1992, November 28, 753–54).

88. In John Paul II 1979, October 2, 265, he describes this incoherence of some governments: "Besides the acceptance of legal formulas safeguarding the principle of the freedom of the human spirit, such as freedom of thought and expression, religious freedom and freedom of conscience, structures of social life often exist in which the practical exercise of these freedoms condemns man, in fact if not

formally, to become a second-class or third-class citizen." See also John Paul II 1987, December 8, 495: "In various countries, laws and administrative practices limit or in fact annul the rights formally recognized by the constitution for individual believers and religious groups."

89. John Paul II 1984, December 8, 493.
90. John Paul II 1979, October 2, 265. Repeated in John Paul II 1980, September 1, 1255; and 1987, December 8, 495.
91. For the ways he moves from calls for religious freedom to denunciations of the imposition of atheistic ideologies, see, for instance, John Paul II 1979, December 22, 1488; 1985, January 12, 60–61.
92. See John Paul II 1979, January 7, 21–22.
93. John Paul II 1979, October 2, 263: "[O]ur modern civilization . . . in the last hundred years . . . has also given rise, both in theory and still more in practice, to a series of attitudes in which sensitivity to the spiritual dimension of human existence is diminished. . . ."
94. John Paul II 1984, March 10, 658. This sentence is actually an unattributed quotation of John Paul II 1979, January 28, 199. There, he continues by saying that hopefully this proclamation will not be hindered by external coercion but, above all, he hopes the church will not cease to do it by reason of "fears, doubts or for having let itself be contaminated by other humanisms, due to lack of confidence in its original message."
95. Hehir 1995, 173.
96. Hehir 1986b, 253.
97. The sentence opens number 22 of *Gaudium et Spes* and is quoted in *Redemptor Hominis,* no. 8. The emphasis is neither part of the original conciliar text nor part of the encyclical's quotation, but it corresponds very well to the theological anthropology of John Paul II.
98. *Redemptor Hominis,* no. 10. See also *Redemptor Hominis,* no. 11: "In Christ and through Christ man has acquired full awareness of his dignity, of the heights to which he is raised, of the surpassing worth of his own humanity, and of the meaning of his existence."
99. *Redemptor Hominis,* no. 21: "Nowadays it is sometimes held, though wrongly, that freedom is an end in itself, that each human being is free when he makes use of freedom as he wishes, and that this must be our aim in the lives of individuals and societies. In reality, freedom is a gift only when we know how to use it consciously for everything that is our true good. . . . The full truth about human freedom is indelibly inscribed on the mystery of the Redemption."
100. *Redemptor Hominis,* no. 13. There is a summary of this argument in John Paul II 1984, December 21, 499: "In becoming flesh so as to dwell among us (cf. Jn. 1:14), the word of God comes to bring us the priceless gift of knowledge of the truth: the truth about him, the truth about us and about our transcendental destiny. Man cannot build himself nor his own freedom except on the foundation of this truth. It is therefore an extremely valuable gift: It must be guarded and defended. Loss of only a part of the whole truth . . . would mean man prejudicing full

realization of himself, to a greater or lesser degree. The church is aware of this. She knows that she was constituted the depository and guardian of such truth. So she feels invested with a special mission, making her duty-bound to a particular service to mankind. . . ."

101. John Paul II 1989, January 9, 543. A short time before, in John Paul II 1988, October 8, 1083, he had advanced an interpretation of the historical genesis of human rights that gives further support to this argument: "[T]he human rights of which we are speaking draw their vigour and their effectiveness from a framework of values, the roots of which lie deep within the Christian heritage which has contributed so much to European culture. These founding values precede the positive law which gives them expression and of which they are the basis. They also precede the philosophical rationale that the various schools of thought are able to give to them."
102. John Paul II 1984, March 10, 655.
103. John Paul II 1980, December 8, 468.
104. John Paul II 1990, December 8, 474.
105. John Paul II 1989 January 9, 543. The English translation of the second clause is ambiguous about the referent of the adjective, but the original French leaves no doubts: "[I]ls devaient trouver dans la foi des croyants et dans leur sens moral les fondements transcendents indispensables pour que. . . ."
106. An example of this ambiguity is found in John Paul II 1983, August 17, 126: "In this, and nowhere else, rests the whole mystery of the dignity of the moral conscience: in its being the location, the sacred space in which God speaks to man. Consequently, if man does not listen to his own conscience, if he consents error to abide in it, he breaks the most profound bond that fastens him in covenant with his Creator." Another example from John Paul II 1985, April 11, 995: "[W]here as a matter of fact the faith in God-made man decreases there begins a crisis for the most profound motive of recognition of the original dignity of every human being."
107. John Paul II 1980, December 8, 470.
108. John Paul II 1987, December 8, 494.
109. John Paul II 1987, September 11, 249.
110. John 8:32
111. *Redemptor Hominis,* no. 12.
112. John Paul II 1990, December 8, 472: "[T]he individual person, despite human frailty, has the ability to seek and freely know the good, to recognize and reject evil, to choose truth and to oppose error."
113. Ibid., 474.
114. Ibid., 472.
115. John Paul II 1984, March 10, 657.
116. John Paul II 1990, December 8, 472.
117. Ibid., 475
118. Ibid.

119. Hehir 1995, 181, doubts it: "[W]hile there are characteristics of religious freedom that do set it apart from other rights claims, it is not clear what the practical or policy importance is of this argument ["that religious freedom is the 'cornerstone' and the 'measure' of other human rights"]. The papal case seems to be that violation of religious freedom inevitably will lead to violation of other rights and will pose a special threat to peace. Even granting the special intrinsic status of religious freedom, it is not clear that the causal connection implied in the papal argument necessarily follows."

120. Francisco Claver, writing from the Philippines about religious freedom in the Asian context, states that "human rights make up an integral whole, and one cannot speak of defending or asserting freedom of religion without at the same time doing the same for freedom of speech, freedom of association and assembly, freedom of movement and the like." He explains that this is a crucially important point "in situations where totalitarian governments systematically violate human rights and the church does not feel any compulsion to act unless religious freedom itself is directly attacked." Claver 1982, 451.

121. In a less-publicized speech John Paul II addresses this question somewhat, denying any claims of merit to a state that apparently respects religious freedom but isolates it from a general context of disrespect for other freedoms: "It is still opportune to mention the problem of religious freedom. You know it, the Church asks no privilege from civil power; with a kind of clarity that, after the Council, shows even better than in the past, she has defined a global position according to which religious freedom is just one of the faces of the unitary prism of freedom: the latter is an essential constitutive element of a society authentically modern and democratic. Consequently, no State may pretend to benefit from a positive esteem, or even more to be attributed merit, just by the simple fact that it seems to grant religious freedom, while it isolates in fact from a general context of freedom." John Paul II 1982, September 18, 486.

122. Interestingly enough, the argument made by Claver about the Asian context quoted above is repeated, in the same collection of essays, by the reporter on Poland, although after a statement of fact that may support the argument of John Paul II. She begins the essay by writing that "for us religious freedom in the 1980s has become the test of all freedoms. The extent to which the state will allow this freedom has been taken as a measure of its attitude toward society." But then she explains that this is due to the social power of the Catholic Church in Poland, a power that can eventually become oppressive. Thus her qualifications about religious freedom: "Religious freedom is a fundamental human right, and the statement as such needs no comment. But I would like to add that a kind of self-respect is needed for this right. Religious freedom is a particular instance of fundamental human freedom. Every fight that is only for *religious* freedom is limited and opened to dangers. I am not especially concerned for a special privilege to have religious freedom, but I want full rights as a citizen, and within those rights, the right to freedom of conscience. Religious freedom cannot be isolated from other freedoms. Religious freedom flourishes to the extent that other freedoms exist within society. We need to insist on the totality-of-freedom principle." Bortnowska 1982, 447.

123. See, for instance, the categorical warning in John Paul II 1985, April 17, 1059: "This structural voluntary character of faith does not mean in any way that believing is 'facultative', and that, therefore, it would be justifiable as an attitude of fundamental indifferentism; it means only that, to the invitation and gift of God, man is called to respond with the free adherence of his total self."
124. John Paul II 1985, April 17, 1060. He followed this exact same sequence of quotations and omissions in John Paul II 1979, October 2, 265, evoked and repeated in John Paul II 1980, September 1, 1255.
125. For instance, John Paul II 1990, December 8, 472: "The right to profess the truth must always be upheld, but not in a way which involves contempt for those who may think differently." A few lines down, however, the ambiguity is again present: "[T]hose who acknowledge the relationship between ultimate truth and God himself will also acknowledge the right, as well as the duty, of non-believers to seek the truth which can lead them to discover the mystery of God and humbly accept it." What about if they, themselves, do not take that duty seriously, or never accept the mystery? Is their right in any way dependent on the fulfillment of the duty? What is the meaning and concrete consequence of that "as well as"?
126. See John Paul II 1987, December 8, 496: "The leaders of religious bodies are obliged to present their teaching . . . in ways that conform to the requirements of peaceful coexistence and respect for the freedom of each individual. . . . the followers of the various religions should, individually and collectively, express their convictions and organize their worship and all other specific activities with respect for the rights of those who do not belong to that religion or do not profess any creed."
127. Ibid., 494.
128. Ibid.
129. Puzzling affirmations like the one that "the right to religious freedom has been present . . . in the life and history of the church since the first times" (John Paul II 1984, March 10, 657) betray a lesser sensitivity to the issues of the first moment.
130. "Human rights are more than legal norms; they are above all values. These values must be sustained and nurtured within society or else they risk being erased from the law as well. Moreover, the dignity of the individual must be safeguarded by custom before the law can do so." John Paul II 1989, January 9, 543.
131. *Centesimus Annus,* no. 29.
132. See, for instance, the reference to Vietnam in John Paul II 1990, January 13, 579; and to China and Vietnam in John Paul II 1991, January 12, 529; 1996, January 13, 528.
133. See John Paul II 1992, January 11, 69; 1996, January 13, 528.
134. John Paul II 1993, December 21, 1522.
135. John Paul II 1989, January 9, 543.
136. John Paul II 1983, August 14, 212.
137. John Paul II 1989, June 5, 1527.
138. John Paul II 1990, January 13, 578. In John Paul II 1991, October 9, 793, he says that the profound transformations that have recently had an impact on Europe

open also "unexpected possibilities for a new evangelical sowing. We are living a 'favorable moment', a true kairos, which we must use with the commitment of faithful servants."

139. John Paul II 1990, January 13, 578.
140. John Paul II 1996, May 19, 561.
141. John Paul II 1991, November 23, 1239.
142. John Paul II 1993, November 11, 1267.
143. We find a clearest formulation of this in an speech delivered in Baltimore, at the end of his 1995 visit to the United Nations and the United States: "The challenge facing you . . . is to increase people's awareness of the importance for society of religious freedom; to defend that freedom against those who would take religion out of the public domain and establish secularism as America's official faith." John Paul II 1995, October 8b, 316.
144. The distinction of these two concepts is not clear in his writings of the second-moment phase. Most of the time they are used concurrently ("freedom of conscience and of religion" is an expression very often encountered); sometimes they even look interchangeable. John Paul II dedicated his message for the 1991 World Day of Peace to an extensive treatment of freedom of conscience. There he refers to religious freedom—defined, for that matter, as "the right to express one's own religious convictions publicly and in all domains of civil life"—as an "aspect" of freedom of conscience; but he also says that there is an "intimate relationship between freedom of conscience and religious freedom." John Paul II 1990, December 8, 472. In spite of this initial attempt to distinguish these two concepts, then, in the development of the message, they are so closely related that they almost seem interchangeable: The requisites of one apply to the other and one cannot be without the other, so in practical terms to defend one means to defend the other.
145. John Paul II 1991, March 23, 630.
146. Ibid., 630–31. We see this same disposition in John Paul II 1990, December 8, 475.
147. John Paul II 1990, January 13, 578. The year after, John Paul II 1991, January 12, 527–28, again gives prominent attention to a critical evaluation of European societies and cultures.
148. John Paul II 1990, January 13, 578.
149. John Paul II 1988, October 11, 1178.
150. See, for a critique of the negative tendencies associated with secularization often turned dechristianization, John Paul II 1985, April 11, 994–96.
151. John Paul II 1980, December 8, 469.
152. *Centesimus Annus,* no. 45: "The culture and praxis of totalitarianism also involve a rejection of the Church. The State or the party . . . cannot tolerate the affirmation of *an objective criterion of good and evil* beyond the will of those in power. . . . This explains why totalitarianism attempts to destroy the Church, or at least to reduce her to submission, making her an instrument of its own ideological apparatus."
153. John Paul II 1991, March 16.

154. *Centesimus Annus,* no. 29.

155. *Centesimus Annus,* no. 46: "[F]reedom attains its full development only by accepting the truth. In a world without truth, freedom loses its foundation and people are exposed to the violence of passion and to manipulation, both open and hidden."

156. *Centesimus Annus,* no. 46. See *Redemptor Hominis,* no. 19 for a more developed statement of how obligation to the truth defines the identity and the mission of the church.

157. "Christian anthropology therefore is really a chapter of theology, and for this reason, the Church's social doctrine, by its concern for the person and by its interest in him and in the way he conducts himself in the world, 'belongs to the field . . . of theology and particularly of moral theology.' " *Centesimus Annus,* no. 55.

158. *Evangelium Vitae,* no. 19. Unless cited as a note, subsequent citations of *Evangelium Vitae* will appear parenthetically in the text with the abbreviation *EV.*

159. *Veritatis Splendor,* no. 35. See also, nos. 4, 32, and 34. Unless cited as a note, subsequent citations of *Veritatis Splendor* will appear parenthetically in the text with the abbreviation *VS.*

160. At the opening of *Veritatis Splendor,* no. 1, John Paul II writes that "truth enlightens man's intelligence and shapes his freedom, leading him to know and love the Lord." However, as a result of original sin, he continues a few lines down, "man's capacity to know the truth is also darkened, and his will to submit to it is weakened. Thus, giving himself over to relativism and scepticism (cf. Jn 18:38), he goes off in search of an illusory freedom apart from truth itself." Nevertheless, "in the depths of his heart there always remains a yearning for absolute truth."

161. *Evangelium Vitae,* no. 19.

162. *Veritatis Splendor,* no. 33.

163. *Evangelium Vitae,* no. 20.

164. In this phase, John Paul II frequently attributes to the protection of the right to life a foundational role similar to the one he assigned to the right to religious freedom at the height of the fray of the second moment, when he developed justifications for considering religious freedom as the first human right. Actually, since the beginning of his pontificate, it is the right to life that consistently comes first whenever he has listed fundamental human rights without setting a special status for religious freedom. See, for instance, John Paul II 1978, December 2, 254; 1989, January 9, 542. Sometimes, as in John Paul II 1980, November 10, 1115, he highlights both the right to life and the right to religious freedom. A curious transitional compromise is found in *Centesimus Annus,* no. 47. When he calls for a strong foundation of democracy on the recognition of human rights, he begins the listing by writing that "among the most important of these rights, mention must be made of the right to life." Later he registers "the right to develop one's intelligence and freedom in seeking and knowing the truth." However, he concludes, explicitly referring back to some of his previous statements, by saying that "in a certain sense, the source and synthesis of these rights is religious freedom, understood as the right to live in the truth of one's faith and in conformity with one's transcendent dignity as a person." In *Evangelium Vitae* he is already making

affirmations like "the fundamental right and source of all other rights which is the right to life" (no. 72); "Only respect for life can be the foundation and guarantee of the most precious and essential goods of society, such as democracy and peace" (no. 101). Even more, in a prepared address for his canceled visit to Sarajevo, he says: "If we want to avoid war, it is necessary to secure respect for the fundamental rights of the human person, among which the right to life occupies the first place, a right that every man has, from his conception to his natural death. There are subsequently the other rights: those, for example, of religious freedom and freedom of conscience, which define the principles for the living together of men in their spiritual dimension." John Paul II 1994, September 9, 882. In John Paul II 1994, April 13, 932, he says that "the right to life is essential, and can be considered as 'the first right, origin and condition of all the other rights.' "

165. *Evangelium Vitae,* no. 18.

166. *Evangelium Vitae,* no. 20. The following sentence from John Paul II 1993, November 19, 1290, summarizes the various dimensions of the problem: "A legislation that contradicts essential moral truths on the supreme gift of life opens the way to those modern forms of totalitarianism, which, by the negation of transcendental truth, destroy authentic human dignity. "

167. *Veritatis Splendor,* no. 101, emphasis mine.

168. *Veritatis Splendor,* no. 34. See also John Paul II 1995, October 8a, 314: "We must guard the truth that is the condition of authentic freedom, the truth that allows freedom to be fulfilled in goodness. We must guard the deposit of divine truth handed down to us in the church, especially in view of the challenges posed by a materialistic culture and by a permissive mentality that reduces freedom to license." And also, for elaboration on this topic commenting on *Veritatis Splendor,* John Paul II 1993, October 15, 1017–23; 1993, October 17, 1045–46.

169. *Veritatis Splendor,* no. 96.

170. "According to Christian faith and the Church's teaching, 'only the freedom which submits to the Truth leads the human person to his true good. The good of the person is to be in the Truth and to *do* the Truth.' " *Veritatis Splendor,* no. 84. The internal quote refers to John Paul II 1986, April 10, 970, an address to a meeting sponsored by institutions affiliated with Opus Dei, in which he reflects on the relation between freedom and truth in morality and anticipates many of the themes and the tone of *Veritatis Splendor.* Actually, almost all of the text of *Veritatis Splendor,* no. 84 is a direct quote from this address.

171. *Veritatis Splendor,* no. 87.

172. One example is a starker affirmation of the priority of the duty to search for the truth over the right to freedom: "Although each individual has a right to be respected in his own journey in search of the truth, there exists a prior moral obligation, and a grave one at that, to seek the truth and to adhere to it once it is known" (*Veritatis Splendor,* no. 34). The footnote groups a curious mix of references. *Dignitatis Humanae,* no. 2 (certainly with great stress on the two sentences that talk about the duty toward the truth) is put in the awkward company of Gregory XVI's *Mirari Vos,* Pius IX's *Quanta Cura,* and Leo XIII's *Libertas Praestantissimum.*

173. *Veritatis Splendor,* no. 63. Shortly before, at no. 62, he had already quoted the whole sentence from *Gaudium et Spes:* "As the Council puts it, 'not infrequently conscience can be mistaken as a result of invincible ignorance, although it does not on that account forfeit its dignity; but this cannot be said when a man shows little concern for seeking what is true and good, and conscience gradually becomes almost blind from being accustomed to sin.' " This sentence of *Gaudium et Spes,* no. 16, is the object of a more extended reflection in John Paul II 1983, August 17, 255–58, in which he stresses that because the conscience may err, it needs to be formed with the help of the doctrine of the church. (The text in *Insegnamenti* mistakenly attributes four quotes to *Dignitatis Humanae,* no. 3, when they are really from *Gaudium et Spes,* no. 16.)

174. *Evangelium Vitae,* no. 21.

175. See, for instance, John Paul II 1996, October 22, 1054. Other examples of his direct appeals to interreligious dialogue and collaboration on the promotion of spiritual values in society are John Paul II 1986, February 5, 597–98; 1987, April 28, 1449–52; 1989, October 10, 834–40. The gathering of representatives of the most important religions of the world in Assisi, for a day of prayer for peace, on October 27, 1986, has been the most eloquent sign of this interest of John Paul II.

176. *Evangelium Vitae,* no. 24.

177. *Evangelium Vitae,* no. 95. See also nos. 21 and 50.

178. *Veritatis Splendor,* no. 99.

179. *Veritatis Splendor,* no. 2. He continues this sentence with his favorite quotation from *Gaudium et Spes,* no. 22: *"[I]t is only in the mystery of the Word incarnate that light is shed on the mystery of man."*

180. *Evangelium Vitae,* no. 29. See also *Evangelium Vitae,* no. 2.

181. *Veritatis Splendor,* no. 36.

182. See John Paul II 1994, November 10, no. 57.

183. John Paul II 1993, September 1, 879.

184. See John Paul II 1993, April 14, 895–97; 1996, October 22, 1053–54; 1996, June 22, 139–41.

185. John Paul II 1994, November 10, no. 36.

186. See, in this line, the diagnosis of the crisis and the remedies suggested in John Paul II 1995, November 23, 6–11.

187. John Paul II 1993, September 1, 879.

188. John Paul II 1993, April 16, 903.

189. *Veritatis Splendor,* no. 106.

190. John Paul II 1993, November 19, 1288. See also John Paul II 1996, June 22, 141: "As the church, we must increasingly fulfill our task of being the moral conscience of society. As Christians we must once more become the 'salt of the earth' and the 'light of the world' (Mt. 13:14). Ecclesial life, which should be exclusively based on the truths of the faith, must remain faithful to Christ and the Gospel message, if we wish to help those members of the church who find themselves in a society that seeks to relativize and secularize all areas of life."

191. *Veritatis Splendor,* no. 107.

192. "The unity of the Church is damaged not only by Christians who reject or distort the truths of faith but also by those who disregard the moral obligations to which they are called by the Gospel." *Veritatis Splendor,* no. 26.

193. "The task of interpreting these prescriptions [moral commandments imparted by God] was entrusted by Jesus to the Apostles and their successors, with the special assistance of the Spirit of truth" (*Veritatis Splendor,* no. 25), "a task which continues in the ministry of their successors" (*Veritatis Splendor,* no. 27).

194. "The Church's Pastors . . . guide and accompany [the faithful] by their authoritative teaching, finding ever new ways of speaking with love and mercy not only to believers but to all people of good will." *Veritatis Splendor,* no. 3.

195. John Paul II 1985, May 11, 20.

196. *Evangelium Vitae,* no. 4.

197. "It is true that history has known cases where crimes have been committed in the name of 'truth.' But equally grave crimes and radical denials of freedom have also been committed and are still being committed in the name of 'ethical relativism.' " *Evangelium Vitae,* no. 70.

198. *Evangelium Vitae,* no. 70.

199. *Veritatis Splendor,* no. 97.

200. *Evangelium Vitae,* no. 71.

201. *Evangelium Vitae,* no. 90. The language here evokes the language of the old "hypothesis" approach to the issue of religious freedom. Politicians are urged not to compromise the ideal ("not to give in") of having legislation in total accord with moral truth, and encouraged to go as far as they can, limited only by considerations of political feasibility ("what is realistically attainable").

202. *Evangelium Vitae,* no. 90.

203. *Evangelium Vitae,* no. 90. At another time he had already declared that "Catholics have a duty to promote legislation which corresponds to the moral law and to seek to reform legislation which does not reflect the truth of man's dignity and transcendent destiny, always by lawful means and rational debate." John Paul II 1993, November 11, 1270.

204. See *Evangelium Vitae,* no. 95: "Too often it happens that believers, even those who take an active part in the life of the Church, end up by separating their Christian faith from its ethical requirements concerning life, and thus fall into moral subjectivism and certain objectionable ways of acting."

205. The way this basic option determines a biased approach to the interpretation of *Dignitatis Humanae* can be seen again in a passage of the section of *Veritatis Splendor* on freedom and the law. John Paul II quotes from the beginning of number 3 of *Dignitatis Humanae* the principle that the "supreme rule of life is the divine law itself" and that God enabled human beings to share in divine law and so they are able, "under the gentle guidance of God's providence increasingly to recognize the unchanging truth." *Veritatis Splendor,* no. 43. His quote stops here, but in *Dignitatis Humanae* this was actually only the premise for the following conclusion: "Therefore all have both the right and the duty to search for religious

truth, so that they may by the prudent use of appropriate means *form for themselves* right and true moral judgments" (*Dignitatis Humanae,* no. 3, emphasis added). The pope puts the emphasis on the recognition of the unchanging truth, while the conciliar declaration's accent was actually on the sovereignty and freedom of the person's conscience, as the remainder of the paragraph elaborates, an emphasis that, to the whole thrust of the encyclical, it is not particularly opportune to highlight.

206. John Paul II 1995, October 5, 295.

207. Ibid., 297: "To cut oneself off from the reality of difference—or, worse, to attempt to stamp out that difference—is to cut oneself off from the possibility of sounding the depths of the mystery of human life. The truth about man is the unchangeable standard by which all cultures are judged; but every culture has something to teach us about one or other dimension of that complex truth. Thus the 'difference' which some find so threatening can, through respectful dialogue, become the source of a deeper understanding of the mystery of human existence."

208. Ibid., 299: "Each and every human person has been created in the 'image and likeness' of the One who is the origin of all that is. We have within us the capacities for wisdom and virtue. With these gifts, and with the help of God's grace, we can build in the next century and the next millennium a civilization worthy of the human person, a true culture of freedom."

Four ❧

Freedom, Dialogue, and Truth: The Presence of the Church in Contemporary Pluralistic and Secularized Societies

Expectations of John Courtney Murray

That *Dignitatis Humanae* was a document with great import for the larger realm of church-society relationships was not missed at the time of its approbation. John Courtney Murray, in spite of his efforts to focus on a narrow approach to the issue of religious freedom, alluded at once to those broader implications. His kind of dual judgment on the declaration, quoted at the opening of this book, aimed at that potentiality of the text. In some other instances he pointed even more directly to that concomitant wider reach. The declaration, he says, "raises a number of serious issues. And it is fraught with theological significance in ways that go far beyond the narrow context of the single problem with which it deals."[1] The plan he will use to start to systematize these implications is announced in the suggestion that this "considerable theological significance . . . will become apparent if the document is considered in the light of the two great historical movements of the 19th century, both of which were bitterly opposed by the Church."[2]

Secularity and Freedom

The first of these two movements was the movement toward secularity, the breaking away from a conception of the sacrality of society and state, both enclosed within the all-embracing church, with the political rulers caring also for the religion of their subjects—a legacy of medieval Christendom that persisted through the ancien régime. The way political and civil society sought to differentiate themselves took, initially, the form of a laicist state of atheistic inspiration, claiming absolute autonomy, and committed to the complete laicization of society—things which the church could never accept, especially its "programmatic denial of public status to religion and its reduction of the Church to the private status of a voluntary society, wholly enclosed within the monist structure of the state and subjected to its omnipotent sovereignty."[3]

However, underneath, there was a movement toward a legitimate secularity of society and state. Only through the first part of the twentieth century was the church able to discern slowly the signs of the times, make the appropriate distinctions, and develop its teaching in the direction of the acceptance of this secularity. For Murray, "this progress reaches its inevitable term in the *Declaration on Religious Freedom*."[4] Taken in its narrow focus on the issue of religious freedom as a particular aspect of church-state relationships, *Dignitatis Humanae* conclusively defines the acceptance by the church of the strict secularity of the function of the state by denying it any competence of *cura religionis*.[5] But, Murray recognizes, "to this conception of the state as secular, there corresponds a conception of society itself as secular. It is not only distinct from the Church in its origin and finality; it is also autonomous in its structures and processes."[6] It is in this way, then, that *Dignitatis Humanae* "has opened the way toward . . . a new straightforwardness in relationships between the Church and the world."[7]

The center of this theological significance of *Dignitatis Humanae* for church-society relationships rests with its consecration of the primacy of the principle of freedom. That this principle was evoked in a confined application to provide foundation for a specific civil right does not prevent the subsequent drawing of its implications for a larger realm. "Though the Declaration deals only with the minor issue of religious freedom in the technical secular sense, it does affirm a principle of wider import—that the dignity of man consists in his responsible use of freedom."[8]

On this basis of the dignity of every human person, the principle of freedom was definitively solidified as a basic standard in the social doctrine of the church.

> Freedom is an end or purpose of society, which looks to the liberation of the human person. Freedom is the political method par excellence, whereby the other goals of society are reached. Freedom, finally, is the prevailing social usage, which sets the style of society. This progress in doctrine is sanctioned and made secure by "Dignitatis Humanae Personae."[9]

The claims of this principle oblige all the institutions and forces within society, from the government to the church. The new statute of religious freedom as a civil right imposed a limit primarily on the power of the state, but, Murray acknowledges, it also constituted "a self-denying ordinance on the part of the Church" as it renounced the instrumental use of the power of the state to further the church's own goals and made freedom its exclusive claim upon the secular world.[10] Now, "it remains for religion itself, by the force of its own truth alone, to recover its public standing and its social influence in an industrial society to which religion has become largely irrelevant and even insipid." In a situation in which estrangement from religion has spread throughout society, the challenge for the church, then, was to open a dialogue able to "embrace the whole of humanity and include all human concerns, both personal and social."[11] This was the present big problem for the church, and so, ultimately, the greatest significance for *Dignitatis Humanae* was to place the church in a position, and with the appropriate principles, to be able to address it effectively.

In sum, Murray's understanding of the relevance of *Dignitatis Humanae* for church-society relationships postulated the extension of the role of the principle of freedom beyond the narrow issue of religious freedom. "The conciliar affirmation of the principle of freedom was narrowly limited—in the text. But the text itself was flung into a pool whose shores are [as] wide as the universal Church. The ripples will run far."[12] The full extent and substance of his expectations can only be guessed. The allusions and suggestions gathered here give only a glimpse of what Murray anticipated as the wider consequences for the church-society relationship following the definite acceptance of the movement toward secularity effected by *Dignitatis Humanae*.

HISTORICAL CONSCIOUSNESS AND TRUTH

While the first of "the two great historical movements of the nineteenth century" was sociopolitical, the second "was intellectual and even more profound in its import. It was the transition from the classical mentality to historical consciousness."[13] The outcome of the first movement was a new prominence of freedom in a society rightly secular. The second concerned a new view of the truth and how this affects the approach of the church to its ministry to the world. Murray offers a summary of the most relevant characteristics of the two opposite views in this second movement:

> [C]lassicism designates a view of truth which holds objective truth, precisely because it is objective, to exist "already out there now" (to use Bernard Lonergan's descriptive phrase). Therefore, it also exists apart from its posses-

> sion by anyone. In addition, it exists apart from history, formulated in propositions that are verbally immutable. If there is to be talk of development of doctrine, it can only mean that the truth, remaining itself unchanged in its formulation, may find different applications in the contingent world of historical change.[14]

This was the old mentality, which the nineteenth-century intellectual movement tried to displace by establishing an alternative approach:

> In contrast, historical consciousness, while holding fast to the nature of truth as objective, is concerned with the possession of truth, with man's affirmations of truth, with the understanding contained in these affirmations, with the conditions—both circumstantial and subjective—of understanding and affirmation, and therefore with the historicity of truth and with progress in the grasp and penetration of what is true.[15]

This movement too was opposed by the church because of its initial term in modernism, which pushed its insights to the extreme of "the destruction of the notion of truth itself—its objective character, its universality, its absoluteness."[16] Again, only a delayed work of discernment, separating the positive insights from their abusive applications, led the church at Vatican II to accept the validity of the direction of this intellectual movement and to start tapping into its richness. Murray sees in the "pastoral" option of the council a sign that the historical mentality was gaining way in the church too. He explains how this approach is not less interested in matters of truth and doctrine; it just puts them within the new perspective characteristic of historical consciousness:

> The pastoral concern of the Council is a doctrinal concern. However, it is illuminated by historical consciousness: that is, by concern for the truth not simply as a proposition to be repeated but more importantly as a proposition to be lived; by concern, therefore, for the subject to whom the truth is addressed; hence, also, by concern for the historical moment in which the truth is proclaimed to the living subject; and, consequently, by concern to seek that progress in the understanding of the truth demanded both by the historical moment and by the subject who must live in it. In a word, the fundamental concern of the Council is with the development of doctrine.[17]

This set of concerns shapes a whole program and method for the church's teaching role in society. It is here that, for Murray, emerges the second theological significance of *Dignitatis Humanae,* for the declaration so embraced historical consciousness that, for that reason, it became itself a breakthrough "pastoral exercise in the development of doctrine"; it effected a development of doctrine that was both more adapted to the historical moment and more faithful to the truth of the tradition.[18]

Promise and Lessons

The end result of these two movements consisted, first, of prominently affirming the principle of freedom, in a new philosophy of society and state founded on the four principles of truth, justice, love, and—the novelty—freedom, as demanded by the acceptance of a legitimate secularity of society; and, second, of a basic change in the view of truth inspired by insights of the intellectual movement of historical consciousness, about the historicity of truth and of the role of the subject in the access and possession of the truth. For the assimilation of the results of both these movements by the church at the council, the role of the declaration on religious freedom was crucial. In their light, thus, the importance, and also the promise, of the declaration becomes more apparent. Murray was keenly aware of the impact already exerted by *Dignitatis Humanae,* and his perception that Catholicism, in the immediate aftermath of the council, was finally in step with these modern tides of human history in Western societies led him to cultivate great expectations for the future of the presence of the church in the secular world.

From the consideration of *Dignitatis Humanae* in light of these two movements of modernity another lesson can be drawn. In both cases, a work of discernment transformed initial intransigent opposition into fruitful distinctions between underlying positive developments and false and unnecessary, but transitory, historical forms of their applications. Murray explains these dynamics in another of his postconciliar essays. The nineteenth-century hostility between Catholicism and liberalism was also due to "a failure on the part of the Church," he notes,

> a failure to recognize the signs of the times, to look beneath the surface of error and deviation and to discern the genuine human aspiration that was at work—man's perennial aspiration to possess his birthright of freedom. Condemnations in abundance fell on the errors to the right and to the left. But there was no effort to discern the truth that always lies at the heart of error.[19]

The lesson to extrapolate, in the language used by Murray,[20] is that the church needs to be careful not to miss the distinction between an immediate "term" of a historical movement, which may have to be rejected, and the "movement" itself with the valid insights that drive it; not to confuse distorted superficial phenomena with the healthy progress growing beneath the surface of history. Attention to the signs of the times and to the profound dynamisms of change in history, and alertness not to crystallize the position of the church in a priori condemnatory attitudes, were proven, by the process that led to *Dignitatis Humanae,* to have become indispensable for a successful relationship of the church with modern ever-evolving societies.

Once again, at the conclusion of this book, Murray was recalled to open the way by framing the questions historically, and by enunciating how he envisioned the import of *Dignitatis Humanae* for the presence of the church in society. This brief recount, besides providing a sense of the anticipations and hopes opened up by *Dignitatis Humanae* in the Catholic Church and in the world outside it for a continued progress in dialogue and mutually enriching encounter, served also to summarize the issues of the first moment, the strategies that eventually allowed the church to overcome them, as well as the traps and equivocations that for so long had prevented the church from surmounting those very issues.

External Challenges of the Third Moment

The first moment of *Dignitatis Humanae* marked a substantial reconciliation of the Catholic Church with the modern movement of secularization. It was made possible by a process of discernment, centered in the area of religious freedom, that distinguished the essential traits of a legitimate and even desirable movement of history from the extreme distortions and abuses of its initial narrow-minded concrete embodiments. However, the finally peaceful agreement on the goodness of the fundamental trend did not mean the end of all extremist inclinations and exorbitant claims. The tendencies whose initial accomplishments had alienated the church have not disappeared and continue to emerge in protracted or new forms. Most of the challenges faced today by the church in its relationship with the Western world—the liberal democratic societies to which the historical-geographical focus of the third moment (as, actually, that of the first) is restricted—continue to show a fundamental similarity with basic issues of the first moment.

In the juridical realm of the constitutional organization of societies, in what regards the attributions of the state in religious matters and its relationship with the church, a mutually acceptable balance was reached by *Dignitatis Humanae,* and it stands. However, while the church-state issues were generally settled effectively, the same basic confrontation has been revived as cultural and philosophical clashes in the realm of church-society.[21] On matters like deeper conceptual views of the human person and of the social order, the recognition of the importance of the transcendent dimension of human life, the role of religion in public life, the assent to an objective moral order, and the understanding of the prerogatives of individual freedom of conscience and the role of authority in morality, there continues to be contention between much of the liberal approach and fundamental values of the Catholic tradition. In another terminology, the church has made peace with political secularization, but cannot accept many features of cultural secularization as this has developed.[22]

From the side of the church, after the resolution in favor of religious freedom, what remained to be clarified was the concrete way the church could, in full respect for freedom, continue its social ministry of intervention in the public life of pluralistic societies in a way that rejects both giving in to the tendencies to privatize religion and any temptations to try to regain privileged positions or return to integralist social projects and triumphalist attitudes.[23]

The expectations of someone like Murray were that *Dignitatis Humanae* had opened the way for a successful negotiation of this tension. The framework of parameters set by the fundamental assertions of *Dignitatis Humanae* offers directions for a practical application of the principles of religious freedom to problems in the larger realm of church-society relationships. The concrete issues in which this presumption needs today to be tested have already been identified. They are the social problems more contentiously engaged by the church's magisterium, as they have been targeted by John Paul II. A brief summing up of them, and of the way the pope has tried to address them, will serve to introduce what *Dignitatis Humanae* has to contribute for this particular instance of the church's public role in pluralistic societies.

SECULARISM AND PRIVATIZATION OF RELIGION

In the third moment, John Paul II has identified and tried to counteract the challenges put to the values of Christianity by the culture of liberal democratic societies at three different levels. At the deepest level, the pope singles out secularism, be it atheistic or of mere indifference toward religion, as the ultimate source of the problems. He had already designated this as the root error behind the totalitarianism religious freedom had to defend itself against in the second moment, but its effects are not less damaging in democratic contexts. In the situation under consideration in the third moment, there is not, in general, repression of religious expression or any state-supported discrimination based on religion, but there is, in the atmosphere of the secularist culture of society, a tendency to consider religion a fading social phenomenon. It is respected, in the name of individual freedom, as a particular option, but limited to a purely private matter with no place in the public sphere. The general climate of society, especially when compared with times past, shows a radical loss of the sense of the transcendent, a devaluation of the religious dimension of human experience, and a great disregard for spiritual values. As a consequence of this general social impoverishment caused by secularism, life both personal and social is more and more guided by a practical atheism, which leaves unchecked the worst human tendencies and thus delivers people to the other great vices of these societies: individualism, utilitarianism, hedonism, materialism, and consumerism.

DISTORTION OF HUMAN FREEDOM

In a second level, John Paul II denounces the derived philosophical views under which this secularist basis presents itself in contemporary culture, namely, the wrongful conceptions of the human person. He emphasizes especially a distorted notion of human autonomy typical of a liberal individualistic ideology that puts freedom as an end in itself, a freedom totally detached from objective truth that claims to construct its own truth in a display of radical subjectivism and relativism. While in the second moment the problem was lack of civil freedoms, now it is the abuses of freedom that most worry him. In the moral sphere, this culture produces a secularist moral relativism based on indifference, if not denial, toward both the truth and God. The pope sees in this culture a threat to democracy when, allying moral relativism with a purely procedural understanding of democracy, it wants to limit what is acceptable in the democratic discussion. The result is marginalization of religious and moral truth from public life and, under the form of a hypertrophy of individual rights, the undermining of any obligation, personal or social, toward objective moral law, natural and revealed.

A MORAL CULTURE OF DEATH

Finally, at the more immediate level, the practical application of this philosophy of ethical relativism leads to widespread attitudes of moral permissiveness, whose worst consequences are seen in what John Paul II describes as a "culture of death." Because of the growing religious indifferentism and of the pressures for the privatization of religion, it has become much more difficult for the church to fulfill in these societies its traditional role of moral formation of consciences and guidance over public morality. The result is a civil law and many socially acceptable behaviors increasingly at odds with the moral law, especially in the areas of the protection of human life. Prospects are even dimmer as, by the conjunction of all these factors, the pope sees people becoming progressively more vulnerable and losing critical resources to help them expose and resist the pernicious moral influence of the dominant culture. This threatens, thus, to let these baneful tendencies achieve even greater domination.

In sum, all these issues have to do with one-sided excesses of fundamental traits of the modern movement of secularization. Just claims of right autonomy for secular society turned into rejection of any public role for religion and active discrimination against the admission of religiously inspired argument in the democratic debate; a legitimate promotion of the freedom of the human person turned into a claim of absolute autonomy for the individual; a correct distinction between the stipulations of civil law and the larger demands of the moral order and the due respect for the freedom of the individual conscience turned into tacit encouragement of moral relativism.

John Paul II's own outlook on the situation may be tendentiously pessimistic. Where others may be inclined to see tendencies and excesses in the midst of movements and developments stirred by good intents and equally filled with more hopeful potentialities, the pope tends to focus almost exclusively on what is regretful and evil. Nevertheless, these challenges from the prevailing culture in Western societies are very much real and the perils they risk for persons, communities, and societies at large are far from being negligible. It can certainly be argued whether or not the pope is too harsh and one-sided in his critique; one can also question the level of the threat and the staying power of resisting positive forces. But none of these qualifications should obscure the substance and distract from the gravity of the challenges.

Some may also think that, especially at the most concrete level, there are, in the area of the relationship of the church with the world, other at least equally crucial and urgent issues calling the church to decisive action. The ones singled out by John Paul II do not cease, for that reason, to be important. Moreover, because of all the attention they have received from the ordinary magisterium, they have become the means by which, in great part, the attitude of the church toward the contemporary world and the perception of the church by secularized societies have defined themselves. This way, these challenges have had a redoubled impact on the whole of church-society relationships, and the concentration on them is doubly justified.

General Goals for the Church's Reply

These are, undoubtedly, great and real challenges. The task for the official voice of the church is to respond to them effectively from the riches of its own tradition revealed and acquired. And it has to do so regarding the three levels of challenge identified by John Paul II: secularism, wrongful conceptions of human freedom, and moral relativism issuing a culture of death. Starting at the last, most immediate level, a successful response by the church implies adaptation to the concrete situations of persons and societies in a renewed commitment to the moral formation of consciences. Such response demands an exercise of reasoning and persuasion that has to go beyond the mere restatement of absolute moral norms. In the liberal democratic context of growing pluralism and increased intercommunication, where competing ideas and worldviews vie for preponderance, the ability to persuade necessitates previously securing a credible and compelling voice in the forums where choices about the public order of society are discussed and the fundamental bases of the dominant culture take shape. From there, either by counteracting or by reinforcing the elements of the overall culture of society more influential in the formation of people's persuasions in moral matters, the church may continue to exercise significant influx on the constitutive values of the social consensus.

At the following level of structuring cultural ideas, the church defends every person and the whole person, denouncing and opposing philosophies and views that are reductionist of the fullness of human dignity and, always attentive to discern in the events of history the deepest hopes and yearnings of humanity, tries to purify and guide the human search for the truth in the direction of the integral truth.

Finally, at the last and most fundamental level, the church hopes to be able to provide the opportunity for everyone to confront oneself in freedom and all honesty with the question of ultimate meaning and transcendent destiny by conscientiously responding to the call to faith implied in a personal, fully revealing encounter with Jesus Christ.

From the description of the issues and the setting up of the general goals, it is easily deducted that any address of the overall challenge will have to deal with topics like freedom and truth; autonomy of personal conscience, its immunity from coercion, and its formation through persuasion and call to responsibility; the role of the political power in the defense of individual freedom and personal rights; and also its obligation to uphold the moral order. These are all topics directly or indirectly touched by *Dignitatis Humanae* in the matter of the civil right to religious freedom. The articulated framework of parameters that the declaration defined can, therefore, provide guidance for these wider issues. Before applying them, however, it is necessary to recall the general orientations of the way John Paul II has himself been responding.

How John Paul II Has Responded

As it was pointed out, in spite of some degree of general ambivalence and even some eloquent counterexamples, the basic attitude of John Paul II toward these challenges is one of denunciation and countercultural separation, much more than seeking mutual encounter and dialogue. With a great sense of urgency he tries to heighten the outrage in the hope of mobilizing more forces against this culture, and to reinforce the determination of those—both individuals and communities—who are resisting. His goal is that an alternative culture, with radically different foundations, may extend itself and overthrow the presently dominating one.

New Evangelization

Following the same heuristic arrangement of the three levels used in the description of the challenges, John Paul II has responded at the most fundamental level to secularism by calling for a "new evangelization." His aim is to mobilize the church into a new great effort to bring back to faith people who live in a culture originally Christian but who have quenched their spiritual senses and fallen into indifferentism and practical atheism. At the same time, this revival will bring these societies, which flourished under the guiding influence of Christian values but which have recently strayed away, to rediscover their roots and traditional identity. The pope is convinced that only religion and the return to God will ultimately be able to overcome the evils induced and permitted by secularism, a conviction that leads him too to a preference for theological argument and greater appeal to revealed sources in his social teaching.

Truth over Freedom

In the more philosophical debate he has been a staunch promoter of what he considers to be authentic human freedom: a freedom dependent on truth. The restoration of the prerogatives of absolute truth against any kind of relativism and the establishment of unequivocal priority of truth over freedom have most probably been the most repeated topics of his pronouncements, across many areas of his teaching, both to the church and to the world. His desire to emphasize truth is such that he seems to shun any formulation of unqualified support for freedom from a fear of unwillingly buttressing erroneous concepts of freedom separated from truth. As we saw, this theme is the main thread of continuity between his approaches to the second and the third moments, and it is essentially connected to his interpretation and development of *Dignitatis Humanae*.

Reinforcement of Authority in Moral Formation

At the level of his advocacy in matters of public morality, John Paul II has opted for a top-down, authority-based approach to moral formation. He has strongly reinforced the role of the magisterium in moral teaching in the church. In civil society too he has endorsed a greater role for political authority in the juridical imposition of moral compliance, especially in the defense of the right to life. He has also alerted Catholic public officials of their personal responsibility to promote greater harmony between civil law and moral law, according to the demands of their religious faith. Here, the struggle against excesses of cultural secularization again raises questions on the edge of the rules of political secularization.

In summary, this is the threefold response of John Paul II to the challenges of the third moment: against secularism, new evangelization; against wayward individualistic freedom, absolute truth; against a culture of death, a civil law enforcing more closely the moral law. At the first level, it is a case of the church announcing its message and looking to induce religious conversion—an action, thus, directly subject to the rules protecting the right to religious freedom. The second level consists of a development of a basic underlying theoretical theme of *Dignitatis Humanae,* and it has determined much of the direction of the interpretation and application of *Dignitatis Humanae* by John Paul II on issues of religious freedom. The same line of interpretation also defines whether, where, and which broader implications of the principles of the declaration are noticed and appropriated in the present circumstance. In the third level, at stake are concrete issues of the relationship of the church with pluralistic societies in the area of public morality, a realm in which the application of those wider implications is suggested and facilitated by a great similarity between the questions of the present and those of the historical problems directly addressed by the conciliar declaration.

The whole response by the present pope stands, thus, within the sphere of *Dignitatis Humanae,* defined by both the symbolic attitudes and the substantive doctrine it prescribed for the action of the church in the world. The exploration of the parameters set by *Dignitatis Humanae* as applied to the challenges of the third moment will show the broader importance of the teaching of the declaration, and, at the same time, it will also become an opportune way to evaluate the strategy of John Paul II before the present predicament of the life and mission of the church, in light of the impulse given to the relationship of the church with secular society by the conciliar teaching on the right to religious freedom.

Dignitatis Humanae, the Public Role of the Church, and John Paul II

Currently, the most contentious problem in the relationship of Roman Catholicism with liberal pluralistic societies—reflected in the intense attention given to it by the institutional church, as the analysis of the teaching of John Paul

II so plainly showed—has been a profound disagreement about standards of juridically enforced common morality in the area of the protection of human life, symbolized and epitomized in the irreducibly antagonistic positions on abortion. For the goal of this book, the question that is to be kept at a level of generality above the specific particulars of such contentious moral dilemmas, is the following: How must the church engage a situation in which its social advocacy in the field of ethics confronts a pluralism of highly opposed views in society? It focuses, therefore, on the public role of the institution of the church,[24] and stays within the confines of social ethics. The attention is given to the methodology followed in this kind of public advocacy, not to the intricacies of the moral positions being advocated. What is under discussion here is not so much the exact appropriateness of *what* the church asserts, but *how* the church goes about gathering public support for it. Because of the emblematic character and especial divisiveness of these particular issues constantly highlighted by John Paul II, the solution suggested for their handling by the approach of *Dignitatis Humanae* will have a general impact on the whole relationship of the church with pluralistic societies in every cause publicly promoted by the church, whatever its ethical realm.

Focusing the issue leaves out many other aspects of the current relationship of the church with pluralistic secularized societies in its entirety. It means also that the evaluation of the stance of John Paul II on this area will concentrate on his teaching in *Evangelium Vitae,* when some positions that appear there in their strongest form are significantly complemented in other pronouncements. However, the encyclical is the place where, in his own perspective, the most contentious issues with liberal societies are addressed more in-depth and with greater authoritative weight. It is also the point of arrival of the evolution of his teaching on the relationships between freedom and truth and where he draws the sharpest social and political consequences from it. Therefore, if the positions strongly reiterated in the encyclical are not everything in his practice and in his views regarding the relationship between church and society, they deal with the most difficult questions in this area at this time, and they have been too the most determining factor in setting the general tone of John Paul II's approach, and, thus, of the perceived attitude of the church. They are, then, the best place to test the potentialities of the parameters set by *Dignitatis Humanae.*

Applied to the most concrete challenge of the third moment as it is seen and approached by John Paul II, the general question of how the church must exercise ethical advocacy in a context of social pluralism may be broken down into two components. One has to do with how the church may go about dealing with people who, in the certain conviction of the church, are in error: What ways may it use to convince them to change, to recognize the moral truth the church offers and to modify their behavior accordingly? The other concerns the role the coercive power of the state is allowed or required to take in order to prevent the spreading of those errors and to uphold the moral law, and whether and how the church can influence the enforcement of this role.

In this format, there is an exact parallel between this particular challenge presently faced by the church and the issue of religious freedom as it was dealt with in *Dignitatis Humanae*. Only now, instead of adherence to the faith of the one true church, what is in question is the recognition and obedience to demands of the objective moral order. The conciliar declaration gave a clear response to each one of the two dimensions of the question for the case of religious faith. For the first, it laid out the constraining demands of human dignity; for the second, it established the incompetence of the state in matters religious. Can these responses be transposed to the case of advocacy for a common morality respectful of natural law?

At the end of chapter 2, the fundamental assertions of the declaration had been systematized in four sets of parameters—around the concepts of truth, freedom, dialogue, and human experience—which define in their completeness the framework of the doctrine on the civil right to religious freedom. A similar framework for the question of public morality can be established by concurrent sets of the same parameters adapted to the contemporary relationship of the church with society. It is an analogous application of that framework, organized in the same fourfold division, that structures this final section of the book.

Affirmation of a Binding Objective Moral Order

As *Dignitatis Humanae* unashamedly affirmed the Catholic Church as the only true religion, so the church in its public advocacy of moral values and norms continues to affirm the existence of an objective moral order based on human nature. This order is knowable by human reason and binding upon all persons and society itself. And the church is commissioned to teach it authoritatively. The church continues to be faithful to its tradition, rejecting any individualistic absolute autonomy of the moral conscience in deciding what is moral or not, as it denies an absolute sovereignty of the individual conscience in religious matters. There is not, thus, any kind of concession to moral relativism, as there is none to religious indifferentism, in the case of religious freedom. *Dignitatis Humanae* itself explicitly affirms all this about individual and communitarian moral duties. In both the case of religious faith and of morality, a universal and absolute order of truth is upheld, with the consequent universal duty to search for its knowledge and to obey it, once it has been encountered.

The recognition of this order of natural law impending upon all and the conviction of the intrinsically social character of the human person ground the traditionally Catholic organic conception of society, significantly different from the liberal model based on a social contract between originally separated individuals. These different conceptions yield different views of the rights and duties of individuals but also distinct understandings of the role of the state in society. Although Catholic social ethics places clear limits on the scope and nature of the power of the state, it still concedes it a broader mandate than a liberal view does.[25] As it was noted, *Dignitatis Humanae* does not endorse a neutralist view of the role of the state regarding religion. Much less does the church defend such neutrality in what concerns issues of public morality.

Public Morality Component of Public Order. At this point of the parallel between the case of the right to religious freedom and the role of moral advocacy by the church, we find a crucial difference in the application of the principles of *Dignitatis Humanae.* While, in the case of religious faith, the basic principle was the total incompetence of the state, in the area of common ethical norms, on the contrary, it cannot be held that there is no place for the state to legislate on issues of public morality. That argument would be, in the extreme, to defend a purely libertarian and anarchist society, which would be based on a radical unmitigated supremacy of the individual over the community. Even a more moderate position—defending the total privatization of morality and the reduction of the role of the state to the arbitration of conflicts between contradictory claims of particular rights—would imply resignation with the possibility of a pulverization of society into groups guided by incommensurable values. In the long run, such a state of affairs would be incompatible with any solicitude for a common good or the continued sustenance of any meaningful social cohesion.

There has to be, in principle, a place for juridically imposed rules of morality, and also, then, for the possibility for the church to advocate their imposition legitimately. The church rightly continues to oppose tendencies toward excessive privatization of moral choices. Nothing in the doctrine of *Dignitatis Humanae* actually contradicts this. This issue of public morality, in the declaration, does not fall under the general principle of state incompetence to use coercion over choices that belong properly to the personal conscience but falls precisely under the exception to that general principle. The state's specific attribution to defend, at the expense of the freedom of particular individuals, personal rights of other people and the public order of society (whose elements are justice, public peace, and, precisely, public morality), legitimates, in the name of these competing values, the resort to coercion, as stated in number 7 of *Dignitatis Humanae.*[26]

Of course, it remains to be determined what can or cannot be included in this public morality component of the public order. Nevertheless, the principle stands, that, in the ethical realm, the obligation to conform to truth is not just a personal moral responsibility, but there is also the possibility that, in particular cases, it may be legitimately imposed by the coercive power of the state.

Full Agreement with Intentions of John Paul II. This first set of parameters, centered on the defense of an objective order of truth, is in full agreement with the ultimate goals that John Paul II has adopted and the fundamental principles he invokes to justify and ground his public advocacy of a restoration of obedient abidance by the truth in matters of personal and common morality. The text of *Dignitatis Humanae* provides explicit doctrinal support and encouragement for the pope's indictment and active opposing of individualism and relativism. Part and parcel of the doctrine of the declaration, in many cases explicitly declared in the text, are an unequivocal affirmation of an objective order of morality accessible to human beings; the duty of moral submission of persons and society to the demands of natural moral law; the avowal of a positive role for political power in enforcing moral norms upon society; and the principle of subjection of civil law to moral law. This first set of parameters affirming an objective order of morality defines the external framework of ultimate ends and nonnegotiable principles within which all the other parameters act. Any following disagreement, therefore, will be limited to the level of the choice of the most adequate means, theoretical and practical, to achieve the same final ends of serving and upholding the living of the truth.

THE CONSTRAINTS OF PERSONAL FREEDOM AND SOCIAL CONSENSUS

The first set of parameters, then, excludes one extreme of the spectrum, namely, the claim that, by reason of the individual right to freedom of conscience, the coercive power of the state can never be used to impose rules of moral practice, and, consequently, that it is never admissible to advocate such action. The state, and therefore the advocacy of the church, is not condemned to inaction. The state and the church are, however, certainly limited by constraints. The opposed, equally unacceptable extreme is one that historically has more easily exercised attraction upon groups of Christian affiliation, especially those committed to social programs directly guided by religious prescriptions. It consists of considering the state the apt instrument to impose full and general conformity of the whole society to demanding and particular standards of morality. If it is part of the social tradition of the church that positive law ought not to contradict moral law and that there is a specific role for the civil law in the defense and promotion of the moral law, it has always been taught, as well, that not all moral law ought to be made into civil law. The demand of non-contradiction in positive substance is far from requiring total consonance and exact coextension.

Between these two extremes, of a state with no role at all and a state enforcer of all, between paralysis and unrestrained intervention, resides, then, the competence of the state to legislate and enforce that minimum of public morality that is an element of the public order of society, and therefore rightly within the boundaries of its competency in society. The exclusion of the extremes is the easy part. The difficult questions still remain. When is the exertion of coercion to uphold moral behavior legitimate and justified? What cases are better left to the moral decision of every person or particular group and what, for reasons of public order, must be upheld by the state even against the will of some people? What basic criteria guide these choices? And then, also in the formulation of those criteria, whose convictions should exercise greater influence? The personal ones of those who happen to hold public office at the time? Those of the majority? Those of recognized "moral authorities" in that particular society? In cases of tension between competing fundamental values, which should (or are in fact) normally privileged: individual rights or the common good, truth or freedom, objective moral rule or subjective conviction? Finally, closer to the restricted goal of this study, what means can groups in society, in particular the church as one of those groups, resort to to influence those decisions in favor of a common morality inspired by Christian values? The task is now to explore the import of the doctrine of *Dignitatis Humanae* for the action and attitude of the church in its public advocacy, in democratic pluralistic societies, of standards of public morality befitting the Christian view of the person and society.

Civil Law and Moral Law in a Thesis/Hypothesis Perspective. The traditional restraint on how much civil law should incorporate moral law, as formulated by Thomas Aquinas, revolves around a prudential evaluation of the positive law's own practical possibility. To the question whether human law should repress all evils, he answers that laws imposed on people should, first, take into consideration the capacity of the majority to refrain from the vices forbidden, both by reason of individual virtue and of the customs of the country; should focus primarily on what may hurt others and would threaten the survival of society; and still take notice that, although human law has also the purpose of leading people to virtue, it should try that only gradually.[27]

It was as an application of this principle to the particular case of religious freedom that the thesis/hypothesis theory was devised. The recognition, in particular historical situations, of the impossibility of establishing juridically the ideal exclusive public status of the one true religion justified settling for a lesser-evil kind of arrangement. This arrangement consisted of tolerance for the existent religious plurality, to be left undisturbed by the state. The theory begins with the absolute truth of an abstract ideal and then, in any concrete historical case, goes as far as possible in the direction of its complete actualization. The driving impulse is the securing of the ascendancy of the truth, the clearly prevailing value. In the stage of social and political development of the time, moral and religious unified conformity was considered to be indispensable to the cohesion of society. The interests of the common good of the community, therefore, heavily trumped the values of personal growth and autonomous personal maturation. That, in turn, prompted an expanded view of the role of the state in the service of the common good, whose care rested with the conscience of political rulers, paternally governing the less than emancipated masses. It was within this social and political mindset that the nineteenth-century Catholic Church resisted the individual right to religious freedom. It maintained the juridical tradition of prudential judgment on the practical possibility of legal enforcement. But the unrestricted goal continued to be the pursuing of a social order reflecting, as far as functionally possible, allegiance to an objective religious and moral truth. The only admitted restraints to the practical implementation of that ideal goal are limitations imposed by accidental historical reasons. And claims of an unconditional individual right of freedom of conscience appeared, in the eyes of the church, clearly beyond this accidental category.

Twentieth-century Catholic social teaching moved away from this paternalistic political model. It centered itself on the concept of the dignity of the human person and began to explore its implications progressively. Such developments only gave renewed significance and larger reach to the traditional principles regulating the relationship of the civil law to the moral law. Incorporating already fundamental political features propelled by modern liberal democratic political movements, especially the principles of a free society under a limited government, Murray classically framed that traditional doctrine in more modern language: civil law should implement prescriptions and prohibitions of the moral law only in as much as those are necessary to guarantee any of the elements of public order, and, even then, "further tests need to be passed by proposed legislation: will the law merit consent? Is the law enforceable? Will the enforcement cause more harm than achieve good?"[28]

***The Advancements of* Dignitatis Humanae.** Still, in official church teaching in the matter of the right to religious freedom, there lacked a definitive break with the traditional mindset of the prudential judgment guided solely by the concept of practical possibility. It was as if, on the part of the church, it continued to be primarily a matter of resignation with extrinsic negative constraints. *Dignitatis Humanae* would complete and crown such development. It effected this clear break in the area of religious freedom and, by the scope of the principles evoked, it brought important new elements into the more general interface between morality and civil law.

In the matter of religious freedom, the declaration changed the official doctrine of the church from forced tolerance—that is a compromise with a lesser evil when, in a particular society, the impossibility to go further in the legal protection and promotion of the true religion was prudently recognized—to religious freedom, which consists of the recognition of a human right based on the dignity of the person to be upheld and practiced in every social and political circumstance. Before, the attitude was one of rationalized resignation with the obstacles imposed by historical accident on the church's commitment to establishing universal recognition for eternal truth. With the declaration, that gave way to the positive undertaking to safeguard first and foremost personal freedom and responsibility, seen as inalienable requirements of the natural dignity of every person. There was a shift from an attitude in which "religious pluralism was acknowledged as a *fact* in Catholic teaching, but never accepted in *principle*," to a clear acceptance and affirmation of "pluralism as a positive possibility the church should not simply resist but should engage in the dialogical style of ministry."[29] From simply tolerated, religious pluralism became normative.[30] The teaching of *Dignitatis Humanae* signified, first, a conclusive endorsing by the church of a legitimate secularity of state and society. Second, in a matter of binding obligation of conscience toward truth, it decisively shifted the starting point and controlling principle from the prerogatives of a disincarnate absolute truth to the freedom of responsible people in their search for truth in history.[31] These two advancements have direct implications for other areas of the whole relationship of the church with society, and, in particular, for its advocacy for a legislated public morality more in accordance with moral law.

Secularity and the Mediation of Social Consensus. Assent to secularity meant that the church renounced any claims of control over the whole society and abandoned any presumption that the power of the state could be an available instrument for direct service of the church in the furtherance of its religious goals. From the constitutionally limited government, the church demands now only respect for its own freedom, as well as for the due freedoms of persons and other social bodies, freedoms which may be restricted only by the stipulations of public order. A secular state serves the will of the people; the legitimization of its actions has to pass through the social consensus at the basis of a stable public opinion in society. In a regime of liberal democracy, with a secular state and a secular civil society, in which the legislative and executive powers depend on regularly repeated elections, only what a sustained majority sanctions can become or remain juridically enforced. These political majorities are determined and supported, in what regards fundamental choices about values in personal and communal living, by a deeper kind of consensus that coalesces and grows at the level of the culture. This consensus evolves through the public debates that constantly take place in dynamic societies and which, in the Western world, have been, in recent times, much broadened and intensified by growing multiculturalism and pluralism.[32] Any goal of influencing or transforming the social consensus that legitimates or not the juridical enforcement of particular moral demands has to address its bases in the cultural sphere of society.[33]

There may be some role also, at least in some situations, for immediate recourse to civil law, used by political power as an instrument to provoke or cement a desired change in the general ethical judgment of a society on particular habits, attitudes, or actions.[34] However, this precocious involvement of the law makes sense only as a way to accelerate change in an already modifying consensus, and, ultimately, it has to be legitimated and sustained by a relatively quick widespread tacit accord with its results and goals. A civil law will not achieve much if it encounters immediate rejection by the great majority, and, under the democratic constraints, certainly it cannot actively subsist if its orientation continues to be sharply at odds with the prevalent direction of the cultural consensus of society. In addition to moral principle, prudential considerations of strategy and tactics are necessary when dealing with the pragmatic dimensions of the political process. Such limitations are even more restrictive in realms of life with a strong private character, often implicating directly a very small number of people, and involving deeply personal options of conscience—as are presently the most controversial issues of public morality advocated by the church.[35]

Public pressure urging the government to use coercive actions in protection of elements of a particular conception of public morality may be democratically legitimate (and politically effective) only if it is formulated (and perceived) in association with a campaign of cultural persuasion and subordinated to it.[36] The action at the political level may serve to sharpen the argument and to provide final orientation for what is primarily (in the order of time and in the order of ends) intended: to induce a generalized change of mentality to the point of bringing the social consensus to include those values within the morality component of public order and, thus, see fit that they be upheld by the coercive function of the state. Direct political petition cannot become an attempt to bypass the social consensus. It is not correct—and, in the long run, it is counterproductive to its own objectives—for a social group, whatever its present or past status in a pluralistic society, to resort to instrumental imposition of its views, taking advantage of privileged influence over political officials, when, by persuasive argument in the public debate, it is failing to gather support for those views in the broader society. The appeal to civil law may be one more means to win in the arena of the moral consensus in a culture; it cannot be a stratagem to overturn the losing of a cultural debate.

The church is one active participant in that cultural debate through which civil society continually strives to define the bases of its organized cohesion and unity of purposes. If it professes respect for the rightful autonomy of society to order itself through democratic processes, it cannot claim privileged ascendancy over the political power. Not the following of a sociological religious majority, the traditional weight in the cultural history of a country, or the evocation of a binding command from an extrinsic superior authority may justify circumventing those democratic processes of a secular society. A church with a strategy of insistent advocacy for the change of the law in matters of public morality, even when justified as the ultimate goal, has to ponder carefully whether in the concrete context it is really helping to promote greater support for the values of the true moral order in society. Or, whether its insistence instead has become counterproductive for the truly effective and realistically sustainable cultural transformation of the common consensus regarding those standards of public morality integral to the public order of society.

There are, obviously, many shortcomings inherent to a system in which fundamental choices about the ordering of social living and the structuring and pursuit of the common good are made through mechanisms of majority agreement and cultural consensus. To sanction it does not mean to accept that public morality is to be decided by majority vote, in the same way as declaring a personal right to religious freedom does not mean the acceptance that all religions or no religion at all are equally valid options. This is no endorsement of a morally relativistic, purely procedural democracy, skeptical about the possibility of any judgment of truth or falsity of each individual view. That view would elevate individual freedom to an absolute and could end up as a tyranny of the majority, with no solidarity for the excluded. This is the kind of totalitarian deviation of libertarian and individualistic notions of democracy that John Paul II denounces and tries to combat by invoking an ultimate place for truth.[37]

Endorsement of the rules of free democracy, in the line of the parameters of *Dignitatis Humanae,* means no giving up on truth or on the possibility of its being recognized in public debate. There is rather confidence that the democratic constraints of a social consensus can actually be, in the long run, the better allies of moral truth, for there is faith in the capacity of the truth to persuade by itself, whenever it is encountered in freedom and confronted in responsibility.

As with the regime of religious freedom for the evangelizing mission of the church, the trust in the power of the truth to transform the culture of a society from within is, in the long run, much more effective for the public mission of the church on behalf of the demands of an objective moral order than any short term instrumental enlisting of the power of the state. The answer to the shortcomings of the democratic culture ought not to be, then, to try to circumvent it, but rather to engage all in the promotion of greater freedom and openness in the search for the truth and the right.

Requirement of the Dignity of Free Persons. These limitations of church action dictated by a culture of entrenched secularity supporting liberal democratic political regimes are not just external impositions, to be reluctantly accepted by the church. They are, actually, intrinsic positive demands of church doctrine, spelled out in consequence of a deeper development of the social teaching of the church effected by the doctrine of *Dignitatis Humanae:* the recognition of the fundamental primacy of the freedom of the human person in the historical search for the truth.

Dignitatis Humanae put an entirely new emphasis on personal freedom as a necessary requirement of human dignity. The truly human way for people to arrive at the truth, it has been asserted by the declaration, is by their own free and responsible search; freedom is a necessary condition for the recognition and embracing of the truth. The mission of the church in the service of the truth was, thus, recentered and became, primarily, a commitment to promote the free development of responsible persons. These persons were enabled, through the help of dialogue and education of conscience, to arrive at the knowledge of the truth and to make a self-determined choice to embrace it because they were convinced by the power of the truth, not coerced by external authority.

What applies to the decision of the personal conscience regarding the act of faith, because it is a fundamental demand of human dignity, applies also to the formation of one's moral convictions. Therefore, the influencing of the social consensus by the public advocacy of the church, on one hand, does not have to renounce the claim that it is an advocacy for obedience to a universally binding absolute moral order. But, on the other hand, it has to respect also the equally fundamental principle of personal freedom. It is, thus, contrived to use means that further promote, and do not hinder or curtail, the responsible autonomy of persons inherent to their natural dignity.

The operative goal set by *Dignitatis Humanae* in the case of religious freedom was a free and responsible decision by every person on his or her religious option. Now, in the area of public morality, the goal set by the same parameters of truth and freedom consists of a culture that promotes a free and open environment in which persons and groups may fully pursue the truth, find themselves ever more engaged and fascinated by it, and, in the free interaction of their findings and responses, form their own consciences according to the truth encountered. Concurrently, that culture will shape a moral social consensus always evolving toward a more faithful historical representation of the moral law. When challenging or trying to sway the moral public consensus, the church can rely on the convincing power of a truth proposed through persuasion and reasonable argument, in full respect for personal freedom of conscience and not on the weight of authority, much less the help of the coercive power of the state. The church cannot try to impose obedience to moral law in society against generalized convictions of the people who form it.

The teaching of *Dignitatis Humanae* determines that, in the church's ministry to the consciences, truth be served inseparably from the keeping of personal freedom, for freedom is the necessary path to attaining the truth in full accordance with human dignity. It is this conjunction of the two that, as the declaration explicitly affirms, defines the personal right and duty to search freely for the truth, so that people, not just for matters of religious faith, may "form for themselves right and true moral judgments."[38] The whole magisterium of moral formation must respect these demands of human dignity.

Public advocacy by the church for coercive enforcement of moral rules through civil law, in the cases where it may be justified, has to give even greater consideration to these parameters, because of the sensitivity of pluralistic societies to claims of that kind. Such civil society can easily harden itself against any perceived attempt of imposition, and retaliate by closing itself a priori to any argument, even if persuasive, coming from the same proponents. And the change of the social consensus through persuasion in the cultural debate is the only means through which, in liberal democratic polities, the church may effectively achieve a greater harmony of civil law with the objective moral order.

The Different Bent of John Paul II. It is here, around the parameter freedom, that the interpretation and application of the doctrine of *Dignitatis Humanae* by John Paul II and the understanding of the wider implications of the declaration's doctrine that is being proposed here distance themselves more distinctly.

As the similarity of language and coincidence of emphases have made obvious, the pope's reading of the document, in what concerns the relationship between freedom and truth, follows the approach of a line of reconstruction of the doctrine of *Dignitatis Humanae* illustrated above by the work of André-Vincent. This interpretation tends to present freedom and truth in competition one against the other. A strong demarcation from the liberal approach to freedom is considered essential, because of the fear that any promotion of freedom in pluralism will actually end up reinforcing the inclination to indifferentism and relativism. So the two counteract that modern trend by an emphatic stressing of the duty toward absolute orders of truth.

A constant insistence on the priority of truth over freedom—especially in affirmations that personal freedom is ultimately grounded on the ontological connection of the person to the truth and, therefore, that freedom can only spring from the experience of the truth—identifies this line of theological interpretation of *Dignitatis Humanae* and appears often in the teachings of John Paul II on personal and social ethics. It stresses the theological point that the fullness of freedom as a human good is something to be attained in the living of the truth, but some of its formulations may leave a certain ambiguity about the relation between freedom and adherence to truth at the political/juridical level.[39]

This approach is in clear tension with the view of Murray and others inspired by him, that, invoking the support of the text of *Dignitatis Humanae,* defends the primacy of the principle of human freedom, a value to be respected always, even when it regards people in error and evil.

In terms of the framework of parameters asserted by *Dignitatis Humanae,* John Paul II favors, thus, a stressing of the parameter truth at some expense of the parameter freedom. The starting point of his teaching is always absolute objective truth, supported in revelation, and he keeps its unqualified primacy all the way. His perspective stays squarely within a classical view of the truth, suspicious of where some insights of the historical mentality may lead. Relativism is what he desires to avoid, and the way he sees to achieve that is by restating immutable, timeless moral norms, the absolute truth as exclusive basis of freedom. The counterpart of this precaution, however, is that this truth remains guarded from a mutually enriching encounter with the human experience of freedom in history, the way tried and proposed by *Dignitatis Humanae.*[40]

This fundamental attitude cannot but have important implications for the church's addressing of the challenges of the third moment in the area of church-society relationships. Molded by the preoccupation to reject anything that may look like a caving in to the dangers of relativism, the church, in its relationship with the world, has been turning itself to a direction different from the one

Murray saw opening before it by the embracing of the intellectual movement of historical consciousness manifest in *Dignitatis Humanae.*

The style of the recent official teaching on public morality, especially in the area of the ethics of life, and the kind of failed reception it has spurred in liberal democratic societies is a telling case of the kind of ambiguities created by the failure to keep the dialectical balance of the two equally fundamental principles of freedom and truth. In this perspective, basic bearings of the substantive progress effected by *Dignitatis Humanae* in the social doctrine of the church appear again under some confusion. The emphasis on the primacy of objective truth culminates in the recommendation of an expanded role for the state in the elevation of morality in society. There are echoes of paternalistic views of political power, especially in the pope's direct appeals to political officials to heed the voice of the church and enforce demands of the objective moral order upon society through legislation. Some of these traits may be reminiscent of ways of thinking and acting that were characteristic of the thesis/hypothesis approach to the deference due toward the truth in situations of pluralism.[41] They put some strain on the perception of full sincerity in the church's embracing of secularity and democracy and leave in the shadow the primacy of the principle of freedom, which are crucial developments brought about by *Dignitatis Humanae.* These developments, in fact, did no more than justify doctrinally what the long experience of the first moment had already unequivocally taught: In its relationships with modern societies, the church is more effective (in the long run, only!) when it resists the easy temptation of trying to pressure governments and increase appeals to arguments of authority, and opts, instead, for persuading people by dialoguing with their culture, denouncing its wrongs but also engaging its progresses.

For the case of religious faith, the declaration held together in harmony the two dimensions of the personal religious quest (the right to freedom and the duty toward the truth) through the demand that, in an exercise of the social and communicational nature of the human person, truth be sought by free inquiry with the help of dialogue and confrontation of experiences.[42] To achieve the same kind of harmony between unwavering advocacy for moral truth and continuous respect for the free evolvement of social consensus, the church, in its public role in society, has to strive for, and decisively contribute to, a public debate that is both fully respectful of the freedom of people and fully open to the truth. Such quality of public dialogue requires honest and exigent commitment both on part of the church and on the part of the prevailing cultural groups in civil society.

The lessons of the first moment of *Dignitatis Humanae* are very important for devising the kind of unique contribution the church has to give to bring about a more accomplished public dialogue. They both emphasize an indispensable carefulness in the interpretation of the position of others, and suggest ways to communicate more effectively the church's own positions. These directions constitute, in the text of *Dignitatis Humanae,* the third set of parameters, around the concept of free dialogue.

Conditions for a Genuine and Fruitful Encounter

An unwavering commitment to respect the general processes of formation of moral consensus in pluralism does not mean automatic settling for whatever a particular culture offers at any time as a common vision. Regard for social freedom does not have to imply resignation with any more or less free choice by society. Any resulting consensus is determined formally by the process of public debate, but even more decisively it is determined by the basic values prevalent in the current culture. The process itself can always be ameliorated in the direction of larger participation and fuller freedom of intervention for all different convictions and visions of human life. It is part of the public role of the church to work for that by voiced claim and practical example. But in order to achieve transformations of the moral social consensus, the church has to work more intensely on the fundamental level of mentalities, cultural values, views of the person, and conceptions of human life and destiny, which are the elements that feed substantially, and determine in great part, the consensus of public debate.

In the direct teaching of *Dignitatis Humanae,* respect for the immunity of the personal conscience did not imply distanced neutrality before any kind of individual decision, but was accompanied, instead, by active and challenging involvement of the church in the formation of consciences. Likewise, solicitous deference for the determination by social consensus of the elements of public morality to be included in the requirements of public order goes hand in hand, on the church's side, with earnest engagement of its public teaching function in the transformation of the basis of that consensus through cultural debate and education for fundamental human values.

This demands, first of all, that the conversation partners recognize the legitimacy and advantage of the participation of the official voice of the church in the public debate. In order for that to be secured, there is a perfectly justified place for denunciations of all arbitrary attempts to exclude religion from the public sphere, be it by the tendency to relegate all religious expression to the realm of the private, or by setting standards of neutrality for acceptable public discourse that are unduly discriminatory of religiously inspired arguments. John Paul II justifiably fights for this right to participate and for a richer quality of the cultural conversation when he decries the emptiness of purely procedural democracy and speaks against the marginalization of religious truth from public life.

Only if permanently subject to the critique of a free discussion in which all views can participate will the cultural consensus be open to transformation. It is very important, then, that the church, in what is within its power, call for and also help create a cultural environment of common responsibility and mutual openness with all other groups in society. This is a condition of possibility for a social moral consensus that is not, in the end, unduly biased because, on the basis of prejudice, it is being kept shielded from confrontation with truths that challenge its dominant defining powers.

There is no question about the appropriateness of such denunciations of undue restrictions on the social mission of the church. Such claims upon civil society to respect the freedom of the church in all its dimensions (including its public advocacy of personal and social moral values) are concurrent with the right to religious freedom concerning communities, understood not just as immunity but also as empowerment.[43] It is here that it is crucial to keep clear the distinction between secularity of the state (approved by the church) and secularism of society (resolutely opposed).[44] Still these are claims upon others, dealing with mostly extrinsic obstacles, and this book wants to focus primarily on the responsibilities of the church, on the ways in which it may, by its own discernment and actions, help or hinder the conditions for success of its public role in the formation of the moral consensus in a pluralistic society.

The direct teaching of *Dignitatis Humanae* recommends an intentional engagement of the church in the formation of consciences, at the same time fully respectful of the principle of freedom. Conditioned this way, its immediate goal is making sure that the truth proposed by the church compels itself upon people by its own power only. There is an equivalent requisite for the church's attempt to inspire the culture of democratic society. In order for a similar moral persuasion over people and the social consensus to be effective, the message of the church has to be in a position to confront genuinely, and also to be confronted by, the other competing cultural positions. For this ever to take place, however, there is a previous condition that needs to be fulfilled: The church needs, first of all, to establish and protect its credibility and pertinence before the other partners in dialogue, so its voice will have a chance to command attention and its proposals be carefully listened to.

The consideration of the process that, eventually, made possible *Dignitatis Humanae* continues to teach lessons about obtaining and keeping this trustworthiness and recognition of competency, lessons which can be ignored by the church today only at the price of falling again into the conundrums the first moment began to resolve.

Careful Distinctions. One of the lessons, discussed at the beginning of this chapter, is unceasingly stressed by Murray in his studies on the development of official Catholic doctrine on religious freedom: the need for the church to be careful in making distinctions and exercising discernment in its reaction to cultural trends or social practices opposed to the truth or harmful to human dignity. It should always resist the temptation of falling into easy dualistic judgments. The church's fault in the past was to rush into wholesale condemnations, including under the same negative look what were undoubtedly inadmissible forms or applications (but which may have been in good part provisional or circumstantial), and the deeper and further reaching underlying historical movements, social, political, or intellectual, which constituted positive developments at the service of genuine human aspirations. In the words of Murray, it consisted in not sufficiently making the "effort to discern the truth that always lies at the heart of error."[45] Then, in the name of a truth abstractly considered, the church stood there immovable in that intransigent opposition to the error more apparent, failing for a long time to respond to the unfolding of that greater truth underneath. The council, in contrast, has committed the church to a mode of public participation characterized by dialogue and persuasion; not regular confrontation, but habitual "mediation of understanding" between the church and the world.[46]

John Paul II systematically refers his condemnations of the moral decadence of contemporary societies to roots in the modern fascination with individual freedom. In doing that, he makes a double return to the problematic of the first moment of *Dignitatis Humanae*. Substantially, he focuses again on the central trend of modernity that originated the claims for religious liberty: the yearning of the human person for freedom. Methodologically, however, the tone of most of his pronouncements often tends to fall, once more, in the same pattern of insufficiently distinguishing deviations of a term from the value of the vital movement.

The pope rightfully rejects the evil consequences of distorted conceptions and bad uses of freedom, the individualism and relativism that ultimately issue the culture of death.[47] In all his condemnations of libertarian or relativistic cultural trends, however, he falls often into general judgments in which everything is negative about the contemporary culture of freedom and seemingly without possibility of reparation. He makes no apparent effort to identify in that culture already hopeful traits that may still be growing, impelled by that truth underneath. Moreover, he does not hesitate to draw from this philosophy practical consequences that further question the prerogatives of freedom, specifically, in his calls for a greater subjection of civil law to the demands of the moral law in society. Within the church, but with equally great repercussions outside, this same willfulness shows in the conspicuous rebuke of theological dissent very strictly defined, typical of this papacy, particularly, again, in moral theology.

Many of these ideas, attitudes, and actions create too much tension between the rhetoric of prophetic denunciation and the purpose of engagement in dialogue and moral persuasion. They cannot help the receptivity to the voice of the church in a culture to which respect for personal freedom has become almost an absolute—to the point of grave distortions and excesses, certainly, but also with a level of inculcation and sense of appropriateness to what it means to be human that cannot be radically put into question. This aspiration for freedom is genuine and legitimate. It has to be unequivocally supported as a minimum token to obtain basic trust by anyone who hopes to engage the debate shaping the moral consensus of contemporary societies. It may be possible to find receptivity to a critique of erroneous expressions of freedom if it is accompanied by respect and a commitment to acknowledge the deeper aspirations for freedom. If it sees that its essential values are honored and its motivations given the benefit of the doubt, a liberal culture may still be persuaded to consider the limitations of its answers. It will never, however, accept the rejection of its fundamental quest. The church has to reassure its partners in dialogue that it takes their yearnings very seriously, first, and, then, considerately suggest that, through honest and open interchange, it is possible to find better answers for them than the ones they themselves have so far developed.

The framework of parameters set by *Dignitatis Humanae,* by upholding the principle of freedom at the same fundamental level of the obligation to the truth, was successful in striking this balance, as proven by its reception from the secular world. It is less certain that the teaching of John Paul II, especially in matters of public morality, fulfills these conditions of credibility and receptiveness to engage contemporary pluralistic cultures successfully. Counteracting the undeniable crisis of conceptual distortions and bad uses of freedom that do not leave space for consideration of the truth does not necessitate a scaling back of the value freedom. Reaffirmation of the value truth can be done without conditioning the prerogatives of freedom fundamentally, much less practically, to the allegiance to the truth. Rather, keeping the greatest regard for freedom as an inalienable principle of human dignity, the crisis demands the promotion of a more and better freedom, which, through energetic striving for the cultural conditions for an increased exchange and discussion, will be more fully open to the truth. This is the way *Dignitatis Humanae* prescribed for bringing people to the true faith, and, expanding the implications of the same principles, it is also the direction proposed for the church's work of persuasion of individual consciences and social consensus of free societies in matters of public morality and, more broadly, in all collaborative promotion of the common good.

Obstacles to Responsive Goodwill. A second lesson of the history of *Dignitatis Humanae* has to do with a correct evaluation of the lasting effects in secular society of past attitudes of the church. These too need to be carefully considered when it is a question of safeguarding good will for the participation of the church in the public discussion. While, in terms of the two historical contexts that defined the first moment of *Dignitatis Humanae* described in chapter 1, the careful attention to distinctions in philosophies and historical movements may be more important today in the American context, this notice is particularly relevant for the social and political contexts of Latin Europe.

A successful promotion, in liberal societies, of the moral values championed by the church demands a style of social intervention that deliberately avoids any hint of arrogance, and relies only on nonoverbearing long-term influence over the social consensus through persuasive dialogue. An unambiguous option for this self-imposed restraint in its public mission is much easier to make in a pluralist context in which the church finds itself in manifest minority. Yet, the legacy of *Dignitatis Humanae* demands the same attitude even in places of overwhelming Catholic majority.

There are two ways in which the declaration does so. First, as a substantive requirement of its doctrine, because its principles assert that, not as a matter of concrete circumstantial possibility (as in the thesis/hypothesis approach) but rather as a basic requirement of human dignity, people ought to be allowed (as well as encouraged) to come to the realization of the truth and decide it for themselves, by the exercise of their responsibility in full freedom, "assisted by teaching and instruction, and by exchange and discussion."[48] Therefore, even where and when church authority could, in a particular context, sidestepping the cultural debate, find assistance for direct political imposition of its views, the church should not try to do so. If the thesis/hypothesis kind of strategy were to be ruled out in religious matters, it should not continue to be operative in issues regarding the social consensus on public morality, since the fundamental principles for the education of consciences that justified the change in the former apply also to the latter.

This first reason in itself suffices. But there is still a concurrent one, from a different nature, that reinforces the constraint upon the church. The second reason is historical and circumstantial and concerns primarily the social political context of the countries of Latin Europe. It basically cautions that the sequels of suspicion and ill will formed by the long animosity, which *Dignitatis Humanae* somewhat finalized, between the church and the historical movement toward secularity still play an important role in people's reception of public interventions by the church's hierarchy. Hence, the church should be especially careful not to discredit its voice by misguided assumptions or indiscreet demeanor.

Although in these societies Catholicism has not lost the position of religious reference for the overwhelming majority and the Catholic Church continues to be the only significant religious institution, the context is today one of considerable cultural pluralism, with deep inroads of secularism, indifferentism, and individualistic privatization of faith beliefs. Civil society has attained a great degree of autonomy and there is a public opinion that prides itself on its independence from the church, with even a bit of resentment against it. Church authorities should not presume, therefore, that they automatically represent the general consensus of society and are, thus, justified to bring the weight of their influence to bear down directly on state authorities in advocacy for the positions they see as right. Moreover, in the area of morals, the church cannot ignore the growing reception gap between the teaching of the hierarchy and the practice of the faithful, even among the most committed ones. Neither can the church hierarchy assume that it has any kind of privileged political mandate, nor think that, on issues of public policy and morality, it does not need to participate in the constantly evolving formation of the cultural social consensus and promote its goals through that transformation. Any other way may well be counterproductive, for traditionally and still culturally, Catholic societies are those more suspicious of undue interference of the church in the political process.[49]

The ability of the church to influence a particular social consensus in favor of a public morality more in accordance with the moral law depends on the generalized recognition and embracing by people of the values of the Catholic tradition. In the case of these nations, such values have been embedded in their characteristically Christian culture and have shaped their imaginations through the centuries in societies religiously homogeneous and reverent to the moral leadership of the church. In modern times, however, there was a split between these civil societies and the church institutional by reason of a very conflictive process of secularization and of its sequels. Since then, too, on the side of the church, the highest magisterium has assumed a more centralized and peremptory role in the formulation and regulation of moral norms for the life of the faithful, and the public voice of the church has often been nonconciliatory in its attacks on the increasing cultural defiance of its moral orientations by social patterns of thought and behavior.

Nowadays, therefore, in this particular historical context, it is still not just the contents, the values in themselves—however connatural and compelling they may still be deep inside one's world view—that determine the reception of the moral message promoted by the church. The style and credibility of the deliverer, its perceived intentions and motivations, the way it awakens or appeases fears and prejudices, are equally important. These cultures may be fundamentally more open than others to the great goals of church moral teaching, but they are also much more sensitive to any hint of attempted control by church authorities. They are more jealous of the autonomy of civil society, because, for them, secularity was gained after a long struggle of emancipation against the church. Where it may be easier to find understanding for the message, it is also where receptivity can more readily be jeopardized by the wrong style of intervention.

Here, the way the goals and means of the new evangelization being promoted by John Paul II end up being perceived in these societies is crucial for the success of his undertaking. He calls the church to a new boldness, to strengthen its witness and renew its presence in society. But aspects of his rhetoric and examples in his teaching, especially on the theology of freedom and on public morality, leave doubt about the fundamental orientation of the re-Christianization he calls for. Will the orientation be a new culture more opened to Christian values, to be shaped by an increased commitment of the church to dialogue with the present culture, as he sometimes says? Or, may his call add force to the efforts of those who attempt to recover an old culture, closer to many values of a premodern social order? May the form of his strong opposition to secularism actually encourage attempts to reverse some of the vectors of a legitimate secularization, under the cover of a denunciation of what is wrongful in secularism?

All through his involvement with *Dignitatis Humanae* (in the process of redaction and, later, in the interpretation and application of its doctrine), the record of John Paul II shows less attention to the characteristic issues and lessons of the crystallization and resolution of the problems of the first moment of *Dignitatis Humanae*. Now, in the third moment, when he is engaging primarily the same societies as in the first moment, his little sensitivity to the historical particularities of church-society relationships in these contexts may be causing him to overlook important aspects that, in reality, hinder the receptivity to his challenges and appeals. In conclusion, falling back on less successful past approaches and overlooking apparently marginal but important aspects may diminish considerably the possibility of real success for the essential goals John Paul II is pursuing with his responses to the moral challenges of contemporary pluralistic societies.

In addition to a careful consideration of the positions and perceptions of the church's secular counterparts, a fruitful encounter in dialogue demands also a particular attention to the way the church situates itself within the larger society and to the type of language in which it presents its own positions. The fourth set of parameters offered by *Dignitatis Humanae,* particularly the valuing of human history as an important resource for the development of moral reasoning, will serve, in the third moment, to guide the church in the search for a truly effective public discourse.

THE DISCOURSE OF A PUBLIC CHURCH

Dignitatis Humanae, in the process of its elaboration and in the final presentation of its doctrine, constituted itself a seminal example for the development of official church teaching done in conversation with ideas and institutions that had evolved separately in the secular world. The text explicitly acknowledges that it was the external shock of a new human consciousness that led the church into a deeper exploration and better understanding of the treasures of revelation and tradition. There it found insights that affirmed and responded to the truth of those aspirations so lively in the world. Accepting the need to start from the concrete historical human experience and opening itself to be guided by the yearnings of people, the council was not afraid to recognize that, in the matter of the human right to religious freedom, clearly the church had been the learning partner in its dialogue with the modern world.

Church-Type Tradition. A firm resolve to involve itself appropriately in the affairs of human history at all levels, and a commitment to maintain continued conversation with secular culture have always been typical of Catholic tradition. These qualities have helped the church define for itself the image of its own identity and role in the world, and have also conditioned the kind of language and the bases of argument traditionally used in the church's social teaching.

The Roman Catholic Church's institutional self-understanding could not be further from that of a group set apart from the world and concerned primarily with preserving itself untouched by the messy concrete reality, especially political issues. Instead, it considers it central to its mission to show a permanent solicitude for all persons, not just Christians, and for the global human community. This leads the church official to assume responsibility for helping to shape the order of social life, including public policy. In this too, it tries to transform society as a whole according to the guidance of gospel values. The church feels itself called to take positions in concrete situations and it is able to live confidently with even certain degrees of ambiguity, if necessary. What is important is that it will always reach out to others and engage them at a level deep enough to make dialogue and argument avenues of persuasion for the truth and the advancement of the common good.

Consequently, the Catholic Church has traditionally shown a constant preoccupation with finding common languages, so that real communication may take place. It has always looked to adjust its message to the cultures of the addressees, without, however, capitulating to those cultures or ever surrendering a critical prophetic stance. J. Bryan Hehir summarizes this typical Catholic historical pattern of relationship with the world under two themes: "a conception of ecclesial responsibility" and "a conviction about the possibilities of public moral discourse."[50] These defining traits are part of what characterizes the Catholic Church as the best representative of the ecclesiological type "church," and, at the same time, the most opposed to the model "sect," in the classical typology of Ernst Troeltsch.[51] Today, other qualifiers that are also used to refer to this dimension of active engagement in the public life of societies, primarily but not exclusively at the institutional, hierarchical level, call the Roman Catholic Church an activist or public church.[52]

In the past, this aspiration to exercise influence upon the secular realm in the concrete of history materialized, in good part, under the form of a close involvement of church authorities with political power. The move to secularity, which culminated with *Dignitatis Humanae,* transferred the search for this consequential encounter to the camp of public debate in democratic cultures. There, the church determines itself to stay locked with civil and political society in a dialectic of difference and commonality, argument and agreement, cooperation and challenge, for the betterment of this world and of the lives of every human person here and now.

Dignitatis Humanae did not just finish relocating this traditional interaction into a different level; it also pulled the church into a qualitatively new realization of this dialogue and a greater commitment to it. The declaration in itself became an emblematic sign that this process is not just about adapting and tailoring the unchanging message of the church to the different audiences and times. It proved, rather, that the influencing is truly mutual; it functions in the other direction too. Open dialogue is a two way road, not just for communication but also for other-induced change in one's views. With *Dignitatis Humanae,* an official position of the church was radically changed under the decisive influence of an advance previously achieved outside of it. Probably as never before, the obliging statement that, when engaged in dialogue, the church is open to learn from the world was backed, on its own side, by the result of a manifest categorical turn in its teaching and practice, a turn presented by the church itself, moreover, as an induced deeper rediscovery of the demands of its own tradition.

Some saw in the new method of moral reasoning that made this development of doctrine possible, and the way the arguments to justify it were crafted, the setting of a new epistemological direction for the church's official teaching. It would have been an authentic change of paradigm, in which the new centrality given to human experience expressed reconciliation with the cultural matrix of modernity. The importance of these mutations and the visibility they obtained augmented significantly the trustworthiness of the church among its secular counterparts and opened hopes for a great step forward in the encounter between the traditional public impulse of the Catholic Church and the modern world, in the line of what, as was recalled at the beginning of this chapter, John Courtney Murray envisaged.

Equivocal Inflections. The optimistic expectation, perhaps exaggerated and a bit naïve, that now everything would be easy and all the obstacles were out of the way, however, soon abated. Secularized society continued to need a strongly critical examination and confrontation, and, in the church, the reflux of the conciliar progressive tour de force did not take long to make itself noticed.

Monsignor Wojtyla, in his collaboration in the redaction of *Gaudium et Spes,* had sided with those who, at the council, raised some reservations about what they saw as an excessive idealization of the world; he himself called for a greater sense of realism. As pope, he has continued to uphold the public role of the church and its legitimacy to express opinion and exercise influence in social and political issues. Under his leadership, the public involvement of the Catholic Church in the affairs of the world, political, social, and economic, has actually increased in visibility and scope of intervention. John Paul II has tried to further affirm the voice of the church and reinforce its influential weight in every public arena. He is, thus, strongly committed to an ideal of church that continues to be unambiguously a public church.

In the particular area of advocacy for standards of public morality in defense of life, however, his strategic preference has been uncompromising denunciation and confrontation in spite of his habitual protestations of interest in fully open dialogue. His perception of the evils caused by secularism, together with a pessimistic anthropology, have often led to statements of negative judgment on the modern world and of a certain suspicion of the capacities of human reason. He seems to have very little expectation that the church may actually learn anything from this culture. Moreover, especially in *Evangelium Vitae,* John Paul II so emphasizes the obstacles to the recognition of moral truth in society created by maleficent liberal freedoms that he depreciates the possibilities of regeneration through dialogue. Instead, he is convinced that *only* from Christ, through the church, can the present world regain direction. His dominant rhetoric conveys an image of the church more of the type "Christ against culture," than "Christ transforming culture."[53] The persistent upholding of the truth is done in a tone of someone convinced of having the truth, the whole truth, accessible in unequivocal propositions. The church, then, teaches that truth magisterially; it does not embark on any shared process of seeking it. It is ready to give answers, but feels no desire to struggle with the questions together with others. On these topics, there is less effort to engage the social consensus in a genuine way than there is merely to denounce it and try to replace it with a radical alternative—the culture of life for the culture of death.

This style of markedly countercultural Catholicism, however, does not avoid some ambiguities of language and argument that weaken the effectiveness of the role of the church as public church. We have seen how John Paul II prefers the use of biblical and theological language in his social teaching. In reaction to previous excesses of a rationally dry, syllogistic moral reasoning based on a propositional understanding of objective natural law, this attempt responds to the enrichment called for by Vatican II,[54] and tried out, in the area of social ethics, by *Gaudium et Spes*. This pope has intensified this methodological orientation.[55]

The better integration of biblical symbols and theological themes with the tradition of philosophical reasoning and natural law in the church's moral teaching is a worthy goal, in as much as it enriches the life of the church and helps to bring more depth and broader, less restricted, participation to the public conversation. It cannot, however, end up being, or at least be perceived as being, an easy way to resort to arguments of authority or to shift the dialogue onto bases not commonly shared. Appeal to revelation in matters of concrete moral norms cannot just be a too easy way to trump the rational argument at the philosophical and theological level.

Often, when John Paul II resorts to the same biblical language and to a style of reasoning distinctly theological, based on the authority of revelation, it seems that he intends primarily to counteract moral theologies that he sees as too accommodating of the contemporary culture. These theologies may be flirting with the errors of historicism and individualistic subjectivism when they stress historical consciousness in the understanding of absolute moral norms, and the roles of experience and personal conscience in moral decision. In response he uses Scripture as an invocation of revealed moral commandments that he presents as objective, unexceptionable, absolute moral norms.[56] Even when speaking of an objective moral order and of a natural law he frequently roots these concepts in biblical texts.[57]

There is a widespread perception that all this is part of his attempt to shape a monolithic church. The confessional language, therefore, is also directed to keep the individual conscience of the faithful shielded from pernicious influences of the culture, and to reinforce the cohesion of the church, which is single-minded in its determination to fight secularism and moral relativism. John Paul II has reinforced in his governance of the church the control by centralized authority in order to promote a unified theology and strict conformity with official moral teaching. He calls all the faithful to witness courageously to values that are at odds with the popular majority. The literal restatement of the biblical commandments is an attempt to proclaim the pure moral truth without subterfuge.

This closing of ranks may impart an appearance of resilience and strength. It galvanizes the most faithful believers, but it also further isolates the church and cuts bridges necessary for its traditional public role. Nowadays, everything that is said and done by the church officials, especially at the highest level of the institutional hierarchy, even when directed only to the inside of the church, is scrutinized by the secular media and influences its image. (It is here that the deficiency in the internal life of the church of practices so honored in liberal societies, and also strongly endorsed in the church's social teaching—like democratic processes of government, respect for personal autonomy and freedom, open due process to deal with dissent—hurt its external credibility.)

According to the balance of the set of parameters of *Dignitatis Humanae,* the church must effectively present its truth, not compromised or watered down, but it has to present it in full commitment to dialogue and promotion of freedom. The sustained growth of a public dialogue realistically capable of transforming the moral consensus of democratic societies sets conditions for the kind of language the church may use with effectiveness in its public role. Because the goal is that all may "form for themselves right and true moral judgments,"[58] its offering of the truth must engage, both at the personal and social levels, the intelligence and the moral discernment about one's own experience.

It is important that the church present its own views in all their specificity. But when the official church becomes too sectarian in tone or its public speech excessively theological there is danger of losing relevance. John Paul II has been criticized for using biblical language and theological reasoning even when addressing society beyond the church. This criticism, especially when dealing with specific contents of civil law, makes his advocacy vulnerable to the accusation that he attempts to impose Catholic views upon the whole society.[59]

For the articulation between the common language of reason and experience and the confessional language of revelation and biblical symbols, *Dignitatis Humanae* offers less than an accomplished example. The philosophical argument and its corroboration by Scripture are more superposed than harmonized.[60] Nevertheless, it made a clear case that openness to insights of secular culture inspired a better appropriation of the church's own tradition, and the use of common discourse and method of reasoning helped the receptivity for its message in the world.

Openness to the culture of the times with a certain degree of interpenetrating influence has always been important for the church. It profited from it in the clarification of its Christology, at the time of the great ecumenical councils, and again for the systematization of its theology with the *summae* of the late Middle Ages. The existence of moral theology was made possible by the integration of the natural-law tradition and all its development owes greatly to the use of philosophical reasoning. More recently, the incorporation of historical and literary critical methods opened an extraordinary development in the understanding of Scripture. And, finally, now with no need for further explanation, there is the case of *Dignitatis Humanae.* There is no reason to think that the church will not continue to learn from this encounter. Such belief is implied by the faith requirement of taking seriously the Incarnation and the continued creative presence of the Spirit of God in the evolving world. God speaks through human history, not just in human history; God speaks not just to history through the church, but also to the church through human experience. This faith-filled conviction demands the acceptance of the fact, with all its consequences, that the church, as a witness to incarnate truth, although with a particular custody of the truth, is a human institution yet, and, as human, still permanently journeying in search of the truth.

In Freedom, through Dialogue, Seeking Truth

The present great challenge for the public mission of the Catholic Church in liberal pluralistic societies is mounted by increasing pluralism and cultural relativism. Within these contexts, and in some aspects over against them, the church has to continue its mission of giving witness to revealed truth and promoting respect for the dignity of every human person in every circumstance. Disagreement has taken place, most visibly, in the area of the rules of public morality for the protection of human life. The articulation, theoretical and practical, at the personal and social levels, of freedom and truth is at the center of the quandaries. Freedom cannot be, of course, the absolute that makes any talk about truth naïve, obsolete, or oppressive—as those in the more libertarian band of liberal society believe. Freedom does not have to be, either, an enemy or a threat to the truth—as many think today in a conservative revisionist approach, which is strong within the church, especially among the hierarchy.

Freedom is an inalienable value and fundamental principle in the process of formation of individual consciences and of the social consensus. It is axiomatic for the liberal bases of the pluralistic democratic social order. And, likewise, it is demanded by the Christian view of an autonomous and responsible natural condition of the human person. But it is also an essential, indispensable means to seek and attain the truth, and, without negating its own ultimate fulfillment, it cannot dispense with permanent and complete openness toward the truth. Promotion of the truth, therefore, has to go hand in hand with preservation of the greatest freedom, inasmuch as this is an inalienable requirement of the dignity of the human person.

After a long struggle with modern liberal philosophies and political practices, *Dignitatis Humanae* set a balance of parameters for the action of the church, in which the church's mandate of service to the truth was harmonized with equal esteem for the modern zeal for freedom. The framework established for the case of religious freedom prescribes also a direction for the wider realm of the relationship of the church with society, particularly for its role of public advocacy for the values of an objective moral order. Central to this harmonious cooperation of freedom and truth is the constitution, careful keeping, and constant betterment of a common place of encounter, an arena of full dialogue and vibrant debate about personal options and the social consensus, in which the truth may permanently be proposed, confronted by all, and allowed to triumph on its persuasive power alone.

The responsibility of the church for the quality of this intercommunication has to be exercised at different levels. First, the church must show a commitment to strive for the conditions that make that insightful mutual interchange and truly consequential encounter possible. This implies supporting and promoting all institutions of public dialogue, leading by the example of sincere and open participation, and, if necessary, denouncing prejudice, arbitrary discrimination, and any totalitarian tendencies. Second, something no one else can do, the church must propose there, as clearly and accessibly as possible, the truth it stewards, offering to everyone, through patient persuasion, the opportunity for a free and responsible confrontation with it. And, third, it ought to do that in a way that does not threaten freedom, but rather elevates it, that does not fear truth's possible rejection, but accepts the possibility of a first rejection of truth itself by others. To sustain this attitude, the church needs to keep its eyes on the long term and constantly rekindle its unfailing faith in the ultimate and lasting convincing power of the truth it serves, as well as in the strength of the interior call in every person to seek the truth and surrender to it. With the fortitude given by this hope, it will be able to live with failures without anxiety, and, above all, to resist the temptation of all times: to resort to other means that promise more immediate apparent success.

John Paul II has revisited the doctrine of *Dignitatis Humanae* often. His personal history, theologies he has adopted, and circumstances he has had to face as pope, have moved him to a particular appropriation of main elements of the declaration's teaching, and a very personal and sustained development of them. John Paul II has distinguished himself as a staunch accuser of the contemporary neglect of the truth. He articulates with effectiveness the sense of uneasiness with the lack of stable referents and of frustration with the nihilism and social fragmentation caused by libertarian notions of freedom, which affect the lives of persons and communities. It has been in this role that he has made greater use of those themes directly and indirectly connected to *Dignitatis Humanae*. However, it may be questioned whether the ways he has undertaken to counteract those evils have always been the most apt. The overall approach he has favored has moved the church in a direction different from the one pointed by the wider implications of the doctrine of the declaration for church-society relationships as this can be systematized in a balanced framework of principles around four topics: equal affirmations of truth and freedom; an option for dialogue; and the valuing of human experience in concrete history. Some of his most extreme positions do not show sufficient appreciation for the values of freedom and dialogue so ingrained in the contemporary culture of Western liberal democratic societies. Instead, they tend to side with groups whose views risk putting the church back on a path of rejection and separation from the movement of history similar to the one that led to the dead end from which *Dignitatis Humanae* finally finished extricating Roman Catholicism.

In order to attain a counterbalanced response to the contemporary problematic of the relationship between church and society, the word to use to talk to a society seduced by relativism is, certainly, truth. The church, and especially the papacy, has been saying it loud and clear. The teaching church, however, in order not to ignore the lessons of the first moment in its zeal for truth, needs to be told, with equal force, another—freedom. *Dignitatis Humanae* charted a framework articulating these two principles in a mutually advantageous way. It worked for the issue of religious freedom, and it was expected to help produce even more considerable results in other areas of the wider relationship of the church with the world. Not everything unfolded that smoothly. The same basic problem is again haunting the church, but the power and promise of the doctrine still stand; that is why there is now the opportunity and the need for a third moment of *Dignitatis Humanae*.

The practical ultimate goal aimed at by this revisiting of the declaration was the attaining of increased credibility and effectiveness for the mission of the church in contemporary society, so that the riches of its message may be acknowledged and their good effects on the concrete lives of people blossom and expand. The preoccupation that has guided this book, therefore, has been to alert the church not to let itself be dominated by only too human individual and institutional insecurities and to invite it to dedicate itself with renewed hope and trust to its mission in the world and to the world. It is a call to the church, that it may see itself evermore as a servant, always attentive to the movements of history in which surface the deepest yearnings of humanity, and always striving to let itself be an ever more apt instrument of God's spirit, who is patiently steering the human community, persons and societies, to their final end—Truth.

NOTES

In citing papal encyclicals and conciliar documents in the notes, short titles have been used. Bibliographic information for the documents listed below can be found in the references under the following entries.

Dignitatis Humanae	Vatican II 1990
Evangelium Vitae	John Paul II 1995, March 25
Veritatis Splendor	John Paul II 1993, August 6

1. Murray 1966d, 576.
2. Murray 1994b, 190.
3. Murray 1966f, 592.
4. Murray 1994b, 192.
5. This is how Murray describes, in what regards the doctrine of the state, the term of the progress reached in *Dignitatis Humanae:* "The sacrality of society and state is now transcended as archaistic. Government is not *defensor fidei.* Its duty and rights do not extend to what had been long called *cura religionis,* a direct care of religion itself and of the unity of the Church within Christendom or the nation-state. The function of government is secular: that is, it is confined to a care of the free exercise of religion within society—a care therefore of the freedom of the Church and of the freedom of the religious person in religious affairs." Ibid., 192.
6. Ibid., 193.
7. Murray 1966c, 673.
8. Ibid., 673–74.
9. Murray 1966a, 687, n. 21.
10. Murray 1994b, 194: "[T]he statute of religious freedom as a civil right is, in reality, a self-denying ordinance on the part of the government. . . . On the other hand, the ratification of the Declaration by Vatican Council II is, with equal clarity, a self-denying ordinance on the part of the Church. To put the matter simply and in historical perspective, the Church finally renounces, in principle, its long-cherished historical right to *auxilium brachii saecularis.* . . . The secular arm is simply secular, inept for the furtherance of the proper purposes of the People of God. More exactly, the Church has no secular arm. In ratifying the principle of religious freedom, the Church accepts the full burden of the freedom which is the single claim she is entitled to make on the secular world."

11. Murray 1965c, 43.
12. Murray 1966c, 673–74.
13. Murray 1966f, 592.
14. Murray 1994b, 194
15. Ibid.
16. Ibid., 195.
17. Ibid.
18. See Ibid., 196–99.
19. Murray 1967b, 322.
20. See Murray 1966f, passim.
21. See Komonchak 1994, 89.
22. The distinction is made by Dulles 1998, 8–10. He points out the following traits of this cultural secularization: Religion has become a private matter for individual choice; it was marginalized into a corner of life, excluded from the other spheres; each person adheres selectively to his or her own religious heritage; the role of authority is greatly diminished and actively questioned.
23. See Hollenbach 1987, 119–21.
24. As it has been the focus of this work, what will be said in this final part about the "church" will have primarily in view the role of the hierarchical structures of the Roman Catholic Church, especially the papacy. Much of it, though, could be applied also to local hierarchies, and in general to all those who, from a position of authority in the church, speak to society. This restriction to the action of the official hierarchy does not intend to mean that the church is to be reduced to them alone. Other voices and activities (e.g., theologians, religious groups lay or vowed, Catholic media, Catholic universities, parishes, and individual faithful) represent the church and are also part of the interaction of the church with civil society. However, the questions raised by the public role of the hierarchy are quite specific and the only ones dealt with here. For economy of language, once again, "church" will be used to refer to this specific role of a particular element of the whole body properly called church.
25. See, for the articulation of the concepts in this paragraph, Hehir 1992, 348–49.
26. See, for an application concerning Cardinal Bernardin's proposal of a consistent ethic of life, Hehir 1988, 227: "[R]egarding the role of civil law in a pluralistic society, the Consistent Ethic should be argued in terms of the concept of public order found in the *Declaration on Religious Liberty* of Vatican II. The public order criterion assumes that the state has positive moral responsibilities, but it sets limits to the use of the coercive power of the state through civil law. The limit is set by the requirement that an issue must be shown to affect directly the core values of public order (i.e., public peace, defense of rights and public morality) before an appeal can be made to invoke the prohibitions or prescriptions of civil law. The use of the public order criterion is first found in Catholic teaching in Vatican II; the previous guide for civil law had been the more expansive concept that the state and the law should be invoked to protect the common good."

27. Aquinas 1981, I–II, q.96, a.2. For a summary of Aquinas's position in the context of a critique of *Evangelium Vitae,* see Kaveny 1997, 141–46.

28. This is the summary, given by Hehir 1992, 350, expands the traditional argument: "The moral law governs the entire order of human conduct, personal and social; it extends even to motivations and interior acts. Law, on the other hand, looks only to the public order of human society; it touches only external acts, and regards only values that are formally social. For this reason the scope of law is limited. . . . Law seeks to establish and maintain only that minimum of actualized morality that is necessary for the healthy functioning of the social order. . . . Therefore the law, mindful of its nature, is required to be tolerant of many evils that morality condemns. A moral condemnation regards only the evil itself, in itself. A legal ban on an evil must consider what St. Thomas calls its own 'possibility.' That is, will the ban be obeyed, at least by the generality? Is it enforceable against the disobedient? Is it prudent to undertake the enforcement of this or that ban, in view of the possibility of harmful effects in other areas of social life? Is the instrumentality of coercive law a good means for the eradication of this or that social vice? And, since a means is not a good means if it fails to work in most cases, what are the lessons of experience in the matter? What is the prudent view of results—the long view or the short view?"

29. Hehir 1989, 210–211.

30. Hehir 1986c, 65.

31. For a systematic exploration of the effects of *Dignitatis Humanae* for church-state and church-society relationships, see Hehir 1986a, 54–74.

32. Murray used this concept of social consensus to designate a convergence of moral direction, which must be created and continually reshaped by argument in order to make it possible for pluralistic societies to find a common basis for the practical structuring of civil public life. See Murray 1960, especially the "Introduction: The Civilization of the Pluralist Society," 5–24. For a more recent exposition of the fundamental features of Murray's concept and of how the complexity of social pluralism has greatly increased since the situation Murray described and addressed, see Hehir 1989, 207–09.

33. I use "social consensus" and similar formulations, not as normative but, rather, as a descriptive concept, as what, in fact, characterizes the views of the majority and directs public opinion in one particular society at a particular time. Hopefully, it will be shaped by the truth (that is what the church in its public role strives for), but even when it is not, even when it is against natural law or the teaching of the church it is still a consensus, a common agreement, a cultural lasting trend or generally shared point of view, in society, which, ultimately, determines the democratic outcome of concrete public choices, electoral or not.

34. Here, different understandings of the relationship between law and culture will yield different preferences. The open question, as formulated by Hollenbach 1997, 42, is: "[D]oes culture shape law, or does law shape culture? It is doubtless true that the relation between culture and law is a two-way street; the values embedded in the *mentalité* of a people will set the direction and the limits for what they think law can accomplish. At the same time, the juridical norms that are operative in a

society play an important role in educating its people about what that society regards as valuable." Practical strategies depend on which direction of influence is stressed. "In the former, law expresses the will of the people; there can be no legitimate legislation that does not reflect some significant degree of consensus on the values held by the people. In the latter view, law has an educative power. It can take the lead in forming the values of the culture and the people." In what regards the preferred strategy to challenge the skepticism and moral relativism denounced by John Paul II in *Evangelium Vitae,* Hollenbach chooses against the encyclical: "My own judgment on this question is that the appeal to law . . . must generally follow the cultural consensus rather than lead or form it. . . . The route of education and persuasion is more likely to improve the moral quality of our culture than is a premature reach for law, which remains coercive even when it intends to be educative" (ibid., 43–44).

35. See Quinn 1997, 151.

36. See Whitmore 1994, 19–20.

37. See, for the characterization and consequences of this libertarian/liberal conception of democracy and individual rights, and for the way John Paul II's call for truth responds to it, Hollenbach 1997, 37–41.

38. *Dignitatis Humanae,* no. 3.

39. See Hollenbach 1997, 42–43.

40. See Hollenbach 1996b, 61–65, 70–73.

41. Griffin 1997, 171, in very strong language not sufficiently nuanced, perhaps, describes the pope's call for the legal banning of abortion as an equivalent to the rejection of religious freedom by the church before Vatican II: "In the years before the Second Vatican Council, Roman pontiffs asked American Catholics to oppose their First Amendment because Catholicism, as the one true religion, was entitled to establishment. In *Evangelium Vitae,* the Polish pontiff asks American Catholics to oppose the constitutional protection of abortion because Catholicism, as the one true morality, is entitled to legal enforcement." Above, on the same page, she describes the position of the pope on the role of civil law regarding abortion as one of "moral error has no rights."

42. See the second paragraph of number 3 of *Dignitatis Humanae:* "Truth, however, is to be sought in a manner befitting the dignity and the social nature of the human person, namely by free inquiry assisted by teaching and instruction, and by exchange and discussion in which people explain to each other the truth as they have discovered it or as they see it, so as to assist each other in their search."

43. See, for this tension between immunity and empowerment for religiously motivated intervention in society in the understanding of the right to religious freedom, Hollenbach 1996a, 129–48, and Whitmore 1993, 149–74.

44. See Hehir 1989, 206. What he says of the First Amendment applies equally to the doctrine on religious freedom: "Although the First Amendment assures the secular character of the state, a secular state is not synonymous with a secularist society that would seek to exclude, in principle, religious insight, values, and activity in public

life." See also Hehir 1986c, 69: "Accepting the separation of church and state should not be understood to mean accepting the separation of the church from society."

45. Murray 1967b, 322.
46. Hollenbach 1987, 124.
47. Even critics of other aspects of his magisterium do not question the pertinence of this undertaking. See, commenting on *Veritatis Splendor,* McCormick, 1994, 25–26: "The papal letter is a strong indictment of contemporary relativism and individualism. It rightly rejects the false dichotomies that lead to these twin errors. There are the dichotomies between freedom and law; the ethical order and the order of salvation; conscience and truth; faith and morality." McCormick, then, justifies the indictment by describing the errors the pope combats (as does *Dignitatis Humanae*): "That the world needs a strong statement of this type is beyond question. There is a school of thought in the contemporary world that makes a double move. First, it moves from the factual plurality of beliefs and practices to the conclusion that there is no truth regarding right (and wrong) belief and practice. Second, from this relativistic premise it concludes that individuals should enjoy all but unlimited freedom in determining what is right and wrong belief and practice. Against this, John Paul II argues that freedom is in the service of truth and that truth is a precondition of freedom (nos. 34, 84, 86–88, 96). In a word, the pope scores radical relativism in moral thinking and radical subjectivism in moral judgment."
48. *Dignitatis Humanae,* no. 3.
49. In the United States the rhetoric about separation of church and state is more a way to keep vigilance over the state so it does not favor any particular religious confession. But religion is ubiquitous in all the American political process. In Europe, secularity of the state means a strict laicity, that is an almost absolute absence of religion or religious references from the political discourse. Especially in the Latin countries, there is a perception, on the secular side, that the state is still very much vulnerable to the pressure of the church, so there is a preoccupation to keep the action of the church constantly under check to inhibit any attempts to explore that situation. For a brief but insightful exploration of some of these contrasts, see Calvez 1998, 645–51.
50. Hehir 1992, 354.
51. Troeltsch 1992.
52. These are the terms more often used by Bryan Hehir, the latter borrowed from Martin Marty, who first introduced them. For an elaboration on the concept, see Hehir 1984.
53. See Childress 1997, 33–35. The typology goes back to Niebuhr, 1951. Childress points to some inconsistency in the encyclical between the dominant rhetoric of confrontation and other instances that point in the direction of withdrawal, and even some aspects more in accordance with the transformationist perspective.
54. See *Optatam Totius,* no. 16, in Vatican II 1987a, 720: "Special care should be given to the perfecting of moral theology. Its scientific presentation should draw more fully on the teaching of holy Scripture. . . ."
55. Hehir 1992, 350.

56. For a critique of the use of Scripture in *Evangelium Vitae,* see Mitchell 1997, 63–70. Conley 1997, 4–8, characterizes his scriptural argument in *Evangelium Vitae* (in continuity with *Veritatis Splendor*) as a phenomenological exegesis focused on the spiritual and moral senses of the biblical narratives, with little consideration of the historical-critical method. For another analysis of his moral methodology that raises questions about his use of Scripture, see Keenan 1997, 45–62. For an earlier discussion of the general use of biblical sources by John Paul II, see Prendergast 1993, 69–91.
57. Grisez 1993, 35–41, exploits this aspect to rule out any possibility of dissent about absolute moral norms as presented by the pope, for even if there may be disagreement with the advanced arguments from reason, the arguments from revelation cannot be challenged.
58. *Dignitatis Humanae,* no. 3.
59. See Griffin 1997, 159–71, especially 160, 171. For locating this critique in the broader context of the habitual criticisms of the options of a public church, see Hehir 1992, 355.
60. No consensus has yet been achieved in the church about this question. Hehir 1989, 212, after setting the terms of the question, and the recent evolution of the historical Catholic approach, concludes: "In a paper on Catholic perspectives on religious pluralism, the most that can be done in 1989 is to note the various attempts being made to be more explicitly biblical and theological in presenting Catholic social teaching without forsaking the insight that a pluralistic society still needs to be addressed in the terms of a shared humanity and rationality, which are the basis of a Catholic natural law thought. It is not clear as yet how the balance will be struck in this recasting of Catholic teaching addressed to civil society."

Appendix

Interventions of Monsignor Karol Wojtyla at Vatican II

1. Letter to the President of the Ante-Preparatory Commission.

First session

2. Oral intervention on *schema de sacra liturgia.*
3. Oral intervention on *schema de fontibus revelationis.*
4. Written observations on *schema de instrumentis communicationis socialis.*
5. First written observations on *schema de Ecclesia.*

Second session

6. Oral intervention on *cap. III schematis de Ecclesia.*
7. Written observations on *schema de B. Maria Virgine.*
8. Written observations on *cap. IV schematis de Ecclesia.*

Third session

9. Second written observations on *schema de Ecclesia.*
10. Written observations on *cap. VIII schematis de Ecclesia.*
11. Oral intervention on *schema de Oecumenismo / libertate religiosa.*
12. First written observations on *schema de Oecumenismo / libertate religiosa.*
13. Second written observations on *schema de Oecumenismo / libertate religiosa.*
14. Oral intervention on *schema de apostolatu laicorum.*
15. Written observations on *schema de apostolatu laicorum.*
16. First oral intervention on *schema de Ecclesia in mundo huius temporis.*
17. First written observations on *schema de Ecclesia in mundo huius temporis.*
18. Second written observations on *schema de Ecclesia in mundo huius temporis.*

Fourth session

19. Oral intervention on *schema de libertate religiosa.*
20. Written observations on *schema de libertate religiosa.*
21. Second oral intervention on *schema de Ecclesia in mundo huius temporis.*

22. Third written observations on *schema de Ecclesia in mundo huius temporis.*
23. Fourth written observations on *schema de Ecclesia in mundo huius temporis.*
24. Written observations on *schema decreti de ministerio et vita presbyterorum.*

References

Writings and Pronouncements of Pope John Paul II

In the references to his interventions at the Second Vatican Council, *Acta Synodalia,* followed by volume and part, and the corresponding pages refer to *Acta Synodalia Sacrosancti Concilii Oecumenici Vaticani II.* Vatican City: Typis Polyglottis Vaticanis, 1970–.

The papal pronouncements are organized chronologically. Each reference begins with its date, followed by a descriptive title and the source from which it was used. The abbreviated location *Insegnamenti,* followed by volume and part, and the pages, refers to *Insegnamenti di Giovanni Paolo II.* Vatican City: Libreria Editrice Vaticana, 1979–.

Wojtyla, Karol. 1959. Letter to the President of the Ante-Preparatory Commission, 30 December. In *Acta et documenta concilio oecumenico Vaticano II apparando, series I (antepraeparatoria), volumen II: Consilia et vota episcoporum ac prelatorum, pars II: Europa.* Vatican City: Typis Polyglottis Vaticanis, 1960: 741–48.

———. 1964a. Oral intervention on *schema de Oecumenismo / libertate religiosa,* 25 September. In *Acta Synodalia,* 3-2: 530–32.

———. 1964b. Written observations on *schema de Oecumenismo / libertate religiosa.* In *Acta Synodalia,* 3-2: 838–39.

———. 1964c. Written observations on *schema de Oecumenismo / libertate religiosa.* In *Acta Synodalia,* 3-3: 766–68.

———. 1964d. Oral intervention on *schema de Ecclesia in mundo huius temporis,* 21 October, with *schema additum.* In *Acta Synodalia,* 3-5: 298–314.

———. 1965a. Oral intervention on *schema de libertate religiosa,* 22 September. In *Acta Synodalia,* 4-1: 11–13.

———. 1965b. Written observations on *schema de libertate religiosa.* In *Acta Synodalia,* 4-2: 292–93.

———. 1965c. Oral intervention on *schema de Ecclesia in mundo huius temporis,* 28 September. In *Acta,* 4-2: 660–63.

———. 1980. *Sources of renewal: The implementation of the Second Vatican Council.* Translated by P. S. Falla. San Francisco: Harper and Row.

John Paul II. 1978, October 17. Address to the Cardinals. *Origins* 8: 291–94.

———. 1978, December 2. Message to the Secretary General of the United Nations. In *Insegnamenti* 1: 252–57.

———. 1979, January 7. *Angelus.* In *Insegnamenti* 2-1: 21–22.

———. 1979, January 12. Address to the diplomatic corps accredited to the Vatican. In *Insegnamenti* 2: 43–51.

———. 1979, January 28. Opening address of Puebla Conference. In *Insegnamenti* 2: 188–200.

———. 1979, March 4. *The redeemer of man: Encyclical letter* Redemptor Hominis. Boston: St. Paul Editions.

———. 1979, October 2. Address to the United Nations General Assembly. *Origins* 9: 257, 259–66.

———. 1979, December 22. Address to the Sacred College of Cardinals. In *Insegnamenti* 2-2: 1479–97.

———. 1980, September 1. Letter to the Madrid Conference on European Security and Cooperation. *Acta Apostolicae Sedis* 72: 1252–60.

———. 1980, November 10. Address to the Judges of the European Court. In *Insegnamenti* 2-2: 1113–19.

———. 1980, December 8. Message for the 1981 World Day of Peace. *Origins* 10: 465, 467–70.

———. 1981, January 12. Address to the diplomatic corps accredited to the Vatican. In *Insegnamenti* 4-1: 54–68.

———. 1981, November 14. Address to the new ambassador of Iran. In *Insegnamenti* 4-2: 634–35.

———. 1982, September 18. Address to the 69th Conference of the Inter-parliamentary Union. In *Insegnamenti* 5-3: 481–88.

———. 1983, August 14. Speech in Lourdes at the end of the torch-light procession. In *Insegnamenti* 6-2: 207–13.

———. 1983, August 17. General audience. In *Insegnamenti* 6-2: 255–58.

———. 1984, March 10. Address to the V International Colloquium of Juridical Studies at the Lateranense Pontifical University. In *Insegnamenti* 7-1: 654–58.

———. 1984, December 8. Message for 1985 World Day of Peace. *Origins* 14: 491, 493–96.

———. 1984, December 21. Address to the College of Cardinals. *Origins* 14: 498–502.

———. 1985, January 12. Address to the diplomatic corps accredited to the Vatican. In *Insegnamenti* 8-1: 53–67.

———. 1985, April 11. Speech to the convention of the Italian Church in Loreto. In *Insegnamenti* 8-1: 989–1005.

———. 1985, April 17. General audience. In *Insegnamenti* 8-1: 1058–60.

———. 1985, May 11. Remarks in the Hertogenbosch Cathedral in the Netherlands. *Origins* 15: 17, 19–20.

———. 1985, December 28. Address to the new ambassador of Bangladesh. In *Insegnamenti* 8-2: 1625–26.

———. 1986, February 5. Address to non-Christian religious leaders in India. *Origins* 15: 597–98.

———. 1986, April 10. Address to the International Congress of Moral Theology. In *Insegnamenti* 9-1: 969–74.

———. 1987, January 9. Address to the new ambassador of Kenya. In *Insegnamenti* 10-1: 66–68.

———. 1987, April 28. Address to the Plenary of the Secretariat for Non-Christians. In *Insegnamenti* 10-1: 1449–52.

———. 1987, September 11. Homily at ecumenical prayer service at the University of South Carolina. *Origins* 17: 248–49.

———. 1987, October 17. Address to the new ambassador of Spain. In *Insegnamenti* 10-3: 876.

———. 1987, December 8. Message for the 1988 World Day of Peace. *Origins* 17: 493–96.

———. 1988, March 26. Address to the participants in the colloquium "Believers in the USSR Today." In *Insegnamenti* 11-1: 771–73.

———. 1988, June 13. Address to the new ambassador of Turkey. In *Insegnamenti* 11-2: 2013–15.

———. 1988, October 3. Address to the new ambassador of Finland. In *Insegnamenti* 11-3: 1021–23.

———. 1988, October 8. Speech to the European Court of Human Rights. In *Insegnamenti* 11-3: 1080–83.

———. 1988, October 11. Address to the European Parliament in Strasbourg. In *Insegnamenti* 11-3: 1171–79.

———. 1988, November 15. Address to the Plenary of the Pontifical Commission "Iustitia et Pax." In *Insegnamenti* 11-4: 1553–58.

———. 1988, December 12. Address to the new ambassador of Mauritius Islands. In *Insegnamenti* 11-4: 1851–53.

———. 1989, January 9. Address to the diplomatic corps accredited to the Vatican. *Origins* 18: 541–44. Original French text in *Insegnamenti* 12-1: 60–71.

———. 1989, March 3. Address to the new ambassador of Cuba. In *Insegnamenti* 12-1: 475–78.

———. 1989, June 5. Speech to members of the "Paasikivi Society" in Helsinki. In *Insegnamenti* 12-1: 1520–28.

———. 1989 October 3. Address to the new ambassador of the United States. In *Insegnamenti* 12-2: 744–47.

———. 1989, October 10. Address to the leaders of the major religious communities in Indonesia. In *Insegnamenti* 12-2: 834–40.

———. 1989, October 13. Address to the Indonesian Episcopal Conference in Jakarta. In *Insegnamenti* 12-2: 881–87.

———. 1990, January 13. Address to the diplomatic corps accredited to the Vatican. *Origins* 19: 577–80.

———. 1990, December 8. Message for the 1991 World Day of Peace. *Origins* 20: 472–76.

———. 1990, December 21. Address to the new ambassador of Czechoslovakia. In *Insegnamenti* 13-2: 1708–11.

———. 1991, January 4. Address to the new ambassador of Pakistan. In *Insegnamenti* 14-1: 33–35.

———. 1991, January 12. Address to the diplomatic corps accredited to the Vatican. *Origins* 20: 525, 527–31.

———. 1991, January 14. Address to the new ambassador of Sudan. In *Insegnamenti* 14-1: 106–08.

———. 1991, January 24. Address to the new ambassador of Singapore. In *Insegnamenti* 14-1: 181–83.

———. 1991, March 16. Speech to the Plenary of the Pontifical Council for the Dialogue with Nonbelievers. In *Insegnamenti* 14-1: 540–44.

———. 1991, March 23. Address to Congress of the International Union of Lawyers. In *Insegnamenti* 14-1: 629–32.

———. 1991, May 1. *On the hundredth anniversary of* Rerum Novarum: *Encyclical letter* Centesimus Annus. Boston: St. Paul Books and Media.

———. 1991, June 17. Address to the new ambassador of China. In *Insegnamenti* 14-1: 1691–93.

———. 1991, October 9. Letter to the Bishops of Europe about the Special Synod for Europe. In *Insegnamenti* 14-2: 792–93.

———. 1991, November 23. Address to the International Forum of Christian Democracy. In *Insegnamenti* 14-2: 1238–43.

———. 1992, January 11. Address to the diplomatic corps accredited to the Vatican. In *Insegnamenti* 15-1: 61–75.

———. 1992, May 9. Address to the World Jurist Association of the World Peace through Law Center. In *Insegnamenti* 15-1: 1374–76.

———. 1992, November 28. Address to the new ambassador of Nepal. In *Insegnamenti* 15-2: 752–54.
———. 1993, April 14. Message to the Meeting of the Council of the Episcopal Conferences of Europe. In *Insegnamenti* 16-1: 895–97.
———. 1993, April 16. Address to the Meeting of the Council of the Episcopal Conferences of Europe. In *Insegnamenti* 16-1: 898–904.
———. 1993, August 6. *The splendor of truth: Encyclical letter* Veritatis Splendor. Boston: St. Paul Books and Media.
———. 1993, September 1. Letter to the President of the Council of the Episcopal Conferences of Europe. *La Documentation Catholique,* no. 2080: 879–80.
———. 1993, October 15. Address to the Bishops from New York and Saint Paul-Minneapolis in Visit "Ad Limina." In *Insegnamenti* 16-2: 1017–23.
———. 1993, October 17. *Angelus.* In *Insegnamenti* 16-2: 1045–46.
———. 1993, November 11. Address to American Bishops from Pennsylvania and New Jersey in Visit "Ad Limina." In *Insegnamenti* 16-2: 1267–73.
———. 1993, November 19. Speech to Canadian Bishops from Ontario in Visit "Ad Limina." In *Insegnamenti* 16-2: 1285–91.
———. 1993, December 21. Speech to Cardinals and the Roman curia. In *Insegnamenti* 16-2: 1516–24.
———. 1994, April 13. General audience. In *Insegnamenti* 17-1: 930–34.
———. 1994, September 9. Address (never pronounced) to the President of the Republic of Bosnia-Herzegovina. *La Documentation Catholique,* no. 2102: 881–82.
———. 1994, November 10. "*Tertio Mellenio Adveniente*: Apostolic letter for the jubilee of the year 2000." *Origins* 24: 401, 403–16.
———. 1995, March 25. *The Gospel of life: Encyclical letter* Evangelium Vitae. Boston: St. Paul Books and Media.
———. 1995, October 5. Address to the United Nations General Assembly. *Origins* 25: 293, 295–99.
———. 1995, October 8a. Homily at Camden Yards in Baltimore. *Origins* 25: 312–14.
———. 1995, October 8b. Address in Baltimore's Cathedral. *Origins* 25: 316–17.
———. 1995, November 23. Speech to the III Congress of the Church in Italy in Palermo. *La Documentation Catholique,* no. 2119: 6–11.

———. 1996, January 13. Address to the diplomatic corps accredited to the Vatican. *Origins* 25: 526–28.

———. 1996, May 19. Speech at the Cathedral of Maribor in Slovenia. *La Documentation Catholique,* no. 2140: 560–62.

———. 1996, June 22. Address to the German Bishops in Paderborn. *Origins* 26: 141–44.

———. 1996, June 22. Address during an ecumenical Liturgy of the Word in Paderborn, Germany. *Origins* 26: 139–41.

———. 1996, October 22. Message to the Symposium of European Bishops. *La Documentation Catholique,* no. 2150: 1053–54.

Other Works

André-Vincent, Philippe I. 1976. *La liberté religieuse: Droit fondamental.* Paris: Tequi.

Aquinas, St. Thomas. 1981. *Summa Theologica.* Translated by The Fathers of the English Dominican Province. 5 vols. Vol. 2. Westminster, MD: Christian Classics.

Aubert, Roger. 1965. La liberté religieuse du Syllabus de 1864 à nos jours. In *Essais sur la liberté religieuse.* Paris: Fayard.

Benoît, Pierre. 1967. La liberté religieuse à la lumière de la Révélation. In *La liberté religieuse,* edited by J. Hamer and Y. Congar. Paris: Cerf.

Bortnowska, Halina. 1982. Religious freedom and the local church's responsibility for mission: The situation in Poland, with some reference to Eastern Europe. In *Mission in dialogue: The SEDOS research seminar on the future of mission,* edited by M. Motte and J. R. Lang. Maryknoll, NY: Orbis.

Braga da Cruz, Manuel. 1991a. A concordata com a Santa Sé cinquenta anos depois. *Communio* 8: 372–79.

———. 1991b. A concordata com a Santa Sé. *Communio* 8: 272–80.

Broglie, Guy de. 1964. *Le droit naturel à la liberté religieuse.* Paris: Beauchesne.

———. 1965. *Problèmes chrétiens sur la liberté religieuse.* Paris: Beauchesne.

Buttiglione, Rocco. 1997. *Karol Wojtyla: The thought of the man who became Pope John Paul II.* Translated by P. Guietti and F. Murphy. Grand Rapids, MI: William B. Eerdmans Publishing Company.

Calvez, Jean-Yves. 1998. Religion et société aux Etats-Unis. *Etudes* décembre, no. 3896: 645–51.

Casanova, José. 1994. *Public Religions in the Modern World*. Chicago: The University of Chicago Press.

Childress, James F. 1997. Moral rhetoric and moral reasoning: Some reflections on *Evangelium Vitae*. In *Choosing life: A dialogue on* Evangelium Vitae, edited by K. W. Wildes and A. C. Mitchell. Washington, D.C.: Georgetown University Press.

Claver, Francisco. 1982. Religious freedom and the local church's responsibility for mission: The Philippines. In *Mission in dialogue: The SEDOS research seminar on the future of mission*, edited by M. Motte and J. R. Lang. Maryknoll, NY: Orbis.

Congar, Yves. 1967. Avertissement. In *La liberté religieuse*, edited by J. Hamer and Y. Congar. Paris: Cerf.

Conley, John J. 1997. Narrative, act, structure: John Paul II's method of moral analysis. In *Choosing life: A dialogue on* Evangelium Vitae, edited by K. W. Wildes and A. C. Mitchell. Washington, D.C.: Georgetown University Press.

Coste, René. 1969. *Théologie de la liberté religieuse: Liberté de conscience, liberté de religion*. Gembloux: J. Duculot.

Delhaye, Philippe. 1969. Préface de Mgr. Philippe Delhaye. In *Théologie de la liberté religieuse: Liberté de conscience, liberté de religion*, by R. Coste. Gembloux: J. Duculot.

Douglass, R. Bruce. 1994. Introduction to *Catholicism and liberalism: Contributions to American public philosophy,* edited by R. B. Douglass and D. Hollenbach. Cambridge: Cambridge University Press.

Dulles, Avery. 1998. Orthodoxy and social change. *America* 178:8–17.

Flannery, Austin, O.P., ed. 1987. *Vatican Council II: The conciliar and post conciliar documents.* Revised ed. Northport, NY: Costello Publishing Company.

Fogarty, Gerald P., S.J. 1986. American Catholic influence on church-state relations. In *Religion and politics in the American milieu,* edited by L. Griffin. Notre Dame, IN: The Review of Politics.

Gleason, Philip. 1994. American Catholics and liberalism, 1789–1960. In *Catholicism and liberalism: Contributions to American public philosophy,* edited by R. B. Douglass and D. Hollenbach. Cambridge: Cambridge University Press.

Gonnet, Dominique, S.J. 1994. *La liberté religieuse à Vatican II: La contribution de John Courtney Murray, S.J.* Paris: Les Éditions du Cerf.

Gorbachev, Mikhail. 1992. My partner, the Pope. *New York Times,* 9 March, A17.

Gómez Mier, Vicente. 1997. *De la tolerancia a la libertad religiosa: Exigencias metodológicas de la Ética Cristiana a la luz del decreto conciliar "Dignitatis Humanae."* Madrid: Editorial Perpetuo Socorro.

Gremillion, Joseph. 1982. Religious freedom and the local church's responsibility for mission: The regional church of North America. In *Mission in dialogue: The SEDOS research seminar on the future of mission,* edited by M. Motte and J. R. Lang. Maryknoll, NY: Orbis.

Griffin, Leslie C. 1997. *Evangelium Vitae:* Abortion. In *Choosing life: A dialogue on* Evangelium Vitae, edited by K. W. Wildes and A. C. Mitchell. Washington, D.C.: Georgetown University Press.

Grisez, Germain. 1993. Revelation versus dissent. *The Tablet* 247: 1329–31.

Grootaers, Jan. 1981. *De Vatican II à Jean Paul II, Le grand tournant de l'Église catholique.* Paris: Éd. du Centurion.

Hamer, Jérôme. 1967. Histoire du texte de la Déclaration. In *La liberté religieuse,* edited by J. Hamer and Y. Congar. Paris: Cerf.

Hehir, J. Bryan. 1984. A public church. *Origins* 14: 40–43.

———. 1986a. Church-state and church-world: The ecclesiological implications. *Proceedings of the Catholic Theological Society of America* 41: 54–74.

———. 1986b. John Paul II: Continuity and change in the social teaching of the church. In *Readings in moral theology no. 5: Official Catholic social teaching,* edited by C. E. Curran and Richard A. McCormick, S.J. New York: Paulist Press. First published as "John Paul II: Continuity and change in the social teaching of the church," in *Co-creation and capitalism,* edited by John Houck (Washington, D.C.: University Press of America, 1983).

———. 1986c. Vatican II and the signs of the times: Catholic teaching on church, state and society. In *Religion and politics in the American milieu,* edited by L. Griffin. Notre Dame, IN: The Review of Politics.

———. 1988. The consistent ethic: Public policy implications. In *Consistent ethic of life,* edited by T. G. Fuechtmann. Kansas City, MO: Sheed and Ward.

———. 1989. Religious pluralism and social policy: The case of health care. In *Catholic perspectives on medical morals: Foundational issues,* edited by E. Pellegrino, J. P. Langan, and J. C. Harvey. Dordrecht: Kluwer Academic Publishers.

———. 1992. Policy arguments in a public church: Catholic social ethics and bioethics. *The Journal of Medicine and Philosophy* 17: 347–64.

———. 1993. Catholicism and democracy: Conflict, change, and collaboration. In *Christianity and democracy in global context,* edited by J. Witte, Jr. Boulder, CO: Westview Press.

———. 1995. *Dignitatis Humanae* in the pontificate of John Paul II. In *Religious liberty: Paul VI and Dignitatis Humanae,* edited by J. T. Ford, C.S.C. Brescia: Publicazzioni dell'Istituto Paolo VI.

———. 1996. Religious activism for human rights: A Christian case study. In *Religious human rights in global perspective: Religious perspectives,* edited by J. John Witte and J. D. van der Vyver. The Hague: Martinus Nijhoff Publishers.

Hollenbach, David. 1979. *Claims in conflict: Retrieving and renewing the Catholic human rights tradition.* New York: Paulist Press.

———. 1987. The church's social mission in a pluralistic society. In *Vatican II: The unfinished agenda: A look to the future,* edited by Lucien Richard, O.M.I., Daniel Harrington, S.J., and John O'Malley, S.J. New York: Paulist Press.

———. 1991. Religion and political life. *Theological Studies* 52: 87–106.

———. 1993. Contexts of the political role of religion. *San Diego Law Review* 30: 877–901.

———. 1996a. Freedom and truth: Religious liberty as immunity and empowerment. In *John Courtney Murray and the growth of tradition,* edited by J. Leon Hooper and T. D. Whitmore. Kansas City, MO: Sheed and Ward.

———. 1996b. Tradition, historicity, and truth in theological ethics. In *Christian ethics: Problems and prospects,* edited by L. S. Cahill and J. F. Childress. Cleveland, OH: The Pilgrim Press.

———. 1997. The gospel of life and the culture of death: A response to John Conley. In *Choosing life: A dialogue on* Evangelium Vitae, edited by K. W. Wildes and A. C. Mitchell. Washington, D.C.: Georgetown University Press.

Hooper, J. Leon. 1986. *The ethics of discourse: The social philosophy of John Courtney Murray.* Washington, D.C.: Georgetown University Press.

Hughey, J. D. 1981. Church, state, and religious liberty in Spain. *Journal of State and Church* 23: 485–96.

Huntington, Samuel. 1991a. Religion and the third wave. *The National Interest* summer: 29–42.

———. 1991b. *The third wave: Democratization in the late twentieth century.* Norman: University of Oklahoma Press.

———. 1993. The clash of civilizations? *Foreign Affairs* summer: 22–49.

———. 1996. *The clash of civilizations: Remaking of world order.* New York: Simon and Schuster.

Jiménez-Urresti, Teodoro. 1966. Religious freedom in a Catholic country: The case of Spain. *Concilium* 18: 91–108.

John XXIII. 1976. *Pacem in Terris.* In *The gospel of peace and justice: Catholic social teaching since Pope John,* edited by J. Gremillion. Maryknoll, NY: Orbis Books.

Kaveny, M. Cathleen. 1997. The limits of ordinary virtue: The limits of the criminal law in implementing *Evangelium Vitae.* In *Choosing life: A dialogue on* Evangelium Vitae, edited by K. W. Wildes and A. C. Mitchell. Washington, D.C.: Georgetown University Press.

Keenan, James F. 1997. The moral argumentation of *Evangelium Vitae.* In *Choosing life: A dialogue on* Evangelium Vitae, edited by K. W. Wildes and A. C. Mitchell. Washington, D.C.: Georgetown University Press.

Kepel, Gilles. 1994. *The revenge of God: The resurgence of Islam, Christianity, and Judaism in the modern world.* Translated by A. Braley. University Park: The Pennsylvania State University Press.

Komonchak, Joseph A. 1994. Vatican II and the encounter between Catholicism and liberalism. In *Catholicism and liberalism: Contributions to American public philosophy,* edited by R. B. Douglass and D. Hollenbach. Cambridge: Cambridge University Press.

König, Franz Cardinal. 1986. The right to religious freedom: The significance of *Dignitatis Humanae.* In *Vatican II by those who were there,* edited by A. Stacpoole. Minneapolis, MN: Winston Press.

Lecler, Joseph. 1953. A propos de la distinction de la "thèse" et de l' "hypothèse." *Recherches de science religieuse* 41: 530–34.

Leite, António. 1970. A proposta de lei sobre a liberdade religiosa. *Brotéria* 91: 467–84.

———. 1978. A religião no direito constitucional português. In *Estudos sobre a Constituição: 2º volume,* edited by J. Miranda. Lisbon: Livraria Petrony.

Marienstras, Elise. 1994. Ambivalences américaines. *Projet* winter: 16–24.

Martina, Giacomo. 1971. The contribution of liberalism and socialism to a better self-conception of the church. *Concilium* 67: 93–101.

McCormick, Richard A. 1994. Some early reactions to *Veritatis Splendor*. *Theological Studies* 55: 481–506.

Mistò, Luigi. 1995. Paul VI and *Dignitatis Humanae:* Theory and practice. In *Religious liberty: Paul VI and Dignitatis Humanae,* edited by J. T. Ford, C.S.C. Brescia: Publicazzioni dell'Istituto Paolo VI.

Mitchell, Alan C. 1997. The use of Scripture in *Evangelium Vitae:* A response to James Keenan. In *Choosing life: A dialogue on* Evangelium Vitae, edited by K. W. Wildes and A. C. Mitchell. Washington, D.C.: Georgetown University Press.

Moody, Joseph N. 1953. Introduction. In *Church and society: Catholic social and political thought and movements: 1789–1950,* edited by J. N. Moody. New York: Arts, Inc.

Murray, John Courtney. 1952a. For the freedom and transcendence of the church. *The American Ecclesiastical Review* 126: 28–48.

———. 1952b. The church and totalitarian democracy. *Theological Studies* 13: 525–63.

———. 1953. Leo XIII: Separation of church and state. *Theological Studies* 14: 145–214.

———. 1954a. Leo XIII: Two concepts of government: II. Government and the order of culture. *Theological Studies* 15: 1–33.

———. 1954b. On the structure of the church-state problem. In *The Catholic Church in world affairs,* edited by W. Gurian and M. A. Fitzsimons. Notre Dame, IN: University of Notre Dame Press.

———. 1960. *We hold these truths: Catholic reflections on the American proposition.* Kansas City, MO: Sheed and Ward.

———. 1965a. Osservazioni sulla dichiarazioni della libertà religiosa. *La Civiltà Cattolica* 116: 536–64.

———. 1965b. Religious freedom. In *Freedom and man,* edited by J. C. Murray. New York: P. J. Kenedy and Sons.

———. 1965c. This matter of religious freedom. *America* 112: 40–43.

———. 1966a. Commentary to "Declaration on religious freedom." In *The documents of Vatican II,* edited by W. M. Abbot. New York: America Press.

———. 1966b. Freedom, authority, community. *America* 115: 734–41.

———. 1966c. Religious freedom. In *The documents of Vatican II,* edited by W. M. Abbot. New York: America Press.

———. 1966d. The declaration on religious freedom. In *Vatican II: An Interfaith Appraisal,* edited by J. H. Miller. Notre Dame, IN: University of Notre Dame Press.

———. 1966e. The declaration on religious freedom: A moment in its legislative history. In *Religious liberty: An end and a beginning,* edited by J. C. Murray. New York: Macmillan.

———. 1966f. The declaration on religious freedom: Its deeper significance. *America* 114: 592–93.

———. 1967a. Declaration on religious freedom: Commentary. In *American participation at the Second Vatican Council,* edited by V. A. Yzermans. New York: Sheed and Ward.

———. 1967b. Freedom in the age of renewal. *The American Benedictine Review* 18: 319–24.

———. 1967c. Religious liberty and development of doctrine. *The Catholic World* 204: 277–83.

———. 1967d. Vers une intelligence du développement de la doctrine de l'Église sur la liberté religieuse. In *Vatican II: La liberté religieuse,* edited by J. Hamer and Y. Congar. Paris: Cerf.

———. 1993a. Arguments for the human right to religious freedom. In *Religious liberty: Catholic struggles with pluralism,* edited by J. L. Hooper. Louisville, KY: Westminster/John Knox. First published as "De argumentis pro iure hominis ad libertatem religiosam," in *Act Congressus Internationalis de Theologia Concilii Vaticanii II,* edited by A. Schönmetzer (Rome, Vatican: 1968), 562–73.

———. 1993b. Leo XIII and Pius XII: Government and the order of religion. In *Religious liberty: Catholic struggles with pluralism,* edited by J. L. Hooper. Louisville, KY: Westminster/John Knox.

———. 1993c. The issue of church and state at Vatican Council II. In *Religious liberty: Catholic struggles with pluralism,* edited by J. L. Hooper. Louisville, KY: Westminster/John Knox.

———. 1993d. The problem of religious freedom. In *Religious liberty: Catholic struggles with pluralism,* edited by J. L. Hooper. Louisville, KY: Westminster/John Knox. First published in *Woodstock Papers,* number 7 (Westminster, MD: Newman Press, 1965).

———. 1994a. Religious freedom and the atheist. In *Bridging the sacred and the secular: Selected writings of John Courtney Murray, S.J.*, edited by J. L. Hooper. Washington, DC: Georgetown University Press. First published as "La liberta religiosa e l'ateo," in *L'Ateismo Contemporaneo* 4 (1970): 109–17.

———. 1994b. The declaration on religious freedom. In *Bridging the sacred and the secular: Selected writings of John Courtney Murray, S.J.*, edited by J. L. Hooper. Washington, DC: Georgetown University Press. First published in *War, poverty, freedom: The Christian response* (New York: Paulist Press, 1966): 3–16.

Niebuhr, H. Richard. 1951. *Christ and culture.* New York: Harper and Row.

Noonan, John T., Jr. 1998. *The lustre of our country: The American experience of religious freedom.* Berkeley: University of California Press.

O'Donnell, Robert J. 1992. The church learning and the church teaching: Vatican II and the liberal tradition of religious freedom. *Journal of Ecumenical Studies* 29: 399–417.

Ottaviani, Cardinal Alfredo. 1953. Church and state: Some present problems in the light of the teaching of Pope Pius XII. *The American Ecclesiastical Review* 128: 321–34.

Papini, Roberto. 1993. Christianity and democracy in Europe: The Christian democratic movement. In *Christianity and democracy in global context,* edited by J. Witte, Jr. Boulder, CO: Westview Press.

Paul VI. 1967. Discours pour l'ouverture de la deuxième session de Vatican II (29 septembre 1963). In *Documents Pontificaux de Paul VI: 1963, I.* Saint-Maurice, Switzerland: Éditions Saint-Augustin.

———. [1969]. Renewal but not betrayal: General audience, 25 April 1968. In *The teachings of Pope Paul VI: 29-12-1967–18-12-1968.* Vatican City: Libreria Editrice Vaticana.

———. [1970a]. Educate ourselves to a more Christian use of freedom: General audience, 5 February 1969. In *The teachings of Pope Paul VI: 1969.* Vatican City: Libreria Editrice Vaticana.

———. [1970b]. Truth is the root of freedom: General audience, 9 July 1969. In *The teachings of Pope Paul VI: 1969.* Vatican City: Libreria Editrice Vaticana.

———. 1972. Liberty rooted in man's dignity: General audience, 18 August 1971. In *The teachings of Pope Paul VI: 1971.* Washington, DC: United States Catholic Conference.

———. 1978. The contribution of the church to the building of a better world: Audience to the College of Cardinals, 22 December 1977. In *The teachings of Pope Paul VI: 1977.* Vatican City: Libreria Editrice Vaticana.

———. 1979. Hope of a more just society in regard to human rights: Audience to the diplomatic corps accredited to the Holy See, 14 January 1978. In *The teachings of Pope Paul VI: 1978.* Vatican City: Libreria Editrice Vaticana.

———. 1992. Apostolic Exhortation *Evangelii Nuntiandi.* In *Catholic social thought: The documentary heritage,* edited by D. J. O'Brien and T. A. Shannon. Maryknoll, NY: Orbis Books.

Pavan, Pietro. 1967. Le droit à la liberté religieuse en ses éléments essentiels. In *La liberté religieuse,* edited by J. Hamer and Y. Congar. Paris: Cerf.

———. 1976. Ecumenism and Vatican II's declaration on religious freedom. In *Religious freedom, 1965–1975: A symposium on a historic document,* edited by W. J. Burghardt. New York: Paulist Press.

———. 1986. *La dichiarazione conciliare Dignitatis humanae a 20 anni dalla pubblicazione.* Casale Monferrato: Piemme.

———. 1989a. Declaration on religious freedom. In *Commentary on the documents of Vatican II,* edited by H. Vorgrimler. New York: Crossroad.

———. 1989b. Il diritto della persona e delle comunità alla libertà sociale e civile in materia religiosa. In *Scritti/1: L'anelito dell'uomo alla libertà,* scelti e presentati da Mons. Franco Biffi. Rome: Città Nuova Editrice. First published as *Dignita della persona: testo e commento della Dichiarazione conciliare sulla liberta religiosa (Dignitatis humanae)* (Naples: Dehoniane, 1980).

Pelotte, Donald E. 1976. *John Courtney Murray: Theologian in conflict.* New York: Paulist Press.

Prendergast, Terrence. 1993. "A Vision of wholeness": A reflection on the use of Scripture in a cross-section of papal writings. In *The thought of Pope John Paul II: A collection of essays and studies,* edited by John M. McDermott, S.J. Rome: Editrice Pontifici Università Gregoriana.

Quinn, Kevin P. 1997. Whose virtue? Which morality? The limits of law as a teacher of virtue: A comment on Cathleen Kaveny. In *Choosing life: A dialogue on* Evangelium Vitae, edited by K. W. Wildes and A. C. Mitchell. Washington, D.C.: Georgetown University Press.

Ratzinger, Cardinal Joseph. 1996. Relativism: The central problem for faith today. *Origins* 26: 309, 311–17.

Regan, Richard J. 1967. *Conflict and consensus: Religious freedom and the Second Vatican Council.* New York: Macmillan.

Riccardi, Andrea. 1987. The Vatican of Pius XII and the Catholic party. *Concilium* 193: 37–51.

Ruggieri, Giuseppe. 1986. Open questions: Church-world relations. *Concilium* 188: 131–37.

Scola, Angelo. 1984. Gli interventi di Karol Wojtyla al Concilio Ecumenico Vaticano II: Esposizione ed interpretazione teologica. In *Karol Wojtyla: Filosofo, teologo, poeta: Atti del I Colloquio Internazionale del Pensiero Cristiano organizzato da ISTRA - Istituto di Studi per la Transizione, Roma, 23–25 settembre 1983.* Vatican City: Libreria Editrice Vaticana.

Sigmund, Paul E. 1986. The Catholic tradition and modern democracy. In *Religion and politics in the American milieu,* edited by L. Griffin. Notre Dame, IN: The Review of Politics.

———. 1994. Catholicism and liberal democracy. In *Catholicism and liberalism: Contributions to American public philosophy,* edited by R. B. Douglass and D. Hollenbach. Cambridge: Cambridge University Press.

Steinfels, Peter. 1994. The failed encounter: The Catholic Church and liberalism in the nineteenth century. In *Catholicism and liberalism: Contributions to American public philosophy,* edited by R. B. Douglass and D. Hollenbach. Cambridge: Cambridge University Press.

Tillard, Jean-Marie. 1986. Final report of the last Synod. *Concilium* 188: 64–77.

Troeltsch, Ernst. 1992. *The social teachings of the Christian churches.* Translated by O. Wyon. 2 vols. Louisville, KY: Westminster/John Knox Press.

Vatican II. 1966. Closing messages of the council. In *The documents of Vatican II,* edited by W. M. Abbott. New York: America Press.

———. 1987a. *Optatam Totius.* In *Vatican Council II: The conciliar and post conciliar documents,* edited by A. Flannery. Northport, NY: Costello Publishing Company.

———. 1987b. *Dignitatis Humanae.* In *Vatican Council II: The conciliar and post conciliar documents,* edited by A. Flannery. Northport, NY: Costello Publishing Company.

———. 1990. Declaration on religious freedom. In *Decrees of the ecumenical councils,* edited by Norman P. Tanner. London and Washington, DC: Sheed and Ward and Georgetown University Press.

Wallace, Marilyn. 1987. The right of religious liberty and its basis in the theological literature of the French language (1940–1980): An analysis and critique of the contributions of Guy de Broglie, René Coste, Philippe Delhaye, and Louis Janssens. Ph.D. diss., Catholic University of America, Washington, D.C.

Whitmore, Todd. 1993. Immunity or empowerment? John Courtney Murray and the question of religious liberty. *Journal of Religious Ethics* 21: 247–73.

———. 1994. What would John Courtney Murray say? On abortion and euthanasia. *Commonweal* October 7: 16–22.

Willaime, Jean-Paul. 1994. La laïcité culturelle, patrimoine commun à l'Europe? *Projet* winter: 7–15.

Wyszynski, Stefan. 1965. Le monde du "Diamat": Intervention du cardinal Wyszynski, archevêque de Varsovie. *La Documentation Catholique* 72: 1783–86.

Yzermans, Vincent A. 1967. Declaration on religious freedom: Historical introduction. In *American participation at the Second Vatican Council,* edited by V. A. Yzermans. New York: Sheed and Ward.

Index